Praise for *Steak* by Mark Schatzker

"*Steak* is well worth reading. . . . An impassioned, cogent, even humble defense of why the steak—and, by extension, meat in general—is worth eating. . . . Through his passion and intellectual curiosity and sheer power of description, Schatzker builds a narrative that reveals a deep relationship between him and the animal whose flanks and haunches and loins he is so fond of consuming. . . . *Steak* is an adept mix of passion, obsession, and what Kipling called 'satiable curiosity.' It is thought-provoking for everyone from the steak obsessive to the vegetarian. . . . To accomplish so much in the context of steak alone is—begging your forgiveness—truly rare.'"
—Ted Anthony, Associated Press

"From the science of what makes for the perfect blade of grass to a look at the work of a Scottish man whose job is retrieving sperm from bulls, the book covers every aspect of what makes the serving of the king of meats."
—Mark Egan, Reuters

"Tasty and entertaining."   —Patrick Beach, *Austin American-Statesman*

"Schatzker, a humor columnist for *The Globe and Mail*, has done an ace job of combining interesting historical facts and stories, dense lessons on food and animal science, and amusing accounts of his steak-seeking travels into an entertaining, story-shaped narrative arc, complete with suspense, clever setups and payoffs, a satisfying steak resolution—this is not a personal redemption memoir about finding oneself through eating, it really is all about steak—and mouth-watering food descriptions. . . . Schatzker delivers some sparkling and playful takes on the food-writing genre."
—Kim Moritsugu, *The Globe and Mail* (Toronto)

"*Steak* isn't just a travelogue or a trot down that Proustian memory lane of lost culinary pleasure. . . . Schatzker writes with wit, pace and grace, and a gentle, self-deprecating humor that makes him the Bill Bryson of beef."
—Richard Vines, Bloomberg News

"Schatzker writes with a discerning eye, an inquisitive mind, and a comedic sense of timing that keeps both shop talk (reading cow pies) and the esoteric (the mysteries of umami) from numbing readers' minds. *Steak* is easily one of the most entertaining and informative non-cookbooks about beef."
—*Publishers Weekly*

PENGUIN BOOKS

STEAK

Mark Schatzker is a columnist for *The Globe and Mail* and a frequent contributor to *Condé Nast Traveler* and *Slate*. He has been a finalist for a James Beard journalism award and lives in Toronto.

STEAK

*One Man's Search
for the World's Tastiest
Piece of Beef*

MARK
SCHATZKER

PENGUIN BOOKS

PENGUIN BOOKS
Published by the Penguin Group
Penguin Group (USA) Inc., 375 Hudson Street, New York, New York 10014, U.S.A.
Penguin Group (Canada), 90 Eglinton Avenue East, Suite 700, Toronto,
Ontario, Canada M4P 2Y3 (a division of Pearson Penguin Canada Inc.)
Penguin Books Ltd, 80 Strand, London WC2R 0RL, England
Penguin Ireland, 25 St. Stephen's Green, Dublin 2, Ireland (a division of Penguin Books Ltd)
Penguin Books Australia Ltd, 250 Camberwell Road, Camberwell,
Victoria 3124, Australia (a division of Pearson Australia Group Pty Ltd)
Penguin Books India Pvt Ltd, 11 Community Centre, Panchsheel Park, New Delhi–110 017, India
Penguin Group (NZ), 67 Apollo Drive, Rosedale, North Shore 0632,
New Zealand (a division of Pearson New Zealand Ltd)
Penguin Books (South Africa) (Pty) Ltd, 24 Sturdee Avenue,
Rosebank, Johannesburg 2196, South Africa

Penguin Books Ltd, Registered Offices:
80 Strand, London WC2R 0RL, England

First published in the United States of America by Viking Penguin,
a member of Penguin Group (USA) Inc. 2010
Published in Penguin Books 2011

1 3 5 7 9 10 8 6 4 2

THE LIBRARY OF CONGRESS HAS CATALOGED THE HARDCOVER EDITION AS FOLLOWS:
Schatzker, Mark.
Steak : one man's search for the world's tastiest piece of beef / Mark Schatzker.
p. cm.
Includes index.
ISBN 978-0-670-02181-9 (hc.)
ISBN 978-0-14-311938-8 (pbk.)
1. Beef. 2. Cookery (Beef) 3. Cookery, International. I. Title.
TX556.B4S35 2010
641.6'62—dc22   2009050994

Printed in the United States of America
Set in Electra
Designed by Francesca Belanger

For my mother and father

CONTENTS

STEAK

STEAK

THE PROBLEM WITH STEAK

O f all the meats, only one merits its own class of structure. There is no such place as a lamb house or pork house, but even a small town may have a steak house. No one ever celebrated a big sale by saying, "How about chicken?" Bachelor parties do not feature two-inch slabs of haddock. Certain occasions call for steak—the bigger the better.

Steak is king. Steak is what other meat wishes it could be. When a person thinks of meat, the picture that forms in his mind is a steak. It can be cooked, crosshatched from the grill and lying in its own juice in a pose suggestive of unmatched succulence, or it can be raw, blood-colored and framed by white fat, the steak that sleeping bulldogs in vintage cartoons dream of.

Steak earns its esteem the old-fashioned way. People don't eat it because it's healthy, because it's cheap, or because it's exotic; it isn't considered any of these things. People love steak because of the way it makes them feel when they put it in their mouths. When crushed between an upper and a lower molar, steak delivers flavor, tenderness, and juiciness in a combination equaled by no other meat. The note struck is deep and resonant. Steak is powerful. Steak is reassuring. Steak is satisfying in a way that only the pleasures of the flesh can be.

The best steak my father ever ate was one of his first. The year was 1952, and the steak was served at an establishment in Huntsville, Ontario, called MacDonald's Restaurant. (Not to be confused with McDonald's, the world's largest fast-food chain.) At $3.95, it was a high-priced item, considering that my father would earn all of $35 that summer as assistant director at a boys' camp. An immigrant kid bent on med school, he found himself with money in his pocket for the first time in his life. On his first day off, he hitchhiked into town and bought himself a steak. It arrived sitting next to a pile of fried mushrooms, and it was huge: a sirloin, an inch thick and a foot wide, its edges drooping over the side of the plate. Nearly half a century after eating it, my father is still moved by memories of the experience. He calls it "the fulfillment of my gustatory dreams."

The best steak my cousin Michel Gelobter ever ate was in the Sierra Nevada during the summer of 1980. He was working at a pack station high up in the mountains, living in a small shack with two other guides. Farther down the slopes, horses and cattle were grazing the summer pastures. He saw the cow alive before it became his meal. It was an unusually tall black-and-white castrated male—a steer—standing in a corral, where it was getting fat on hay, sweet sagebrush, and grass. A few weeks later, his boss delivered meat up to the cabin, and the men started with the tenderloin, which is known in fancy talk as the filet mignon. They put it in a pan with salt and pepper, then placed the pan inside a propane stove set to broil. Michel doesn't remember cutting the steak or chewing it, but he does remember the flavor. "It tasted buttery," he says. "It was just slightly tougher than pâté and unbelievably juicy." The steak brought all three men to the same level of extreme astonishment. "I don't think any of us had ever had anything like it," Michel recalls. "It felt like a freak of nature. It was the best steak we'd ever had." When the steak was finished, Michel went over to inspect the remaining raw beef. It was a dark brownish red, with lots of streaks of white in it. Since then, my cousin has been searching. He has eaten "a fair amount of steak," some of it very good, but none of it equal to the Sierra Nevada steak of 1980.

The best steak I ever ate gave way between my teeth like wet tissue paper under a heavy knife. There was a pop of bloody, beefy steak juice and I had to close my lips to keep any of it from escaping. The problem is, this steak lives only in my imagination. I haven't actually tasted it— not yet, anyway. It's a false memory, of the culinary variety.

There have been, certainly, remarkable steaks in my past, most notably one at a Peruvian chain restaurant in a suburban mall in Santiago, Chile. It was served on its own plate, separate from the French fries, allowing the juice to pool in a manner that seemed premeditated. It was not the most tender steak I have ever eaten, but its deliciousness floored me. When I was done eating it, I raised the plate to my mouth, tipped it up, and gulped the juice in one long, excellent sip. I was ready to order another one, but I had a plane to catch.

Steak came to me the same way consciousness did. One day I woke up, and it was there. My father started grilling it when I was around nine, as I recall, which is to say that's when he started *sharing* steak with his youngest son, because he had been buying it and cooking it regularly ever since the trip to MacDonald's Restaurant. By the age of eleven, I knew the difference between a New York Strip and a T-bone (the bone). When my parents visited their three boys at summer camp, they would bring cold steak, black cherries, and icy cans of Coca-Cola.

My relationship with steak started getting, as they say, complicated in the early 1990s. My eldest brother, Erik, moved to South America and began sending regular dispatches on all the great steak he was eating. Every time I spoke to him on the phone, he evangelized about his latest filet or rib eye, and I would hang up jealous and hungry. One day he told me the secret to a great steak: season it only with salt and pepper. I went out and bought the most expensive steaks I could find and did as he said. The piece of meat on the end of my fork tasted like textured salt water.

I did not give up. Most of the steaks I cooked resulted in textured salt water, but occasionally there was a standout. I bought a strip loin at an above-average grocery store one day and pan-fried it according to a Julia Child recipe, and it tasted so good I felt like taking to the streets and raving about its deliciousness through a megaphone. The next day, I returned to the same store and bought an identical-looking strip loin. It was terrible.

I began chasing steak in earnest the year I got married. My wife and I went to Tuscany for our honeymoon, and on our second night there we ate at a restaurant in Florence called Del Fagioli, a cozy little spot with checkered tablecloths and big flagons of Chianti. The waiter did not recommend pasta, veal marsala, or anything else I had, until actually visiting Italy, thought of as Italian food. His advice: "Get the steak." We did, and when I swallowed the first bite, I let out a string of four-letter words and fell silent for a duration lasting more than a minute. Then I swore some more. The steak was that good.

A few years later, I found myself on what may turn out to be the greatest journalistic assignment of the century. To celebrate its twentieth anniversary, a glossy travel magazine called *Condé Nast Traveler* asked me to travel around the world in eighty days, the sole condition being that I wasn't allowed to fly. I saw it as a well-funded steak excursion, and the first night I found myself driving through Chicago, a city famous for its excellent and huge steaks. I went to one of the pricier steak houses, one that claims to keep its own perfect bull down in Kentucky who has the enviable job of siring every one of the cows that provide the restaurant's steaks. The rib eye they served me looked perfect: black on the outside and red in the middle. It tasted like grilled tap water. A few days after that, still heading west, I drove over the Sierra Nevada—not too far from my cousin's pack camp—and dropped thrillingly down into California. That night I ate in the Napa Valley, and the steak was so good I decided to have a look at the local real estate prices, which ended up spoiling an otherwise perfect evening.

A cruise across the Pacific Ocean and a train ride north through China brought me to Mongolia, where I ate the worst steak of my life. It was a T-bone, half an inch thick, grilled over a gas flame and so tough that mid-chew I had to pause and let my jaw muscles rest. But it was only slightly more disappointing than a steak I once ate in Las Vegas at an old and hallowed steak house recommended by a hotel concierge who assured me it was better than all the others. The strip loin I ordered turned out to be more than an inch thick and looked too big to ever fit inside my body. It was expertly crisscrossed with gridiron marks, and as I cut into it, red liquid poured onto my plate. The level of expectation approached the dramatic, but that's where the story ended, at expectation. The meat had a watery texture and hardly any beef taste. It was one of the most expensive steaks I had ever ordered, and also among the most insipid. I took bite after bite, incredulous that something that looked so beefy could taste so limp. Eventually, I gave up. The waiter removed my plate and said, "It's a big serving." I nodded sheepishly and paid the bill.

Steak was now a problem. It had become a culinary version of the weather in England: occasionally beautiful, but on the whole depressing.

Unlike the weather, however, steak was something no one paid any attention to. At steak house dinners, people would spend a minute, tops, deciding on what cut to order before turning to the wine list, which they studied like it was scripture. The meal would inevitably degenerate into an ad hoc seminar on grape varieties. *Should we go with a California cabernet? No, a big zinfandel for sure. But not too oaky—I hate oaky.* The steak itself enjoyed the same status as a napkin or the ice water: people just accepted what was given to them.

Why was it that, in steak houses all over North America, people were talking about grape varieties and not cattle breeds? Why was there an entire aisle at my magazine store devoted to wine magazines, but not so much as a newsletter about steak? Everyone loved steak, and yet no one seemed to know a thing about it. What was going on?

What is it about steak, for that matter, that makes people want to eat so much of it? Why did my father continue to grill it on a near-weekly basis, even though no steak ever measured up to that one he ate in 1963? I suffered from the same disease. Like some pale-faced slot machine addict, I kept exchanging money for steak, hoping to strike gold, but steak after steak said, "Better luck next time."

Why was the meat all so bland? And what could account for those rare standout steaks? What made the Sierra Nevada steak my cousin ate in 1980 so different from those he's eaten since? I couldn't find any answer—not at my local butcher, not in the pages of cookbooks, and not, incidentally, among wine connoisseurs, all of whom are undiscerning steak eaters.

The world, it seemed, reserved its gustatory passion for things like single-cru soft-filtered olive oil, hundred-year-old balsamic vinegar, rare and exquisite Japanese sake, single-malt Scotch, fine port, and so forth. I knew of Italians who get into raised-voice arguments over buffalo-milk mozzarella versus cow-milk mozzarella, Spaniards who feed acorns to pigs to make the ham more delicious, and Americans who take barbecue so seriously it has become a competitive sport.

So what was going on with steak? Had modern agriculture bled the flavor out in the name of efficiency and profit margins? Was steak just one more thing that wasn't as good as it used to be? Or was the reverse true? Had steak been improved and perfected to the point that we were all eating the red meat equivalent of single-cru soft-filtered olive oil, and I was just some gustatory outlier, someone who preferred Italian or Chilean steak the way others prefer French cars or Japanese vacuum cleaners?

Given that at any moment, I could step out my front door and within minutes find myself consuming beer from Germany, mushrooms from Croatia, fish sauce from Thailand, cigars from Cuba, or rum from Guatemala, the latter, surely, seemed more likely. If there was great steak out there, surely the forces of globalism would have found a way to put it on my plate. Like every other fine and expensive thing on the planet, it was just a matter of coming up with enough money.

But as I discovered in Mongolia, globalism missed the boat on mutton. This is the meat from a mature sheep, which the Western world gave up on long ago. (The only place it's ever eaten these days is in nineteenth-century British novels.) The reason is that mutton is tough, with a taste so pungent as to be off-putting. Or so I was told. But two days after gnawing my way through that boot-tough steak in Mongolia, I found myself in a ger camp deep in the Mongolian hinterland preparing for a feast of mutton, which I presumed would be much worse than that steak. As the sky darkened, I sat in a tent and watched three Mongolian women prepare it in a traditional manner. They threw mutton chops into a huge wok, added potatoes, carrots, and salt and pepper, and then opened the door to a wood-burning stove and retrieved several intensely hot rocks, which were tossed in with the same nonchalance as the carrots and potatoes. The rocks were so hot that where they touched mutton bone, the bone burst into flame. Some water was added. A lid came down, and as the mutton cooked, I braced myself for awful meat. But that's not how the mutton tasted. The chops were as tender as any lamb I'd ever eaten, but the flavor was richer, deeper, and better.

Mongolian mutton, I realized, was flying below everyone's radar. Despite a world of meat eaters numbering in the billions and communication and distribution networks wrapping the planet like spider's silk, I had to travel to Outer Mongolia to discover the joys of mutton chops.

Could the same be true of steak? Was there a land where all the beef was bursting with deliciousness, and the people ate nothing but good steak? Somewhere, there had to be someone who knew the secret to creating it.

That's the day my search for steak became a quest. That's the day I set out on a journey that would cover some sixty thousand miles of this planet's geography, taking me to seven countries on four continents, and sending more than a hundred pounds of steak into my grateful mouth. That's the day I booked a flight to Texas.

CHAPTER ONE

TEXAS

exas is the beefiest state in America. Even my cabdriver, who was from Pakistan, knew that. He was driving me to the airport for my flight to Dallas and, talking at the rearview mirror, asked why I was going. "To eat steak," I said. He thought I was joking and let out a fake but courteous little chuckle. When he realized I was serious, he had this to say: "Sir, I think Texas has the very best steak in the world."

"Really?" I said.

"Of this I am sure." Like all pontificating cabdrivers, he sounded sure.

The Plains Indian felt the same way. Before Europeans ever set foot in what we now call Texas, grass grew as tall as a deer's head, and the land was thick with bison, which the Plains Indians loved to eat. Long ago, these people had been cultivators of corn, but when they learned how to ride the horses that escaped from the white people, they gave up corn farming so they could trail the bison herds and make eating their meat a way of life.

The first cattlemen in Texas spoke Spanish. Their cattle roamed not far from present-day San Antonio in tall grass prairies and salt marshes. These *vaqueros*, as they were known, invented the word *ranch* and other standout examples of the cowboy lexicon—lariat, lasso, mustang, corral. English-speaking cowboys didn't get to Texas until around 1815, where they discovered a feast of grass waiting for their herds. Within ten years, cattle outnumbered people twenty-two to one. By midcentury a visitor traveling by stagecoach could peer out the window and see nothing for miles in every direction but cattle grazing on prairie, their heads lowered, their tongues ripping grass and pulling it into their mouths.

In the early 1880s, a Welshman named David Christopher Jones became a cowboy. He had left his home in Pontypool, crossed the Atlantic Ocean, and made his way to the Texas Panhandle, where he bought a chunk of hard land on the banks of Palo Duro Creek. His cattle had red blotchy faces, grazed on buffalo grass, and sipped water out of the creek. When they got big enough, they were driven north to the Flint Hills, way up in Kansas, where they spent the summer eating the better grass that grew there. Come September, the cattle were fat, the technical term for which is "finished." A cow getting fat is "being finished" the same way that a pie in the oven is "being baked."

At one time, the only way a cow could get from Texas to New York was to walk. But by the 1880s, David Christopher Jones's cattle were driven to the Kansas City Stockyards, slaughtered, and sent by train to cities. The very best parts of those cattle were cut into steaks, which were served at better restaurants or sold at high-dollar butcher shops.

The D. C. Jones Ranch is still owned today by some of his descendants, but they don't live there anymore. A hundred and eleven years after Jones set foot in Texas for the first time, the family was driven off the homestead for good, and it was because of steak.

The trouble occurred on May 3, 1995, when D. C. Jones's great-great-grandson, John Bergin, who was two, had to be airlifted to a hospital in Amarillo because there was manure in his lungs and he could not breathe. The manure was inhaled in the form of a windborne substance called fecal dust. John's dad, David Bergin, believes that it came from a feedlot on the other side of the creek called Palo Duro Feeders. Bergin is so sure, in fact, that he has brought a lawsuit against Palo Duro to recover damages for the injuries he claims that his son and family have suffered from the feedlot's operations.

Palo Duro Feeders had been raising cattle since the 1960s, but in the early 1990s, a new owner had expanded the operation considerably. Thirty thousand head of cattle now live huddled together in its open-air pens, and all are there for a single purpose: to gorge themselves on flaked corn. Nothing gets a cow finished like flaked corn, which is made by blasting whole corn kernels with steam and passing them through giant rollers, which flatten them into thumbnail-sized scabs of starch. Flaked corn looks, smells, and, I am told, tastes something like cornflakes, but cows do not relish it because of its crunch. Being flat and thin, flaked corn has a high ratio of surface area to mass, which means a cow's digestive system can process the starch quickly and efficiently. A feedlot cow eats about twenty-five pounds of flaked corn feed every day, and what is not absorbed exits the digestive tract as a wet, dark slop.

Something in the order of two million pounds of this slop was splatting onto the ground every day at Palo Duro Feeders. The evening is cooler than the sun-blasted day in West Texas, and according to David Bergin, that's when the cattle at Palo Duro Feeders like to get up from their corn-fed stupor and stir. They walk over to the feed bunk and gulp down more mouthfuls of flaked corn, or they mosey over to the water trough for a drink. In their wake, clouds of baked manure get kicked up and are carried north on the breeze.

From the D. C. Jones Ranch, the fecal dust would appear as a dark fog advancing over the creek. Late at night, David Bergin would stand outside with his flashlight pointed skyward and track its beam through the cloud. The next morning, he would have to wipe down the windshield on his pickup truck.

In John Bergin's first two and a half years of life, respiratory and sinus problems sent him to the doctor fifty-eight times. The night of May 2, 1995, was especially dry. It hadn't rained in a week, and during the previous month less than an inch of precipitation fell. Dust was blowing, and John Bergin couldn't breathe. Toxins found in the cell walls of bacteria that live in cow manure are known to trigger an immunological response in asthmatics. John's airways were swollen, and he spent the night wheezing and coughing in his mother's arms. The next morning, David Bergin drove his son to the hospital in nearby Spearman. John was placed in an oxygen tent, but he couldn't achieve air exchange, so an air ambulance took him to Amarillo, where doctors admitted him to intensive care. When he recovered, the family moved into a house up the road in the town of Gruver. The Bergins haven't lived on the D. C. Jones Ranch since.

As soon as the Bergins left the homestead, John's health improved. He's a teenager now and plays basketball and football. On weekends he visits the old family homestead and keeps a few longhorn and Corriente cows, descendants of the state's original Spanish cows. "If ever there was a kid born a hundred years too late," David Bergin says, "it was John."

You can smell Palo Duro Feeders before you can see it, and it does not smell like steak. On the drive north from Amarillo to Gruver on Highway 136, you hit a wall of shit-stink, a zone of mind-boggling reek that took over the interior of my rental car and defeated all traces of what had been, an instant earlier, pungent new car smell. A mile later, the cows appear—thousands of cows, most of them black, as far as the eye can see, lined up in rows and watching the passing cars and trucks like spectators at Wimbledon. One would dip its head into the concrete feed trough and come up with a mouthful of flaked corn feed, then return its gaze to the road. On the other side of Highway 136 was an empty field where, right out of a Texas postcard, horses were galloping. They would gallop in one direction, neigh, kick their hind legs in the air, shake their gorgeous manes in a manner suggestive of freedom, then gallop off in another direction.

A little ways ahead, but still well within the epicenter of stench, there was—unbelievably—a picnic area. I pulled over, opened the car door, and came face-to-face with the olfactory wallop of 32,000 defecating cattle. A wind was pelting my face with tiny particles of dust, and I stood there, awestruck by the magnitude of the aroma.

What I wanted to know was: How did these cows taste?

Delicious, you would think. And with good reason. History is replete with incidents of humans devising ways to make animals more delicious. Somewhere, sometime in ancient Egypt, someone figured out that merely feeding geese wasn't sufficient—you had to force the grain down their throats, causing their livers to become large and tremendously fatty. More than four thousand years after that eureka moment, millions of geese and ducks the world over have grain funneled down their throats twice a day so that humans may enjoy their ultra-creamy livers, which are known as foie gras. Before a French chef cooks a crayfish alive, he grasps the middle segment of its tail and pulls it off, ripping out the creature's digestive tract, thus removing any unsavory crunchy bits. The Chinese dispatch fleets of ships to pull sharks out of the oceans and cut their fins off for soup. No other part of the shark, apparently, can be used to make soup, so the sharks are returned to the sea alive but finless, and they sink and die. The greatest instance of cruelty in the name of gustatory pleasure may be found in an unfortunate songbird called an ortolan. The French catch them wild and pluck out their eyes. A night feeder, the blinded bird gorges itself on a diet of millet and figs. Once fattened, it is drowned in cognac and sent to the oven.

The nearest restaurant to Palo Duro Feeders is the El Vaquero. You find it eight miles north on the main street of the town of Gruver, near a Dairy Queen, a Phillips 66 gas station, and a salon called Shear Style. Within the first thirty seconds of your arrival at the El Vaquero, the probability is high that someone within earshot will say, "Y'all." It has a marvelous terrazzo floor, each square of which is inlaid with the brand of a local rancher. David Bergin was sitting across the table from me, and he pointed out the D. C. Jones brand, which is a D and a C with a line running beneath. (Spanish cowboys tend to have the fancy-looking brands, but you don't find many of those up in the Panhandle.) Years ago, the floor belonged to a hotel lobby where ranchers came to smoke cigars and talk rancher talk. In between their laconic, hardscrabble sentences, they fired bullets of dark saliva into spittoons on the floor.

The El Vaquero's menu gets right down to business and lists the steaks at the top, where you'd expect to find salads or soups. Sirloin Steak. Club Steak. Rib Eye Steak. Chicken-Fried Steak. David Bergin recommended the rib eye. It arrived on a small silver platter—regal, festive, suggestive of a Spanish influence—next to a heap of French fries and a grilled hot pepper.

The steak was not from Palo Duro Feeders. On the southern edge of Gruver, there is a hobby-sized feeder called Bob Cluck Pens, but the steak didn't come from there, either. It was, rather, delivered by refrigerated truck from Amarillo, which is a hundred miles south, by Ben E. Keith Foods.

The Ben E. Keith steak looked the way steak is supposed to: big, gray, and crosshatched with black grill marks. Nestled next to it was a little plastic cup of dark steak sauce, but I opted to eat the steak "dry." I was there to taste steak, after all, not steak sauce.

I took a bite. It was hot and tender enough, with the merest suggestion of beefiness. After a second or two of unmemorable but easy chewing, an undertone of sweetness became present, but, as undertones go, it wasn't easy to detect.

In terms of shape, the steak looked like a crude version of Africa, and somewhere near Cape Town was a curl of white fat that was comically easy to cut and glistened on the fork, but didn't taste of much, either. Still, it was soft and succulent. With each morsel of meat I would include a little wedge of fat.

Halfway through I succumbed, taking the little cup of sauce and drenching the steak. Now it had taste. Now it was meaty. Now it was juicy.

David Bergin poured sauce over his steak before taking a single bite. He was born in 1958, and he can remember some of America's last cattle drives. Considering the distances Texas cattle once covered on hoof, these were tiny efforts—only eight miles. He and his father would get on horseback, round up the cattle that were ready to be sold, and herd them up Highway 136 to Gruver, where they were prodded onto scales and loaded on a train bound for the Midwest.

David Bergin hasn't raised cattle since he left the ranch, but he is no enemy of corn-feeding. Before the dust, he had his own little feedlot with fifty cattle, and later managed a feedlot for a huge company called Cargill. Today he is president of a bank, and some of his clients run feedlots. He still wears cowboy boots and a Stetson and carries a six-shooter in the cab of his truck to shoot coyotes and skunks. David Bergin is still a cowboy.

After dinner, on the drive south out of Gruver, I crossed back into the zone of reek and passed Palo Duro Feeders again. It was lit up by bright lights and shrouded in a dark fog of dust. The lights stay on late so that the cattle can feed long into the night.

Bill O'Brien is not a cowboy. He drives a sporty Lexus and does not wear a Stetson, and he lacks the heft of a cowboy. He is spry and has a big-toothed grin and the charm and confidence of a senator. But like cowboys, O'Brien does raise a lot of food for the folks back east. He owns

Palo Duro Feeders along with another feedlot called Texas Beef, which holds twelve thousand more cattle than the one on Palo Duro Creek. He took me out to Texas Beef to have a look.

O'Brien is soft-spoken and upbeat by nature, but as we drove, he told me about how big-city attitudes toward steak make him angry. The *New York Times*, he said, kept printing stories claiming that corn isn't a "natural" feed for cattle. "If that isn't the biggest bunch of bull," he said, sounding disbelieving and hurt. To prove those urban journalists wrong, one day O'Brien opened the gate in the back of one of his feeding pens, giving the cows inside the option of leaving their corn-filled feed bunks for open pasture. The cows continued to eat their corn, but then they wandered out and ate grass, and then, later still, they would wander back in and return to their corn. This, O'Brien said, proved that corn was a natural food. O'Brien printed his findings, calling his study group "The International Center for the Study of Bovine Happiness," and mailed it off to a writer he considered one of the more egregious *New York Times* offenders, Marian Burros. "She just doesn't like me," O'Brien told me. "She's an urban food writer. She's never been to the country. I debunked the mythology she's created, which is that it's unnatural for cattle to eat grain. She doesn't like it." His study received no response. When the experiment was completed, the cattle were sent to the slaughterhouse. No one recorded how they tasted.

Like Palo Duro, Texas Beef stank from at least a mile out. We pulled in and drove down one of the wide alleyways between pens. O'Brien stopped and opened the windows. The cows were frightened by the car and backed away from the feed bunk. They stopped and stared at us, wide-eyed, blinking, ears twitching, then began inching forward. "Do these cattle look unhappy to you?" O'Brien asked.

The truth is, I couldn't say. They were crowded together, fifty thousand of them, in numbers and concentration you wouldn't ever find in nature, standing in textbook filth next to an open-air sewage lagoon, eating a yellow powdery substance that was dispensed by a truck. And yet, no cows were moaning. There weren't any dead ones covered in swarms of flies. No cow was lying on its side, panting and glassy-eyed. One cow, which I could hear but not see, was coughing.

We stepped out of the car for a better look. West Texas is a windy place, and for the second time in twenty-four hours—and also the second time in my life—my face was pelted by fecal dust. I put on my sunglasses, certain of one fact: I would not be happy living in a feedlot. But many of the things that bring me comfort—high-thread-count cotton, watching hockey and baseball in HD, fishing, eating steak—would not make a cow happy. A few cows stepped up to the feed bunk, dipped their heads down, and took in mouthfuls of food. I stepped back into O'Brien's Lexus.

O'Brien has big plans for Texas Beef. He wants to build a biodigester, which is a big high-tech fermentation tank that will somehow derive electricity from the tons and tons of manure. He just spent $6 million on a new feed mill. I walked into one of several shiny aluminum bays, large enough to park a dump truck, where O'Brien will store ingredients—mainly corn. The mill itself is a small industrial complex of tubes and silos where whole kernels of corn are steamed, flaked, and mixed with other feed additives. It takes eight hours to manufacture enough feed for nearly fifty thousand cows to eat in a single day.

Cows spend about five months at Texas Beef eating and crapping, after which they walk out five hundred pounds heavier than when they arrived. Every week, two thousand graduate. They step onto a semi and are shipped to a slaughterhouse fifteen miles away in Cactus, Texas, which is owned by a large corporation called Swift, which is itself owned by a much larger Brazilian company called JBS—the biggest meat pro-cessor in the world. There, they are killed, de-hided, and sliced into cuts. The cuts are sealed in plastic, packed in boxes, and loaded onto trucks that fan out from the Pacific to the Atlantic.

Not far from Texas Beef, O'Brien has an eight-thousand-acre farm where he grows wheat. A herd of wild pronghorn antelope had recently discovered that wheat and started helping themselves. We pulled into one of his fields and found pronghorns grazing on profit margins. Compared with corn-fattened cattle, pronghorn antelope are a vision of elegance. They are have dainty hooves, shapely bodies, and delicate, aerodynamic faces. As good as pronghorn antelope are at eating O'Brien's wheat, they are even better at running. Up until about twenty thousand years ago, they lived a high-strung life, getting chased on a daily basis by the now extinct American cheetah. No animal on the continent can run as fast. If a pronghorn buck bolted through the nearby town of Dumas, he would get pulled over for speeding.

O'Brien demonstrated. He pulled onto the wheat field, which had been baked to an asphaltlike hardness by the Texas sun, and gunned the Lexus. The pronghorns dispersed, trotting this way and that. Bill nosed the car forward, and now they took off, their hind legs flicking back and forth at a rate reminiscent of an industrial sewing machine's. We kept up for a few seconds, but the antelope would dart in one direction and then another, and it didn't take long until they were behind us, the herd reformed, all of them back to an easy trot. As far as handling goes, a sporty Lexus has nothing on an extinct cheetah.

O'Brien pulled back onto the highway, and the pronghorns returned to their eating. There wasn't a mammalian heart that wasn't beating faster. I asked O'Brien how pronghorn antelope taste. "Gamy" was his answer.

Some twenty miles southwest of Texas Beef is the O'Brien family ranch. Centuries ago in Andalusia, Spain, a *rancho* referred to a hut where a cattle herder could grab some shut-eye. In America, the word became "ranch" and came to denote something considerably grander. O'Brien's is situated next to a formerly rough-and-tumble old town called Tascosa, which used to boast no fewer than four brothels. Nearby is a cemetery, and one of the headstones contains the following epitaph:

> *Frenchie McCormack*
> *Aug 11 1852*
> *Jan 12 1941*
> *Madame at Whore House*

The ranch sits on a hilly and parched section of land near the Canadian River, which has carved out moments of inspiring grandeur from the West Texas limestone. Not far away is a box canyon where Billy the Kid used to hide stolen horses, and we rode out there on ATVs to have a look. O'Brien's granddaughter accompanied him while I followed along behind, nearly tumbling over a small cliff. We stopped at the top of the canyon on an outcropping of smooth rock and took in the fine view. In the rock beneath our feet, I noticed some peculiar holes. They were a few inches deep and almost perfectly round. O'Brien said they were made by Indians, who would grind flour by spinning a cylindrical piece of wood over corn placed in a rocky depression. He has seven thousand cattle running on the ranch, and when they're a year old he ships them to Texas Beef or Palo Duro Feeders to eat flaked corn. I looked at the Indian grinding holes and pondered how long it would take to mill a day's worth of feed for fifty thousand cattle with a cylindrical piece of wood.

The ranch house is big and comfy, the kind of place a sun-weary Spanish cowherd could take the nap of a lifetime. Next to it is a creek-fed pond, and we sat on the bank and ate a lunch of ham and cheese sandwiches on white bread with mayonnaise and mustard. As we ate, O'Brien warned against the dangers of letting the superficial trappings of wealth—fancy cars, society balls, yearly kitchen renovations—go to one's head. He had bought the ranch from a man who'd wasted a lot of money on just that sort of frippery.

My hope was to taste some of O'Brien's steak, but he didn't have any available—or at least, none that he knew for certain was his. He gets his steak from his son, Alex, who is a former pro tennis player and owns a business selling premium-quality steaks, which he buys from Swift. Some of the steaks originate in O'Brien's feedlots, and some in other feedlots, but no one knows which ones come from where exactly. On a single stretch of Texas highway, I saw four Swift trucks, all filled with boxed beef. Some of those boxes may have been O'Brien's. Every day, all over the country, people are eating Palo Duro steaks, but no one is aware of it.

Ben E. Keith Foods, I later found out, buys beef from big companies. Sometimes Ben E. Keith buys its steak from Swift, though, according to their customer service representative, "not very often." It is possible, then, but not likely, that the steak I ate at the El Vaquero came from just down the road. I will never know. The only Palo Duro product I can say with certainty that I ingested was a small amount of fecal dust, though not enough to taste.

.   .   .

Two cowboys were standing out front of the Big Texan Steak Ranch when I pulled in, one big and one small. The big one was wearing a white Stetson, chaps, and a red bandana around his neck and was so tall you couldn't miss him from I-40. He was the restaurant's sign—big enough to do battle with Godzilla and as perfect a specimen of Americana as the iconic "Welcome to Las Vegas" and Hollywood signs. The other cowboy, who had just walked down the restaurant's patio steps, was wearing dark blue stovepipe jeans with a tight crotch, a big gold belt buckle, and a black Stetson. His lips were thin, his eyes were beady, and his face looked as though it'd seen its fair share of bad weather, real and metaphorical. A gimp leg gave the cowboy, who appeared to be in his sixties, a slow, clopping amble. You could almost hear dry desert earth crunching under the leather soles of his boots, even though he was walking over tarmac. Full of steak, he heaved himself into the cab of a Ford minivan and drove off.

Inside, the steak house is done up to look like a rickety old saloon (though it seems doubtful that any Old West saloon ever got so big). A young woman in a sexy cowgirl outfit called me "honey" and took me to my table. Country music was playing, and the heads of dead ungulates— deer, moose, elk—were mounted on the wall. I took a seat at a table on the balcony, which wraps around the main dining room. It occurred to me that if there were a shoot-out and I got hit, I would crash through the wooden picket railing and fall onto one of the tables below, just like in the movies.

A waitress appeared wearing the same sexy cowboy outfit as the hostess, though she was less sexy. "What can I get you, honey?" she asked, enthusiasm bubbling over. One thing Texans have realized is that men enjoy walking into restaurants and being addressed as "honey."

The Big Texan serves a steak called "The Texas King" that weighs a whopping seventy-two ounces. To appreciate a piece of meat of that magnitude, consider that a twelve-ounce steak qualifies as big at most restaurants. There are babies born—viable, long-lived babies—who weigh less than a Texas King. What is most remarkable about that steak, however, is that if you order it, you don't have to pay for it.

The catch is that you have to finish it. According to my waitress, most do not. "We had a couple of guys in yesterday who thought they could do it," she said. "They didn't make it."

Finishing a Texas King is not just a matter of eating, but of eating under pressure. Challengers are seated at a table set on a raised plat-form—a stage, basically—so that the other patrons can take in the drama. They have sixty minutes to transfer the steak from their plates to their stomachs, and a clock above them counts down every second. If they encounter any fat or gristle, they may set it aside, but they must eat every edible bit of steak, along with the shrimp cocktail, roll, potato, salad, and ranch beans that come with the meal. A garbage pail sits at the end of the table. The day before, a man midway through a Texas King lowered his head into it and vomited. Vomiting gets you disqualified.

And yet, many have bested the Texas King. Out of the more than fifty thousand people who have attempted the feat—collectively order-ing almost a quarter million pounds of steak—almost ten thousand have succeeded. The record for eating a Texas King the fastest was held for twenty-one years by a former Cincinnati Reds pitcher named Frank Pastore. He downed one in nine and a half minutes but was dethroned by a professional hot dog eater named Joey Chestnut, who beat him by more than thirty seconds. A Texas King was once fed to a Bengal tiger, who swallowed it all in less than ninety seconds, which included a fair bit of sniffing and licking, but he was spared the shrimp cocktail, bread, and other accompaniments, so the record does not stand. A Canadian pro wrestler named Klondike Bill, now deceased, once ate two Texas Kings in under an hour. That works out to an average-sized steak every six minutes.

I asked for an average-sized rib eye and gave myself more than six minutes. The Big Texan sprinkles Montreal steak seasoning on its steaks, but I wasn't in Texas to taste food from Montreal, so I ordered it dry. It arrived, nevertheless, soaking in a half inch of dark liquid, which the waitress explained was "au jus." To the French, *jus* is the precious intense, brothlike liquid that drips off beef as it roasts, but it didn't seem likely that what was being billed as *au jus* was genuine *jus*, given that the steaks were grilled and that the liquid tasted strongly of powdered beef broth.

The steak itself was mildly worse than the one at the El Vaquero:

somewhat drier, somewhat tougher, and a little sour, though in the end similar enough to be its first cousin. The only way to guarantee a succulent morsel was to carve a thin slice off and bathe it in the "au jus." The best part, again, was that nub of fat.

I asked the manager where he got his steaks. In the thickest Texas twang I'd heard yet, he answered, "From a var-ah-ety of prov-ah-ders." He singled out one in particular that does a lot of business with the Big Texan: IBP. Once known as Iowa Beef Processors, IBP is today part of an unimaginably huge company called Tyson Foods, the country's largest marketer not only of beef but of chicken and pork, too. Tyson processes about 150,000 cattle *per week*, and each Texas King, at four and a half pounds, represents a small fraction of what the company churns out in a single *second*.

I pulled out of the Big Texan and back onto the interstate, which struck me as a slow-moving river, with fast-food restaurant signs reminiscent of overhanging foliage. America's steak heartland wasn't living up to its billing. So far, the steak just wasn't that good. Another question formed in my mind: What makes a good steak good, anyway?

In Texas, there are people who know how a steak will taste just by looking at it. Even children have the gift. And on yet another sun-dried West Texas morning in the city of Lubbock, fifty or so thirteen-year-olds were competing to see who could do it best.

Gawky and acne-challenged, they were gathered in a refrigerated room, dressed in long white lab coats and hard hats and staring intently at six sides of beef. The deliciousness of each side was determined in silence because talking is forbidden. Each competitor noted his or her findings on a clipboard, and after ten minutes a whistle blew and a woman yelled, "Rotate!" The group moved into another cold room where more meat of indeterminate quality was waiting. When it was over, they handed in their score sheets for evaluation. The winner was a young man named Markus Miller, who scored 713—28 more than the boy in second and 37 more than the top-ranked girl. Coming in last, with 149 points, was a boy from Hereford, Texas—a town named after a breed of cattle.

The Texas Tech Invitational Meat Evaluation Contest is one in an entire season of high school meat-judging events. Texas Tech itself is a university, with NCAA football, baseball, and basketball teams, all of which are known as the Red Raiders. It also fields a meat-judging team, and its contingent of Red Raiders is one of the best. The university hands out more than $50,000 every year in meat-judging scholarships. The team practices Tuesdays, Wednesdays, and Thursdays for two hours, starting at 6:00 a.m. On Fridays, they get together after lunch and go to a nearby meatpacking plant to practice on fresh carcasses. Saturdays are called Super Saturdays. The team meets in the meat science lab at four in the morning, where coaches set up carcasses and cuts of meat to simulate the conditions of an actual competitive event. At noon, eight hours after arriving, they leave the meat lab. In a normal season, each member of the team will appraise thousands of pieces of meat.

The Invitational gives high school meat judgers a glimpse of a big-league venue. But do not make the mistake, as I did, of assuming the high school squads are manned exclusively by novices. Competitive meat judging can start as early as seventh grade, and in a group of fourteen-year-old judgers, veterans may be found. A Red Raider named Matthew Morales—a junior when I met him—was twelve when he judged meat for the first time. He was competing against high school students that were older than he was, and he had to squeeze in front of bigger kids just to see the carcasses. When he found himself face-to-face with the raw meat, he got butterflies. "I was looking at four big old pieces of meat," he remembers. "I didn't know what to do. The coach told us to relax, to turn around and not look at the meat, then look at the meat again and focus. And it worked. I came fourteenth out of sixty or so kids." By his twenty-first birthday, Morales estimates, he had judged carcasses numbering in the hundreds of thousands.

Just as a varsity football, baseball, or basketball player who turns enough heads in college can turn pro, so can a meat judger. The U.S. Department of Agriculture employs 200 meat graders, 140 of whom specialize in beef. In a single day, a USDA grader can judge as many as 1,200 beef carcasses, each carcass requiring no more than six to eight seconds of the grader's time. Like high school and college meat judgers—

and just like the twelve-year-old Matthew Morales—the USDA grader is looking mainly for one thing: marbling.

Marbling consists of the grains, spots, and streaks of fat within a steak. The rim of fat around a steak is not marbling. The nub of fat in a rib eye is not marbling. But the small white dots and curls of fat spread throughout a steak's red flesh *are* marbling. To a USDA grader, there is no greater quality that a piece of beef can possess. Steak with the highest amount of marbling is the best steak, period. It is called Prime. Next down in ranking is Choice, followed by Select, followed by Standard, which is "practically devoid" of marbling. A Standard steak is red through and through, with its only fat on the edges. It sells for a fraction of what Prime sells for. A Prime steak looks as if someone took a Standard steak, hung it on a wall, and fired a shotgun loaded with fat into it.

Peter Luger, the famous New York steak house, claims that it has been serving "the finest USDA Prime steaks since 1887." This cannot be true because the USDA didn't grade its first beef carcass until 1927. And the reason it did so then was because, by 1927, beef was being produced in the same way as cars, furniture, and clothing—it was being churned out of factories.

It hadn't always been. Up until 1850 or so, beef was killed locally. Cowboys delivered cattle on the hoof to cities, where butchers would turn each animal into steaks and roasts. Quality control was in the hands of the cowboys. During a cattle drive from the Flint Hills in Kansas, or the Sand Hills in Nebraska, all the way to Chicago or New York City, it was their job to keep the cattle calm, move them at a moderate pace, and graze them the whole way. The cowboys would clop into town sore, bowlegged, their spines herniated, but if the weather had cooperated and luck had been on their side, their cattle would be plump and delicious.

The railways put cowboys out of business. Instead of being shepherded to market, cattle started taking the train. And then a great American industrialist by the name of Gustavus Swift went and changed everything. The appearance to this day of the Swift name on refrigerated eighteen-wheelers on West Texas highways is a testament to one man's vision and legacy.

Henry Ford gets all the credit for inventing the assembly line, but the truth is that he borrowed the idea from Gustavus Swift, although in Swift's version it was a *disassembly* line. Cattle arrived intact and fully operational at his packing plant at Chicago's Union Stockyards. There they were killed, and their carcasses were carried by an over- head trolley system to various workstations, and at each one a cut was sliced or an organ removed until the entire beast was fully dismantled. Once "dressed," the beef was sent by refrigerated railcar—another Swift creation—to New York, Boston, Philadelphia, or anywhere else beef was in demand.

By the early twentieth century beef was getting cheaper, but it wasn't always good. Butchers, restaurateurs, and hoteliers ordered beef without ever setting eyes on it or the person who raised it. Some of that beef was excellent, but some was terrible—tough, with a gamy, almost rancid taste. Years earlier, if a customer bought a lousy steak, she could take up the matter with her local butcher. The butcher, in turn, could make sure not to buy any more of those scrawny brown cows with the twisted horns from the cowboy with the heavy beard.

Now beef was coming via Chicago from who knows where. Some came from dairy cows that had spent the last decade getting milked. Some came from emaciated, poorly cared for cows fed on bad pasture. And some came from well-bred steers that had been grazed on lush pasture and, maybe, were fed a little grain, too. So the USDA decided to step in. Starting in 1927, they decreed what beef was delicious and what beef was not.

These pioneering USDA graders were faced with endless lines of beef carcasses of indeterminate quality funneled in from all over the country. How did they determine which ones were the good ones? The best, if most impractical, method would have been to fry up at least a medallion of beef from every cow to see how it tasted. Instead, they determined the quality of a side of beef simply by *looking* at it. They looked for plump animals that weren't too old. They looked at the inside of the ribs for fat, which they called feathering. They looked for fat on the flank, which they called frosting. The choicest, fattest, younger animals—amply feathered and frosted—received a grade of Prime.

By the 1960s the USDA was no longer interested in feathering and frosting. Now they would take a side of beef, make an incision between the twelfth and thirteenth ribs, and peer at virgin rib eye. They were looking for little dots and curls of fat. They were looking for marbling. They still are today.

Marbling equals deliciousness. Every meat scientist I spoke to at Texas Tech sang the same refrain, and study after study has proven the point. Fat is flavor. Because it is softer than muscle, fat is also tenderness. Fat is juicy, a quality that has given rise to the "lubrication theory" of marbling. As the droplets of fat melt, the muscle fibers are lubricated, and so too are the teeth and tongue and the warm, wet cave that is the mouth, making for a moist and satisfying chew. Fat, furthermore, triggers salivation. A marbled steak goads the mouth into joining in the festival of juiciness.

Marbling is one of many topics that grip the imaginations of meat scientists. Here is a discipline that craves the certainty of physics and the penetrating insight of psychology. There are factors meat scientists can talk about at the level of micrograms: amino acids, moisture content, monounsaturated fats. They can measure tenderness to a minute degree using a Warner-Bratzler device, a contraption that adds weight to a cutting blade to determine the exact resistance of cooked steak. (The more weight required to cut the steak, the less tender it is.) But meat scientists also wrestle with the mysterious, intangible qualities bound up in meat— flavor, satisfaction, succulence—and attempt to render them into numbers, too.

A not unusual day at the lab will see a meat scientist slip into a white lab coat and eat steak. These sessions, which can occur five times in the course of a single day at Texas Tech, are known as Beef Sensory Evaluations. They take place in a long, narrow, dimly lit space called the Sensory Evaluation Room. On the left wall is a row of seven booths separated by dividers so that a person sitting at one cubicle has no idea what the persons on either side of him think of the meat they're eating. Red lights cast a trance-inducing glow that cancels out any potential cues of visual appeal. The ugly steak, after all, may be more delicious than all the others.

Evaluators face a blank wall. On the other side of the wall is another room where someone takes cooked steak—prepared on an industrial belt grill in a nearby kitchen, unseasoned—and slices it into morsels, then passes them through a series of hatches to evaluators in the Sensory Evaluation Room. Each evaluator puts the steak into his mouth, chews it, and records his sensory impressions on a score sheet. He may spit out the beef into an expectorant cup, as is common at wine tastings, but most of the steak is swallowed. After each sample, an evaluator takes a sip of apple juice to clear the steak residue from his palate, and then he clears the apple juice with a sip of water. He is now ready to evaluate again.

Using the senses of taste, smell, and feel, evaluators break each steak down into attributes, each of which gets a number. Juiciness ranges from extremely dry (1) to extremely juicy (8), and it comes in two forms: "initial juiciness" and "sustained juiciness." The same is true of tenderness—initial and sustained, which likewise ranges from extremely tough (1) to extremely tender (8). There is also cohesiveness; springiness; beef flavor; flavor intensity (extremely bland to extremely intense); overall beef mouthfeel (extremely non-beeflike mouthfeel to extremely beeflike mouthfeel). "Off flavor" goes from 1 to 3 (none to strong off flavor). The most interesting category is "characterization"—1 is sweet; 2 is acid; 3 is sour; 4 is rancid; 5 is warmed over.

Sensory evaluations have proven the supremacy of marbling time and again. American meat scientists believe in marbling the way American physicists believe in atoms and American biologists believe in cells. It's at the leading edge of research where things get more interesting, where beneath the refreshingly hard-and-fast truths like marbling awaits a world of intrigue and complexity. Take this "in-home beef study," sponsored by Texas A&M University, which, incidentally, also fields a meat-judging team. It compared the preference for clod steaks—known to some as shoulder steaks—among residents of Chicago and Philadelphia. The study divided each geographic group into Beef Loyals (people who eat a lot of steak); Budget Rotators (cost-conscious meat eaters who buy chicken as well as beef); and Variety Rotators (rich, well-educated meat lovers who divide their meat consumption between beef, chicken, and other meats).

The study describes the Beef Loyals as follows: "They were average in age, income, education and household size. They were not particularly concerned with diet and health issues. Their food preferences were not driven by budget concerns. They had positive attitudes about beef and considerably fewer positive attitudes about chicken." The Beef Loyals, unsurprisingly, enjoyed clod steaks more than the Budget and Variety Rotators. (They are nothing if not loyal.) Philadelphians thought fried clod steaks tasted better than grilled clod steaks. But in Chicago, respondents felt just the opposite, preferring grilled to fried. In both cities, flavor was considered more important than tenderness or juiciness.

Beef Loyals of the world, there is good news. Achieving marbled beef is easy: what you need is corn. You need steamed, flaked corn, and you need a lot of it. None other than the chair of the Texas Tech Meat Science Department told me so. He happens to have the same name as the thirteen-year-old who won the high school meat-judging competition I witnessed—Markus Miller—because that boy is his son. I sat in his office, next to shelves filled with published findings on the science of meat, where he put it thus: corn equals marbling, and marbling equals flavor.

Few things in life reduce to such a simple formula, but steak is one of them.

American cattle didn't always eat corn. When the Spanish first moved their Mexican herds up into Texas, they grazed on grass. When British settlers arrived, they pastured their animals in meadows and forests. The first American cattle to eat corn did so in eighteenth-century Appalachia, and they ate the whole plant—leaves, cob, everything.

According to Markus Miller Sr., American beef has never tasted as good as it tastes right now. It started improving after World War II, when a meat scientist at Texas Tech named Ralph Durham helped develop bovine meals that included enormous quantities of starchy corn. (A meat pioneer to the max, Durham also invented a method of injecting melted beef fat into steak to "create" marbling.) Before World War II, roughly one in twenty steaks came from a grain-fed cow. Today, just about all of them do.

In the modern industrial system, steak has effectively become a widget. The industry refers to its own product—unironically—as "commodity beef." Beef is a commodity in the same way that corn, gravel, rubber, soybeans, uranium, Brent crude, copper, and palm oil are commodities. It is mass-produced, uniform, and predictable. USDA-graded live cattle are traded as "cattle futures" on the Chicago Mercantile Exchange. A cattle future lets you buy live beef at a particular price at a future date; a single contract consists of 40,000 pounds of live cattle. The Chicago Mercantile Exchange trades roughly 45,000 contracts a day, which amounts to roughly 1.8 billion pounds of live beef. Some of the people making trades are pure speculators, men and women who make or lose entire fortunes on cattle without once inhaling the smell of manure. Some are big chain restaurants looking to hedge a commodity whose price could go up.

A big steak house chain might buy cattle futures as a hedge against a possible rise in the price of beef, then sell the contract to a meatpacker like Swift or Tyson. A week later, that steak house chain could phone up the very same meatpacker and buy thousands of pounds of beef. In all likelihood, that beef would not come from the same cattle whose futures the steak house had so recently owned. There is no way of knowing. Live cattle futures are traded anonymously in a pit or online. Buyers don't know sellers, and sellers don't know buyers. But it hardly matters. Feedlots churn out identical fleets of cattle, and the packers churn out boxes filled with identical steaks. One load is interchangeable with another. Beef is what economists call fungible.

So it doesn't matter that I never tasted a Palo Duro Feeders steak, because a Palo Duro Feeders steak is fungible. By tasting a USDA-graded corn-fed steak, I already had. Bill O'Brien's steak is the same as the steak being produced by feedlots all over Texas, Kansas, Nebraska, and the rest of the country. They're fed the same, killed the same, and shipped via the same trucks. Beef is beef is beef. It comes in different grades: Select, Choice, and, the very best, Prime.

My problem, as any number of Texas seventh graders could have told me, is that I wasn't eating Prime. The steak on my plate wasn't marbled enough. I now planned on remedying the situation, and turned my rental car onto Interstate 40, heading east for the oldest steak house in America.

When you get to Oklahoma City, look for the bronze statue of a cowboy lassoing a steer, and when you find the emporium selling an impressive variety of cowboy boots, walk across the street. You'll find yourself standing at the front door of the Cattlemen's Steakhouse, which has been open for business continuously since the year 1910, when it went by the less cowboy-sounding name of the Cattlemen's Café. The current owner is a man named Dick Stubbs. He bought the establishment from Gene Wade, who won it in a craps game from Hank Fry in a smoke-filled hotel room in 1945. In a display case at the front of the restaurant sits a collection of old menus that are kept, like precious relics, behind glass. One lists a small filet mignon with a baked potato and small salad for a dollar. Another features a painting of a cowboy sitting on a dusty prairie, eating steak and gazing thoughtfully at a covered wagon, behind which a herd of cattle are grazing. Black-and-white photos hanging on the wall attest to a more authentic time, when people walked into the Cattlemen's and sat down on stools at a counter, under a tin ceiling, watched over by mounted deer's heads as they ate their steaks. The interior was updated to tragic effect in the 1970s, by the looks of things, and now it features booth seating, ceiling tiles, and fluorescent lights.

When the waitress asked, "What can I get you?" I answered with two words: Prime steak. Like the Big Texan, the Cattlemen's Steakhouse dusts its steaks in seasoning before they hit the grill and pours on some "au jus." But I was there to sample the marbled glory of Prime, not seasoning or concentrated broth, so I asked for the steak dry. Minutes later I was presented with another charred rib eye. I put the first bite in my mouth, and the lubrication theory became more than just a theory. There was a burst of thick, tongue-coating liquid. The grease made for a moist chew, but as chews go, I wouldn't call it more or less satisfying than the steaks I had eaten at the Big Texan or the El Vaquero. From a flavor point of view, it was almost identical to the steak in Texas. There was a suggestion of beefiness, but it was dwarfed by an arc of bitterness coming off the charred exterior. In a sensory evaluation, I'm not sure I'd have been able to tell the steaks I had consumed on this trip apart. The taste of all the steaks was fungible.

I got in the car, pulled back onto the highway, and drove. Nothing was making sense, marbling least of all. Fat, everyone insists, is flavor. But there was a problem with that idea. I had eaten several slices of fat at the Cattlemen's, just as I'd done at the Big Texan and the El Vaquero. It was soft, succulent, and buttery, but it wasn't what you would call flavorful. If anything, the fat tasted milder than the supposedly flavor-challenged muscle next to it. Does marbling *really* equal flavor?

Despite the assertions of everyone at Texas Tech, however, the science on that subject—like a lot of science—is inconclusive. While a group of studies has indeed found that more marbling equals more deliciousness, a slightly smaller group of studies concludes otherwise. As far back as 1963, some meat scientists found *no* relationship between marbling and flavor. Other studies have found that the issue isn't black-and-white. In 1980, a panel of eighteen sensory evaluators at Texas A&M didn't like steaks with no marbling, and they liked steaks with "modest-plus" marbling. But the steaks they judged the most tender and tastiest of all had "modest-minus" levels of marbling. The supposed relationship between marbling and tenderness was long ago refuted by scientific experiment. As one Texas Tech grad student put it to me, "Marbling isn't acting the way it's supposed to." And as for the study of clod-steak-eating Beef Loyals in Chicago and Philadelphia, for them deliciousness had nothing to do with marbling.

I was struck by a thought: *Elk*. Not only elk, but moose and deer, too. These animals are, just like cattle, ruminants. They predigest all their food in the first of four stomachs, called a rumen. I have eaten deer, moose, and elk several times, and they definitely have flavor. (Sometimes they have way too *much* flavor.) But I have yet to lay eyes on a deer, moose, or elk steak that marbles anywhere close to Choice, let alone Prime. There is only the faintest streaking of fat to be found in the loins of a wild ruminant. So why is their meat so flavorful? Elk, deer, and moose, furthermore, all taste different from one another. You can raise an elk in a pen next to a moose, feed both animals the same food out of the same bucket, and they will taste different. Something of their *essence*—whatever it is that makes a deer *a deer* or a moose *a moose*—can be detected and appreciated by the tongue. Cows, by comparison, seemed lacking in character. What was going on?

Two hundred miles north, I found a man who claimed to have the answer. Allen Williams is a former varsity meat judger for Clemson University as well as a former NCAA wrestler, and though he is decades removed from the ring, he appears every bit as compact and sure-footed as he must have been in college. He is also a PhD meat scientist, though he abandoned the ivory tower more than a decade ago, his exit fueled partly by disgust at what was happening to his profession.

Williams met me in Sedan, Kansas, one of the prettier versions of small-town America that sits plunk in the middle of the Flint Hills, where David Bergin's great-grandfather's cattle used to come to get fat. Little and big bluestem grasses still grow as thick as the fur on a dog in fields next to the highway. In the distance, the rising and dipping prairie looks to be upholstered in suede. I told Williams I'd been driving through Texas and Oklahoma, eating steak. "How was it?" he asked.

"Disappointing," I said.

"I'm not surprised."

Williams said he could tell me precisely what was wrong with the steak I'd been eating and suggested we go out and talk about it over steak. I hopped in his pickup truck and we drove back over the Oklahoma border and pulled in to a local steak house that, many years ago, had been demolished by a tornado—a legitimate risk for any long-lived Oklahoma business. We sat down in a low, comfy booth and ordered rib eyes. As they cooked, Williams told me about the steak I was about to put in my mouth.

"There is a ninety-nine-percent chance—perhaps even greater—that your steak was raised in the conventional manner," Williams began, in a tone that wasn't what you would call appetizing. "What we cannot know is the ranch it originated from," he continued, "or how old it was. There is no traceability." Here's what we did know: it was probably born on a ranch, implanted with a growth hormone—most likely Ralgrow or Synovex—when it was two or three months old, taken rudely from its mother at seven or eight months and sold at an auction barn, and then removed to one of two places: a stocker operator, which is basically a big farm or ranch, where it would have eaten grass for the next few months; or a grow yard, which is like a feedlot for young cattle. (A grow yard is to a feedlot as juvy is to prison.) More hormones were injected. When the calf reached 750 to 850 pounds, at around twelve to sixteen months of age, it was taken by truck to a feedlot to start eating corn, where it would have received two more hormone implants along with something called a beta-agonist—likely Optaflexx—which caused it to gain even more muscle mass.

Bill O'Brien believes flaked corn to be a perfectly natural thing for cattle to eat. Allen Williams does not. I presented him with O'Brien's study, the one put out by the International Center for the Study of Bovine Happiness, which concluded, "The proposition that grain is an unnatural and unintended foodstuff for cattle is proven plainly wrong." Williams looked it over carefully. "These guys aren't scientists," he said. "They're idiots. They are bloomin' idiots." You might say the study was abundantly marbled with experimental flaws. After enumerating those flaws—no university attached, no evidence of review of previous literature, sample sizes skewed, on it went—Williams made a more general point about corn: "It doesn't exist in nature." Before humans came along roughly ten thousand years ago, there was no such thing as grain. Humans coaxed grasses into growing abnormally big and starchy seed heads—rice, corn, wheat, and barley are all big, starchy seed heads— which they then harvested and ate and, eons later, steamed and flaked and fed to cattle. Before that, cattle would have only ever eaten the comparatively smaller seed heads that grow on wild grasses, and then only in mouthfuls that would have included lots of grass. He concluded the critique thus: "Where does nature provide a concrete trough full of flaked corn?"

Corn, it so happens, can actually kill cattle. It contains such a concentrated explosion of starch that, when fed in sufficient quantity, it can result in all sorts of mortal ailments. Corn can cause a cow's liver to abscess, which can lead to death. Its rumen can become gassy and inflate like a balloon, ultimately pressing on the lungs to such a degree that the cow suffocates and dies. A cow's rumen can become extremely acidic, a condition called acidosis. "In bad cases," Williams said, "what you'll notice is a very nasty anal discharge. There will be blood, and a loose, discolored discharge with a foul odor. The animal is passing the endometrial lining of its gut."

Roughly 98 percent of cattle do live to see the day the truck from the packing plant pulls up because antibiotics are mixed in with the feed to keep livers and guts from failing. A certain number are fated to die, however. Feedlot nutritionists, Williams explained, actually want to see a small percentage get sick, as "that way, they know they're pushing the feed ration to the edge." The ones that aren't dying are getting fat fast.

The survivors don't taste particularly good. All those hormones don't help, and neither do beta-agonists, both of which conspire to bulk up cattle and make beef cheaper. According to sensory evaluations, their meat is less palatable and tougher. Corn is also a problem, according to Williams. "It's just bland, empty starch. It doesn't produce a rounded flavor profile."

Perhaps gravest for the steak eater is the fact that the cattle are stressed. "They're on a ration that's pushing them to the edge," Williams said, "living in muddy conditions—if it isn't muddy, it's dusty—and living day after day in a confined pen. They can't run or jump. Men on horseback called pen riders come into their pens and pick out the ones that have gotten sick or died. Every day, they see their buddies get dragged off. Their endocrine gland is producing cortisol, the stress hormone. They're full of adrenaline. Lactic acid is building up in their muscles. Their guts are acidic. It all has an effect on flavor."

I then posed what felt like either a very smart or a very stupid question. "Do cattle feel stress?"

"Of course they do," Williams replied. "We know that they can feel fear, and they can feel anxiety. Cattle can sense fear and anxiety in other cattle. It's stupid of us to say that they don't."

The rib eyes arrived. Like so much commodity steak, each bite started with a pleasant burst of warm fat that was followed by an abrupt absence of flavor, followed by a gentle but undeniable sour note that lingered on the tongue. This particular restaurant flavors each steak with seasoning salt, and without it our two rib eyes were drab and boring.

Williams wasn't interested in eating his steak so much as looking at it. By its size, he could tell it had come off a cow with at least some continental genetics, because cattle breeds from continental Europe—which all have exotic-sounding names like Charolais, Simmental, and Limousin—are bigger and grow faster than cattle from the British Isles. He stared at his plate, and then at mine. "My rib eye was cut closer to the chuck, and yours was cut closer to the loin," he said. "Always take the rib eye closer to the chuck." The reason for his preference is that there's more spinalis and multifidus at the chuck end. (The chuck is butcher talk for the shoulder.) A rib eye consists of a circle of muscle called the longissimus, which runs all the way along a cow's spine. Sitting on the longissimus like a thatch are the cap muscles, the spinalis and the multifidus lumborum thoracis. The two latter muscles, Williams claimed, are among the most tender and flavorful on a carcass. "The fibers are flat, and flat fibers have lower shear force tests."

When Williams finally bit into his steak, he had this to say: "My longissimus is pretty chewy." But if chewiness is a consequence of low-cost beef, there is a low-cost solution. It's called tenderizing, and Williams described the surprising number of ways in which chewiness can be removed from beef. One method is called blade tenderization. A steak is sent on a conveyor belt and, at a certain point, slammed from above by a bed of needles. It still looks like a steak but is now as perforated as a kitchen sieve. Sometimes entire sides of tough beef are electroshocked, which likewise destroys muscle fibers. "They give it a good jolt," Williams explained, "and the whole side of beef will jump." Another way around the problem is to soak the steaks in enzymatic brine. (I later came across a frozen steak from Walmart with a label that read, "tenderized with ficin and bromelain," both of which are enzymes that break down protein.)

Williams despises all such methods. "If you've ever eaten a steak that tasted mushy, it was because it was tenderized." He had nothing good to say about the major steak house chains, either, and pointed out that all of them—even the expensive ones, which supposedly serve steaks of unparalleled quality—use commodity beef.

And yet, for a man so appalled by the current state of steak, it remains his favorite meat. He is as beef loyal as they come, eating steak three times a week, with no plans to stop. Unprompted, he began talking about how much he loves the rib eye's cap muscles. "I've always wanted to take the cap, unwrap it from the longissimus, and make it its own steak," he said, sounding as dreamy as a former college wrestler can sound. "That would be the best steak. There's no question about it."

The discourse on terrible steak continued at a nearby sports bar called Hoops, where nine television screens were displaying all manner of competitive team activity, none of which involved meat judging. We sat on stools at a round table in the glow of televised women's college basketball. "Now comes the part I hate about eating a grain-fed steak," Williams said. "I feel heavy, almost sick. We have just consumed a lot of saturated fat. Now that absorption has started, we're feeling the impact. I want to cleanse my mouth."

I decided to cleanse mine with a glass of red wine. At a sports bar in small-town Oklahoma I was offered a choice of merlot, cabernet sauvignon, or zinfandel. As I sipped cabernet sauvignon, Williams talked. He told me that beef was symptomatic of an agricultural sector gone wrong. "We're trying to grow everything too fast. Not just beef, but chicken, pork, fruit. The new varieties all grow too quickly to ever develop a flavor profile. Peaches are all rock-hard and have no aroma. A peach with no aroma—what the heck is that? You should be able to smell it from a ways away."

As his accent attests, Williams grew up on a farm in the foothills of the Blue Ridge Mountains, and he can reminisce as well as anyone about the way fruit used to taste. As a boy, he would walk down the road to visit his uncle—"all the houses up and down the road were all family"—to eat scuppernongs, an American species of grape. "I would stand under the vine and eat for hours and hours. I would go to the edge of the woods and eat muscadines—another kind of grape—that grew on the trees like trellises." He told me about a tomato farmer in California, a man with tomato acreage that feeds thousands. The farmer grew technologically up-to-date commercial varieties that were big, plump, and red. But he kept none for himself. Instead, he had a separate garden where he grew old, slow-growing varieties. These tomatoes had flavor. These tomatoes were reserved as the family's personal stash.

Williams's disillusionment with food set in around the same time as his disillusionment with academic life. In the 1990s, he noticed that government funds had started drying up, and meat scientists began getting more and more of their money from large food and drug companies. "The research is bought and paid for," Williams told me. "They're taking agribusiness dollars and regurgitating back to agribusiness what agribusiness wants to hear about its products."

By the mid-1990s, Williams was an associate professor, with publications in journals that meat scientists deem impressive—the *Journal of Animal Science*, for example, and the *Journal of Heredity*. A pharmaceutical company had developed a new pregnancy detection product for dairy cattle and was eager for it to be tested by universities in the hopes that positive results would lead to FDA approval. The company offered grant money, and Williams bit. When he performed his experiment, however, the results suggested the product did not work, and Williams wrote an abstract saying as much, and planned on presenting the results at an upcoming conference. The head of his department dropped by his office one day, sat Williams down, and told him to pull the abstract. "It was very matter-of-fact," Williams recalled. His boss reminded Williams that the company had paid for the research and it was the firm's data. Williams argued that the university was a public institution, funded by taxpayers, and that it was in the interest of science for the data to be made public. "My argument didn't win," he said. In 2001, he left academia.

"So how *do* you grow good steak?" I finally asked.

"Feed them grass."

With that, Williams launched into an encomium to grass-fed beef that was as all-encompassing as his critique of grain-fed beef had been. Grass, he said slowly, deliberately, is the kind of food cattle would eat—

and did eat—in a state of nature. Grass does not cause their livers to abscess, or their rumens to turn acidic. When a cow eats grain, the fat in its body becomes saturated—greasy and artery-clogging. When a cow eats grass, on the other hand, its fat is more like the fat you find in wild salmon, and is generally considered healthier. Grass-fed beef, furthermore, tastes the way beef is supposed to taste. "It should have a slightly sweet and sort of nutty flavor," Williams told me. "But with a discernible beefy robustness."

Grass covered the Flint Hills the way peel covers an orange. It had drawn Allen Williams north from his home in Mississippi just as it had attracted cowboys and cattlemen back when the Welshman from Pontypool named David Christopher Jones moved to Texas to raise cattle. Williams had cattle, and they were feeding on that sacred range. They were eating big and little bluestem, gamagrass, Indian grass, buffalo grass, crested wheatgrass, and needle grass.

Unfortunately, those cattle weren't anywhere close to being fat. The grass was ready to be eaten, but the cattle were not. Like the California farmer's private reserve of tomatoes, grass-fed cattle take longer to ripen. In cowboy parlance, they just don't finish all that quickly.

My chances of finding grass-fed beef, I reasoned, would be better back in Texas. Since that state has more corn-fed cattle than any other—some 2.5 million—it might also have at least a few cattle that still ate grass. I tested that presumption on the Internet and eventually found a chain called Saltgrass Steak House. Judging by the description on its Web site, it was perfect.

Our story goes back to the mid 1800s, when millions of Longhorn roamed freely throughout Texas. With the taste of beef becoming a newfound favorite in the North, Texas ranchers prospered as never before. Each winter the Longhorn were driven to the Texas Gulf Coast to graze on the rich coastal saltgrass. And when they headed for market, they followed the legendary Salt Grass Trail, known far and wide for the best beef in the whole Lone Star State.

After consecutive days of eating steak, the prospect of grazing on salt grass—fibrous, colon-cleansing salt grass—seemed appetizing. But the prospect of beef that was, as Williams put it, sweet and nutty but with a discernible beefiness sounded even better. I pictured a herd of longhorns on a salt marsh, the sun shining, a breeze blowing through their fuzzy ears. They would lift their great horned heads upward and chew, gazing out into the gulf, listening to the sound of surf crashing on the shore. I was salivating.

The man who answered the phone at Saltgrass Steak House could not say precisely what salt marsh the cattle were grazed on, so I asked to speak to someone who did know the answer. Another man soon got on the line and told me that Saltgrass Steak House used feedlot beef.

I wasn't totally out of luck, however, because 250 miles south in northeast Texas was a man named Ted Slanker growing cattle on historically significant grass. He was situated almost on the banks of the Red River, the very same river that stars, with John Wayne, in the movie *Red River*.

I drove to Slanker's farm, which is near the town of Paris, Texas, parked the car, and waited for him under a spreading oak tree. A red-and-white bull stood on the other side of an electrified fence, the wire no thicker than string. I couldn't help but notice the size of the bull's testicles, and in keeping with their magnitude, he didn't take the slightest interest in me. His nose was glued to the ground, tearing off clump after clump of green grass, not even pausing to chew. The air smelled clean and herbal. Birds were singing. A chicken goose-stepped across the gravel path in front of me, hunting insects.

Slanker came into view, seated behind the wheel of an electric golf cart that was bobbing up the gravel drive, its wheels sloshing through small puddles. He pulled up wearing a blue shirt, rubber boots, and a baseball hat, and invited me into the golf cart for a tour of the farm.

Slanker got right to the point. "Grain," he said, "is the atomic bomb of the American food system. There is no worse food you can eat than grain." As Ted Slanker sees it, the human race's fall from paradise can be traced to a particular time and place: ten thousand years ago in the Middle East, when it figured out how to grow grain. Up until that point, all the food that had sustained humans came in the form of green leaves or animals that ate green leaves. "See all this green stuff growing," Slanker said, gesturing to a grass-covered field. "That's the foundation food for animal life. . . . The first sustainable life-form," he told me, "was a one-celled green plant in the oceans. The first animal to come along to eat this one-celled plant would have picked up certain fatty acids from the plant and put them in its own membrane. These are called essential fatty acids, and they're critical for cell function. Animals have been eating plants for probably a billion years. That's the way it's been, and that's the way it's going to be," he said with a tone of grand finality.

It is a life-and-death issue. A green leaf, Slanker said, is alive. A seed head is dead. A seed head is an inert package of starch intended to feed a sprouting blade of grass. Grain farming, as he sees it, is a distortion of nature. "You have to gather a bunch of seed heads and plant them. Then grass comes out of the ground, and you can't let any animals graze it. You wait till the grains appear, then you run out there and gather them all up, store them, and eat them year-round. That is just a huge distortion."

The result of eating grain, or eating animals that eat grain, is disease. "The minute a man deviates from green leaves, he's going to have dysfunctional cells, a damaged immune system, and vitamin and mineral deficiencies. Every single body failing—they call them 'chronic diseases'—can be traced to eating foods that don't follow the green leaf, grain being the number one.

"Grains have a terrible fatty acid profile," Slanker continued, in a tone that was more pulpit than soapbox, "and are universally contaminated with fungi. There are all these mental disorders these days—attention deficit disorder, schizophrenia, autism—and it's because kids are grain-fed from conception."

"What about arthritis?" I asked.

"Osteoarthritis is an autoimmune disorder—anything to do with immune dysfunction is tied to grain."

"What about cancer?"

"Absolutely. That's body failure."

Slanker is also a raging Beef Loyal. He consumes ten to twelve pounds of beef every week, and often two pounds in a single day. His loyalty extends only to his own beef, however, which is raised on green leaves and usually sits on his plate next to a pile of green leaves in the form of salad. He won't touch commodity beef and hasn't touched it for ten years, before which he was "a typical grain-fed American."

Judging by appearances, he is in fine health. The morning we spoke, he was sixty-three years of age, though if he'd told me he was forty-eight, I wouldn't have questioned it. He is lean and fit, the skin on his face is clear and wrinkle-free, and he zooms around his farm with the energetic bearing of an army colonel. From time to time, his joints give him trouble, but only when he eats starchy, grain-based foods.

We had spent more than an hour talking about grain, and I was now convinced never to eat the stuff again. But I wasn't in the mood for green leaves; I wanted steak. I wanted to eat Slanker's grass-fed, sustainable, as-nature-intended steak. "How does it taste?" I asked.

This is not the kind of question a person should ever put to Ted Slanker. "Right there," he answered, "you're immediately off track. Flavor," he told me, "is meaningless."

I tried again. "What would you say is the best steak you've ever had?"

"That's like asking, 'What was the most memorable time you filled your car with gas?'" When people eat steak, he explained, they shouldn't be thinking about flavor or juiciness, but should instead look at it the same way they approach buying fuel. "Maybe your car needs gas with eighty-seven octane? Maybe the air-to-gas ratio needs to be this or that? You should have the same concern about what you're dumping in your own body, which is what carries your brain around."

My ridiculous and unhealthy concern with flavor was nothing new to Ted Slanker; it was a mistake common among the grain-fed masses. "My daughter," he said, "who's coming on sixteen and thinks she's thirty-five, doesn't like seafood. I look at that as being childish and ignorant. Fish contains some fatty acids that go directly into the brain and are necessary for optimal brain function. You want to make sure there's no shortage whatsoever."

Slanker was not able to say whether or not I would like grass-fed beef—which, of course, was beside the point. "Some people," he said, "love it on the first bite, and some people can't stand it." It all depended on conditioning. Like everyone else, I'd been accustomed to corn-fed beef, which to Slanker tastes "like cardboard and glue." Some people think grass-fed beef tastes gamy, he said. Others say it's fishy, an attribute that Slanker attributes to the high amount of omega-3 fatty acids, which you find a lot of in fish like mackerel and salmon. And others consider it delicious.

I wanted to buy a steak. Slanker handed me a one-and-a-half-pound sirloin, saying, "This is one night's meal," and followed with a dissertation on how it ought to be cooked. The Slanker philosophy of cooking steak, it will come as a shock to nobody, also flies in the face of convention. "Low and slow," he said. "Warm it up to a palatable temperature. Charred meat is carcinogenic."

"Is a little char marking okay?"

"No. You don't want any sizzle. When my grill gets to two hundred degrees Fahrenheit, I know it's gotten too hot." He suggested I use a pan over low heat. He also suggested I cook the steak in macadamia nut oil, which contains more monounsaturated fat even than olive oil, as well as palmitoleic acid, which is said to lower cholesterol.

I left the farm. I had grass-fed steak. I had macadamia nut oil. What I needed was a pan and a source of gentle heat.

Deeming it unlikely that any steak house, restaurant, or diner would be willing to lightly heat a one-and-a-half-pound sirloin in macadamia nut oil, I found myself accommodations with a kitchen. The stove was electric, and on the smallest burner the lowest setting was one. I set it to three, placed the pan on the burner, and poured in a wide puddle of macadamia nut oil. I laid Slanker's grass-fed steak in the oil. Raw, it had a green, fecund smell, the smell of a just-mowed, well-fertilized lawn after a thunderstorm. A few minutes later, I discovered that three was too hot a setting. I could hear sizzle, and the side of the steak was gorgeously browned, caramelized, and carcinogenic. I flipped it and turned the heat down to one. The odor coming off was swampy. Ten minutes later, it was ready.

Ted Slanker said that people either love or hate his grass-fed steak. I fall into the latter demographic. The first bite was sour and tasted like algae. It was so tough as to seem bulletproof. I chewed and chewed, transferring it with my tongue from one set of molars to the other. Eventually, the swampy juice had all been wrung out of it, and I was rolling a wad of pulpy protein between my cheeks. After I swallowed, a metallic taste crept into my mouth. This, I thought to myself, is what healthy eating is all about.

After four bites I threw the steak into the garbage. Five minutes later, a swampy aftertaste floated into my mouth like a stubborn green fog. Coffee could not cut through it. Orange juice could not undo the damage.

As I drove to the airport in Wichita, Kansas, the next day, I gave some thought to my quest. It wasn't going well. I had always thought of myself as a Beef Loyal. Was I, really? I didn't much like the steak in Texas. I didn't like the Prime steak I ate in Oklahoma City. And Ted Slanker's Red River swamp beef was awful—even worse than the Mongolian bootleather steak. I asked myself, What do I feel like eating right now? Not steak. I pictured fish grilled in a pan with lemon and herbs, boiled new potatoes, and a fresh green salad. I was starting to sound an awful lot like a Variety Rotator.

There was a time in my life when the best news I could have heard was my father saying, "We're having steak for dinner." He used to go to the butcher shop and pick out different cuts so we could cook both and decide which we preferred. But as miles of midwestern highway ticked along, I came to the realization that my youth had been filled with foods I don't like anymore. Most vividly, I could recall an intense love of McDonald's Big Macs. I remember being ten years old, on a rainy canoe trip at summer camp—wet, cold, hungry—and almost weeping over the thought of a Big Mac. Now, I don't eat them. Now, a Big Mac tastes to me like salty-sweet mush, like something designed to be squeezed through a feeding tube to someone with impaired taste buds. Was the same thing happening with steak? Was I turning into one of those people who goes to a nice restaurant and orders the sea bass?

Did I even *like* steak? After five days of eating nothing but, not a single steak struck me as good. The best steak I'd eaten was also the cheapest—at the El Vaquero. Unlike the others, it wasn't sour, but you'd hardly call it beefy. I had only one culinary reason to return to Texas, and that was for the El Vaquero's grilled hot pepper.

I had another question: Is there *other* steak? Is steak universally fungible? Does the rest of the world think of steak as a widget? Is a Texas steak the same as steaks in other countries? What about the steak I ate on my honeymoon in Tuscany? Would I still consider it to be good? Or did the Italians mask it in some masterful sauce? People talk a lot about Japanese Kobe beef, the raising of which, they say, involves the Japanese massaging their cattle with rice wine and giving them cold beer to drink. Only a few people I know have actually eaten Kobe beef, and they are all in agreement that it is sublime. Is it? And what about France? People accuse the French of thinking they know everything, but when it comes to food, it isn't so much an accusation as a statement of fact. What does a French steak taste like? And what about an Argentine steak? The best steak my brother ever ate was in Argentina, and when he talks about it, he enters a state verging on delirium.

Maybe my Pakistani cabdriver was wrong. Maybe the best steak in the world wasn't in Texas. Maybe the best steak in the world was even now being fattened, cooked, or eaten in some other country, on some other continent. As Kansas prairie drifted by, acre after acre after acre, it seemed to be telling me this: *The world is very big. There must be quite a lot of steak out there.*

It couldn't hurt to go out and have a look.

CHAPTER TWO

FRANCE

In the beginning, there was no steak. For more than four billion years, the world got on just fine without it. Steak did not become a possibility until sixty-five million years ago, when a six-mile-wide chunk of rock hurtled past Jupiter and kept right on hurtling until it plunged into the Gulf of Mexico and, a fraction of a second later, butted heads in a most severe way with Earth's crust. The subsequent boom was equivalent to three hundred million nuclear bombs going off all at the same time in the same place. It caused earthquakes and thousand-foot tsunamis. It sent rocky debris up in the air that hurtled down as fireballs and ignited unimaginable wildfires. It lifted a fog of hot dust and ash into the atmosphere and choked off the sun's life-giving rays.

When the dust cleared, the dinosaurs were no more, but one life-form's loss is another's gustatory gain. By that point, carnivorism had already been raging for hundreds of millions of years, but the movement reached its all-time peak during the Cretaceous with the meat-loving dinosaurs like *Tyrannosaurus rex*. The meat they ate came from other dinosaurs, mainly, and it probably tasted something like chicken. A few of them may have gobbled the odd mammal, but mammals had yet to distinguish themselves. The biggest one was no larger than a groundhog, and you don't get much steak from a groundhog.

Not until fifty million years after the great impact did a mammal worthy of the grill first appear. It was the size of a dog, it had horns, and it may have tasted something like beef, or possibly deer, bison, lamb, or elk—its flavor is forever buried in the geological strata of evolution. This mammal had a special skill. It was capable of digesting a flowering plant that was new on the scene: grass. Back then, there was a lot of grass, but eating it was usually out of the question because the cell walls of grasses are made out of cellulose—wood, basically—which enjoys the twin distinctions of being the most abundant organic compound in the world and one of the most difficult to digest. If a human, dog, cat, or monkey eats grass, it comes out the other end looking a lot like it did on the way in, having yielded almost none of its energy.

The only living beings that are truly adept at breaking down cellulose are microbes, and these tiny organisms are the secret to the success of those dog-size grass-eating mammals, which invited microbes to live rent-free in their stomachs. They accomplished this by evolving four stomachs, the first of which is a dank cavern called a rumen, which you can think of as a big fermentation vat. Chewed-up plant matter goes in, and microbes contentedly attack it, breaking it down into digestible forms of energy. An animal with a rumen is called a ruminant. Cattle are the most well-known ruminants, but it's a big club, including moose, elk, gazelles, giraffes, sheep, antelope, and bison as members. Horses eat grass, but they are not considered ruminants because they don't have rumens; their microbes live at the other end of their digestive tracts.

A half million years ago, a new ruminant appeared in the grazing lands of Asia and Europe, and it was enormous. It stood six feet at the shoulders and weighed 1,800 pounds. The males were black with a gray stripe running down their spines called an eelstripe. On their massive heads, they carried a set of horns—crescent shaped, forward pointing, and turned up at the ends. In a dead sprint, a big, angry male could reach thirty-five miles per hour, horns first, followed by a ton of galloping bone, hide, and muscle.

This was a fact that a hungry Paleolithic human, cowering in the bushes and staring at a herd of 1,800-pound beasts, could not help but have been mindful of. Even so, Paleolithic humans hunted and ate these fearsome creatures, which are called aurochs. They chased them, ambushed them, trapped them, or lured them into pits and then speared them. Around ten thousand years ago, somewhere in the Middle East, humans tamed the aurochs, herding them and goading the mothers into sharing their milk. There is a word for tame, milk-sharing aurochs: cattle.

Humans now owned herds of plump cattle, but they kept on hunting their wild forebears, and over the millennia, aurochs' numbers dwindled. They achieved a kind of mythical status among Europe's hunting-obsessed aristocrats and were tracked to the remotest corners of the continent, where they could still be found and killed. Finally, in the year 1620, on a game reserve in Poland, the sole remaining aurochs bull died. Seven years later, the last female joined him. The wild aurochs, forever extinguished, was cursed by a characteristic that proved to be its undoing: it was delicious.

Despite the veggie-friendly urgings of lentil-eating university coeds and the grumblings of bearded vegans who lurk at the edges of cocktail parties, there is zero doubt that humans are designed to eat meat. Our digestion is too speedy, for one thing. It takes about thirty-five hours for a meal to pass through a gorilla, whose long digestive tract is designed to break down fibrous plants. A human, on the other hand, passes food in around twenty hours, which, digestively speaking, is only enough time to handle ripe fruit, certain vegetables—and meat.

Meat contains a great deal of protein, which humans require just to stay alive—to make new muscles, hormones, cells, hair, skin, eyelashes, fingernails, and so forth. Proteins themselves are constructed from amino acids. There are many different amino acids, but eight are considered essential for humans—not eating them causes problems ranging from lethargy and emaciation to impaired wound healing, reduced intelligence, and death. All eight essential amino acids can be found in plants, but almost never in the right balance. Wheat, for example, lacks the amino acid lysine. Legumes lack tryptophan, and pulses (beans) lack methionine. Steak, on the other hand, features all eight essential amino acids, as do chicken, pork, eggs, cheese, lamb, goat, rabbit, and so on.

Meat also contains the vitamin B12, for which there is no known vegetable source. (Vegans must take supplements to obtain it.) Vitamin B12 is required for the splitting of cells and the formation of blood. Without it, a human will show symptoms ranging from itchy tongue and migraine headaches to facial pain, mouth sores, memory loss, cognitive impairment, and spinal cord degeneration, which results in death. Primitive humans, it's worth remembering, couldn't take vitamin B12 supplements any more than they could peruse the produce aisle. They ate what they could pick or catch, and that often meant meat. From a nutritional point of view, nothing beats a dead animal.

As a species, we are in near universal agreement on this matter. Less than one-tenth of 1 percent of the world's population is willing to suffer through life as a vegan. Not a single major religion promotes veganism. There are parts of the world where people eat very little meat, but that is almost always because there is very little meat to be eaten. In every society, the rich eat more meat than the poor, but the poor nevertheless spend a disproportionate amount of their income on meat. They eat what's good for them.

The human brain stands as its own compelling argument for our need for meat. When parents raise their children as vegans, they put them at higher risk of slow growth and mild cognitive impairment. The human brain is extremely large, relatively speaking, about five times bigger than it ought to be, if you go by the brain-to-body mass ratios of typical mammals. A big brain is expensive, physiologically speaking. Like the engine in a sports car, it consumes a lot of fuel even when idling. Getting that much fuel from plants is a tall order, especially given our short digestive tracts. Somewhere along the road of evolution, a trade-off seems to have taken place. As our brains got bigger, our ancestors supported them by getting rid of their slow-moving, energy-hogging digestive tracts. This substitution has occurred elsewhere in nature: South America's capuchin monkeys are accomplished and intelligent hunters, and have big brains and small guts. So do dolphins. Cattle, by comparison, have small brains and enormous guts. From a design point of view, a cow is a grass-fermenting vat perched on four legs, while a human is a big, brain-stuffed head perched on two.

Some anthropologists believe it was the turn toward meat eating that set humans down the evolutionary road to intelligence. Consider this: humans still forage for plant food much the way chimps do. They go out and pick it. Hunting is a different story. While chimpanzees—our closest living relative among primates (our DNA is 98 percent identical)—hunt, they are known as "opportunistic" hunters. They will set out in search of ripe fruit, but if they happen to come across a colobus monkey or a newborn antelope hiding in the bushes, they will rip it apart with their bare hands and eat it with skin-tearing, bone-crunching glee.

Humans, by comparison, do not start their day looking for berries and just happen to kill a moose on the way home. Humans set out to find big game, and once they do, they stalk it and kill it. Humans hunt game with advanced tools, like spears or a bow and arrow (or, more recently, the Remington Model 700 BDL hunting rifle, which can fire a 7-millimeter-wide bullet at a speed of 3,110 feet per second). A hunt is a highly social event. It calls for strategy, planning, and cooperation. It requires some understanding—intuitive or learned—of how a hunted animal behaves. And it requires communication. If one human is trying to explain to another human the concept *I'll step out from behind that tree and start shouting. When it runs in your direction, jump out from behind the bush and throw your spear at its chest, at which point Larry here will toss the net over its head, whereupon, if your spear hasn't found its heart or lungs, all three of us will commence bashing its head in with rocks,* it certainly helps to have the benefit of subject-predicate sentences and at least a basic vocabulary.

When a human kills a big animal, he does not keep the meat all to himself but shares it with the rest of his tribe. While this gesture may seem altruistic and noble, a mark of the beginnings of civility—perhaps even the earliest stirrings of Scandinavian socialism—big-game hunters got something in return for their generosity: *prestige.*

The late anthropologist Marvin Harris coined a term for the human craving for meat: *meat hunger.* Ancient humans, who lived a calorie-burning outdoor lifestyle, would have experienced epic bouts of this longing. Being ancient, they're not around to describe the intensity of that hunger, or how they satisfied it. But some hunter-gatherer cultures, amazingly, have managed to run the gauntlet of history and come out standing. In some of the planet's more remote regions, people can be found who have not taken to planting seeds or milking ruminants but eat much the way early humans did, by foraging for plant food and hunting animals. Meat is an obsession shared by them all.

For the Kaingang of southern Brazil, meat is real food, and everything else is just a garnish. Bolivia's Siriono people feel the same way.

The Amazon's Canela people have one word for meat hunger and another word for regular hunger. When the !Kung of Africa run out of meat, they sit around talking about how much they miss it, no matter how great the abundance of mongongo nuts. In the jungle villages of Peru, Sharanahua women will refuse to have sex with the men if they don't bring home meat. Instead, they taunt them by wearing beads, putting on face paint, and cornering each man individually, tugging on his shirt or belt and singing, "We are sending you to the forest, bring us back meat." For the Sharanahua, the hunt is an "economic structure in which meat is exchanged for sex," according to the anthropologist Janet Siskind. She may as well have been talking about the Aché of eastern Paraguay, whose women cheat on their spouses with the hunters who've brought home the most meat. Prestige, it would seem, counts for a lot.

A human in the throes of meat hunger craves the hit of flavor and texture we are designed by evolution to relish. One of these flavors is umami, the so-called fifth basic taste, the mysterious sibling to sweet, salty, bitter, and sour that most people outside of Japan don't understand. There is no word in the West to describe umami, so we use the Japanese word, which means "deliciousness," though a more apt definition might be "meatiness." Put simply, umami is the taste of protein. The problem is that it's not quite that simple. Protein on its own has no taste. (Some proteins found in rare tropical plants *do* have a flavor—sweet.) But amino acids, which are the building blocks of protein, taste of umami, as do nucleotides, which are the structural units of DNA. (Strictly speaking, nucleotides don't taste of umami so much as amplify that taste.)

One amino acid is notably good at triggering the umami taste receptor: glutamic acid, which was discovered in 1908 by a Japanese scientist searching for the ingredient that made seaweed broth so perfectly savory. All humans like the way it tastes. When a clear vegetable soup adulterated with glutamic acid is dropped on the tongue of a newborn baby, it causes an acceptance reaction: there is lip licking, smacking, and sucking. Sweetened water causes the same reaction, but bitter and sour water do not.

Glutamic acid does not occur only in seaweed. There is quite a bit of it in your brain, for example, where it functions as a neurotransmitter.

There is also a huge amount of glutamic acid—not to mention many other types of amino acids—in live muscle and, hence, dead muscle, which is what meat is. If you take glutamic acid and turn it into a salt, you are left with a crystalline powder called monosodium glutamate, which is such a popular flavor enhancer that the world eats almost two tons of it every year.

A person afflicted by meat hunger also craves fat, which may turn out to be the sixth basic taste. (The research is pending.) Nothing adds mouthfeel to a piece of meat like fat. If there's an evolutionary basis to the USDA's fixation with marbling, it is that humans are programmed to crave and relish fat. Without fat, meat can be poisonous. When humans eat too much lean meat, they die.

This condition is called rabbit starvation and was experienced by nineteenth-century explorers in the Canadian arctic who attempted to live on wild rabbits, which are extremely lean. Explorers ate huge portions of rabbit meat, and yet, no matter how they stuffed themselves, they constantly fought a gnawing hunger. Seven days into their all-rabbit diet, they were eating three or four times as much rabbit meat as at the start of the week. By day ten, their guts would be so distended with rabbit meat that the bulge was visible through layers of clothing. Diarrhea, fatigue, and headaches followed. Expelling reeking breath, they would speak of a constant craving for fat. After a few weeks, they died.

As much as humans crave and relish meat, we are not as skilled at digesting it as true carnivores, such as cats. If cats had explored the Canadian arctic, they could have eaten as many lean rabbits as they desired because cats have livers that are designed to handle lots of lean meat. Humans do not. If more than 40 percent of our dietary energy comes from protein, our livers begin to buckle under the load, and toxins accumulate in the blood.

The calories in meat that matter come from fat. A gram of fat contains nine calories—more than double what a gram of protein or carbohydrates packs. No one is more aware of this than hunter-gatherers, who obsess over the quantity of fat in their food even more than the most neurotic, body-obsessed Pilates instructor. When they take down big game, they eat the fat around the organs, they render the fatty marrow out of the bones, and they eat the fat-rich brain. Unlike true carnivores, humans don't prey on the sick, the old, or the weak, because the sick, the old, and the weak are lean. Humans pick out the healthiest members of the herd—the biggest, fattest animals—as the wall of any hunting lodge will attest. When faced with the decision to choose prey, a lion or wolf chooses the diseased, the weak, and the scrawny, but a human is looking for specimens in their robust prime.

We like to believe that hunter-gatherers, ever attuned to and respectful of the pulse of the land, use every last bit of the carcass. This is often not true, and in cases of extreme leanness, they might not use any of it. The Pitjandjara people of Australia, to use one among many examples, will abandon an entire kangaroo carcass if no fat is found in the tail.

In the early 1800s, the American explorers Meriwether Lewis and William Clark set out on an epic voyage overland to the Pacific Ocean, and their journals feature a veritable subplot recording their encounters with fat. When an animal is killed, the level of fattiness is invariably noted. They find fat catfish, fat bears, and fat deer. One particularly fat buck, which was killed on Tuesday, July 31, 1804, had an entire inch of fat on its ribs. If anything, however, this obsessive reporting of fattiness is a testament to its scarcity. Some bison were so skinny, they didn't bother shooting them at all. Others proved to be so painfully lean that they harvested only the tongue and marrow and left the rest for scavengers, whose livers were up to handling that much protein.

Plains Indians killed their fair share of bison, sometimes by stampeding whole herds of them over cliff faces. Despite the pleasant mythology to the contrary, they, too, did not always consume the entire carcass. (Fossil evidence of not using an entire bison carcass dates to before European contact.) Bison meat composed up to 85 percent of the food they ate. It nourished them so fully that during the mid-1800s, Plains Indians were the tallest people on earth—almost a full inch taller than the comparatively undernourished white Americans at the time. Above all other cuts, they prized the bison hump, which is full of fat. White Americans prized it, too, once upon a time. During the nineteenth century, they served buffalo hump as a Christmas roast.

• • •

Humans have been hunting aurochs for as long as we've been human, but it took the French to make them fashionable. Modern humans, with our high foreheads, smooth brow ridges, pointy chins, and delicate frames, appeared for the first time about 200,000 years ago. But it would take another 170,000 years before humans set down a permanent reminder of the fundamental difference between the animals and us, when Stone Age people living in Europe began making paints out of earth, stone, and charcoal and drawing pictures on cave walls. What did art look like when, after 170 millennia, it finally stepped out of the void? What did our earliest artists paint?

Pictures of steak.

The steak was still on the hoof, as it were, in the form of paintings of aurochs and other meaty animals, including horses, bison, reindeer, an enormous deer called *Megaloceros*, and a variety of large four-legged game. In the most famous prehistoric cave—that of Lascaux—the aurochs are placed front and center. They even have their own room: the Hall of Bulls.

The caves sit so close to the present-day town of Montignac that it's hard to believe it took until the autumn of 1940 for modern, crop-harvesting humans—in this case, four teenagers and a dog—to have found the caves and those amazing paintings. Montignac sits in a picturesque patch of French countryside called the Périgord that looks tailor-made for aurochs. My train from Paris chugged through dense pockets of forest that opened into spreading valleys carpeted in pasture. Out in the fields, cattle, stooped over and grazing, looked like little lumps.

Finding parking at Lascaux is astoundingly easy considering that, in Europe, the amount of parking is inversely related to the age of a monument. Swaths have been cleared in the woods large enough to accommodate tour buses that lurch through the greenery like mastodons. From the ticket counter, I walked down a ramp, and a left turn took me inside the earth's crust and sixteen thousand years into prehistory.

The Hall of Bulls was dark and cool, a tranquil refuge from the world above. The sloping cave walls put the paintings right in front of you and connect the viewer to the painted subject more intimately than most art galleries do. It seemed as though Stone Age people were calling out to the natural world, saying, *Hey, we can paint you!*

The aurochs at Lascaux are so big, the sight of them made me flinch. Their form was both crude and masterful and captured the unnerving heft of these taller-than-a-human beasts. Technically, there are more horses than aurochs depicted, but proportionally the aurochs are three times larger than the other animals. They have the lead role, appearing almost as objects of worship. But in truth, these ancient images that had reached across the chasm of history to touch me were all certifiable fakes, according to the guide. The genuine caves sit two hundred meters away and have been sealed off from visitors, whose moist exhalations infected them with mold.

The guide was a friendly middle-aged Frenchman named Denis Tauxe who described the present caves as "a true reproduction" and felt that, from an experiential point of view, visitors weren't missing much, other than an always-sought-after sense of authenticity, which is something I hadn't been missing until I learned the apparently ancient cave I was standing in had been molded out of concrete in the early 1980s.

When the tour concluded, I invited Tauxe out for lunch. We headed down the hill to a little restaurant across the road from a herd of grazing cows. The special of the day was flank steak, which we both ordered, eating marinated mushrooms from the salad bar while the steaks were cooking. Within the hierarchy of Europe's many prehistoric painted caves, Lascaux is considered the Sistine Chapel, according to Tauxe. It dates from the Magdalenian Period, making it around fourteen thousand years younger than the oldest painted cave in Europe. This makes cave painting—however passé—the world's longest-lived artistic movement.

In France, discussions of art invariably turn toward the thorny subject of meaning, and Lascaux is no exception. Interpreters have long had a funny habit of asserting that nothing can be known about the beliefs and artistic intentions of an unknown people who spoke an unknown tongue more than ten thousand years before the beginning of history, and then they tell you precisely what the paintings mean.

One of the first theories about Lascaux was that the paintings were an attempt at a sort of hunting magic: depicting lots of animals in caves would cause more to appear out in the forest. (This is the prehistoric equivalent of writing in extra zeroes to the left of the decimal point on your paycheck.) Another theory held that the animals represented different clans, and that the caves depict an epic struggle between them. A more analytic approach revealed that horses tend to appear beneath aurochs, and stags above them, and that the color of their coats corresponded to their mating seasons, which led to the idea that the cave was all about fertility, creation, and cosmic cycles.

Dennis Tauxe, who has spent a considerable portion of his waking life in the fake Lascaux and even a little time inside the real one, thinks the paintings were inspired by their artists' religion. "The walls are not the story of their life," he told me. They are, he believes, a reflection of a long-lost people's dreams and myths. "The cave was a metaphysical place," he said, and it struck me as very French to associate the word *metaphysical* with prehistoric paintings. "It was almost like the first church," he added, popping another mushroom in his mouth. "Lascaux," he grandly announced, "is the memory of the culture of Lascaux."

The flank steaks arrived. They were a bit tough and a little thin in the flavor department. As I chewed, I wrestled with doubt. Were the paintings about hunting? Tribal warfare? The cycle of creation? Did the Stone Age hunters of Lascaux worship animal spirits?

Maybe. But maybe not. No one can say for sure.

But the paintings must have meant *something*. One unusual panel features a bison with its intestines spilling out of its gut charging a man with the head of a bird sporting an erection. If the man or woman who painted that painting didn't think it meant something, then all art is meaningless. The problem is certainty. Lascaux meant something to the people who painted it. But what?

I looked at the steak on my plate. The ancients probably contended with a fair amount of tough meat. Steak, it seemed to me, might have something to do with the images on those walls. The Siriono, !Kung, Sharanahua, and Aché, after all, are all hunter-gatherers, and they are all obsessed with meat. Could Stone Age hunter-gatherers have been any different?

Consider that predators make up a scant 3 percent of painted animals in European cave art. Seven lions and one bear inhabit Lascaux, as compared to around six hundred non-flesh-eating animals. Lascaux is about prey. Lascaux is about tasty-looking prey. There is not a scrawny or diseased aurochs on Lascaux's walls, even though scrawny, diseased aurochs were certainly roaming the forests of primeval Europe. Looking at the walls is not all that different from flipping through the pages of a hunting magazine: both are rife with picture-perfect specimens. The aurochs are all fat, vigorous, and in the prime of life. If there is a suggestion of fertility, perhaps it has less to do with the ancient obsession with the cosmic cycle of creation and more to do with the fact that big, four-legged mammals like deer and aurochs mate in the autumn, after months spent grazing on prime forage. The fat males are prepared to expend expendable calories battling it out to prove who is the mightiest. The females carry heavy reserves of fat to support fetuses, which gestate over the winter and hit the ground in spring, with a summer's worth of good foraging ahead of them. To a meat-hungry, fat-craving Stone Age hunter-gatherer, an autumnal aurochs is the best kind of aurochs there is.

So add the following theory to the pile: Lascaux is indeed a holy place, but it comes from an era when the line between church and steak house was not so easily drawn.

I asked Denis if any bones had ever been found at the caves. He said yes—reindeer bones. Reindeer are widely thought to have been the most common meat consumed by Europe's Stone Agers, because a lot of their bones have turned up at archaeological digs. More recent research suggests that the equation may not be quite that simple. The French biologist Dorothée Drucker, who teaches at the University of Tübingen in Germany, and who enjoys her steak rare, analyzed the skeleton of a young woman who lived during the Magdalenian Period in southwestern France, close enough to Lascaux that she may have even visited it. The remains of Magdalenian Woman were found in the banks of the Dordogne River underneath a limestone cliff, ringed by deliberately placed rocks. She was adorned in seashells and deer teeth that accompanied her into the grave sixteen thousand years ago—an archaeological indication that Magdalenian Woman was "socially privileged."

Nearby, the remains of prey animals were discovered—saiga antelope, horses, bison, and aurochs—all marked by signs of "intense butchery." The saiga antelope remains outnumbered the others, and the thinking had always been that Magdalenian Woman's people hunted saiga antelope regularly and deliberately, and hunted aurochs, horses, and bison the way chimpanzees hunt colobus monkeys—when the opportunity presented itself.

Drucker tested the theory by analyzing isotopes in the collagen in Magdalenian Woman's bones and comparing them with isotopes found in the remains of Magdalenian prey animals. The results were surprising: Magdalenian Woman, Drucker discovered, ate hardly any fish. She didn't eat much saiga antelope, either, because there wasn't evidence of much saiga antelope consumption in her bone collagen. What she did eat was a tremendous amount of steak. Sixty-eight percent of her protein came from large bovids—either aurochs or European bison. Given that Paleolithic humans ate huge amounts of meat—probably as much as three and a half pounds a day (though a Paleolithic serving probably included as much fat as lean muscle)—that means that during an average week, Magdalenian Woman downed almost four Texas Kings' worth of aurochs or bison meat.

Was Magdalenian Woman one of prehistory's greatest Beef Loyals? Did she eat better than the other women? Was she privileged? It is possible, especially given all that jewelry. In France, a wealthy husband is still sometimes referred to as his wife's *bifteck*. If she goes to a cocktail party and starts spreading unpleasant rumors about the man who got the promotion her husband deserved, people will say, *"Elle défend son bifteck"*—she's defending her steak. Maybe the hunter who flattered Magdalenian Woman with seashells and deer teeth also dragged home plenty of dead aurochs and bison and lavished her with back fat, bone marrow, and rib eyes.

Why would Stone Age hunters have prized large bovids? Because they were large, for one thing. Killing a big animal results in a great deal of meat, to say nothing of the prestige accorded the thrower of the winning spear. Fat had everything to do with it. During a Paleolithic winter in France, fruit and vegetables were scarce. If Magdalenian Woman didn't get a little over half her caloric intake from animal fat, she would have died. Fat was a winter-long obsession. And for a fat-obsessed hunter-gatherer, a bigger carcass is always preferable to a smaller carcass. Other things being equal, a bigger carcass will have more fat on it than a small one. There is a fine strip of back fat beneath the hide of a saiga antelope, but the strip of back fat underneath an aurochs's eelstripe is thicker, wider, and more filling.

Some evidence suggests, furthermore, that the larger a mammal is, the higher the percentage of body fat it will have. It is the consumption of small, ultra-lean rabbits that leads to protein poisoning, after all—though if you want lean, try eating a shrew. Blue whales, on the other hand, come wrapped in thick layers of blubber. When you consider that a big male saiga antelope tops out at 140 pounds and a big male reindeer at 700 pounds, an 1,800-pound aurochs would have provided hundreds of pounds of fat—fatty brain, fatty marrow, fatty organs, and fatty steaks—that could feed a tribe of cave-dwelling humans for weeks. An 1,800-pound aurochs, it hardly needs saying, would have earned its killer unimaginable prestige.

The aurochs painted on the walls at Lascaux, it comes as no surprise, look fat. None of them appear remotely scrawny, which, as far as portrayals of actual forest-dwelling ruminants go, is wishful thinking. As modern-day Texas cattlemen would put it, the aurochs look finished. (To get a better understanding of just how fat the Lascaux aurochs are, I later e-mailed some images to Allen Williams, the meat scientist I met in Kansas. Here is his response: "There is no doubt that the animals depicted in these cave drawings are fat animals. Their briskets are distended and full of fat, they have excellent fat cover over the ribs and in the rump area. They also have full 'barrels' or midsections.")

Denis Tauxe was almost done with his steak. In broken but usable French, I articulated my theory, ending on the thought that the biggest animals painted on the walls at Lascaux were the most delicious ones. He wasn't buying it. He countered, explaining that in some caves you find paintings of abstract shapes, which are neither edible nor delicious.

He warned me not to take a painting of an aurochs too literally. The caves, he said, do not depict "the everyday" and rarely feature representations of the weapons that did the killing, just the animals themselves. I parried, pointing out that modern hunting lodges are much the same: you see the heads of deer, elk, moose, and so forth mounted on their wood-paneled walls, but rarely will you find a Remington Model 700 BDL mounted next to them.

With an air of finality, Tauxe declared, "You can represent Christ without eating Christ."

"That's true," I replied, and we both sat there in silence for a few seconds until I was struck by the obvious and ironic flaw in what he had just said. "But people *do* eat Christ," I said, pointing out that good Christians eat his body and his blood on a weekly basis. Tauxe laughed—briefly—but was unswayed. The steaks were finished. Across the street, cows were still grazing.

The roads near Lascaux are old. Not Paleolithic old, mind you, but old enough that they're not bound by the straightedge of some government planner. They wind through forests and next to rivers, and burst suddenly and gloriously over the crests of hills where you can catch panoramic snapshots of the up-and-down. More than 250,000 people visit Lascaux every year, and spillover demand has helped other Stone Age tourist attractions take root. I stopped in at Préhisto Parc, where an open-air walking tour takes visitors past dioramas of Neanderthals and prehistoric humans killing animals. Neanderthals are typically cast as the inveterate morons of the prehistoric world, but Préhisto Parc sheds light on their superb skill as hunters. They were intelligent enough to invent the bola, which they twirled above their allegedly crude-looking heads and hurled at the legs of stampeding prey, which, after tumbling into the ground, were speared. Dorothée Drucker conducted some isotope analysis on Neanderthal bones and found that they were, as she put it to me, "hyper carnivores," eating everything from woolly rhinoceros and woolly mammoth to deer, horses, aurochs, and reindeer. Some believe they ate almost as much meat, proportionally speaking, as cats, and if so they must have had livers that could handle such massive amounts of protein. A Neanderthal pang of meat hunger is something a modern human cannot conceive, though it is nevertheless fun to try.

I came upon one diorama of a Stone Age human with a dead rabbit slung over his shoulders entitled *The Hunter Returns with a Hare*, though it could have easily—and more accurately—been called *If This Hunter Doesn't Watch It, He's Going to Give Himself Protein Poisoning* or *Good Luck Getting Laid with That Pathetic Amount of Lean Meat*. Farther on, a sign addressed the prehistoric fondness for cave art by announcing: "The main motivation for this seems to have been the symbolic and not the aesthetic dimension." The aloof tone and fixation on the metaphysical seemed, once again, characteristically French. *How the hell do they know it was symbolic?* I mumbled to myself, more convinced than ever that the images at Lascaux were—at least in part—some early version of the still life, which is to say, *aesthetic*.

I got thinking about aurochs again. When European aristocrats hunted aurochs, the meat was considered a delicacy. It would be wrapped in aurochs hide and sent, as a gift, to the king. No one ever did that with a dead rabbit. An old Polish poem speaks of roasting a red aurochs calf for a wedding feast. Did aurochs taste exactly the same as modern cattle? Were they gamy, rich, strong, sweet? It's been almost four hundred years since the very last aurochs keeled over in Poland, and history has not left much in the way of adjectives.

Hours later, I drove north to a town called Nanteuil-en-Vallé, which, like so many small towns in rural France, was built to fairy-tale specifications hundreds of years ago. After refrigerating my insides with a beer at the local bistro, I stepped back into the greenhouselike interior of my car, headed down a country road past fields and woods, and pulled into a driveway where I was greeted by the most stylish-looking farmer I have ever seen. He had a trim haircut and was wearing green, svelte-cut overalls, the only such pair I have ever encountered. He shook my hand and smiled. His name was Xavier Chanssard, and he had something he wanted me to see.

We walked over some fields to the base of a small hill and found the first set of droppings: fresh, but no longer glistening. A good sign. We set off up the incline, and were not yet at the summit when horns came into view, skyward pointing and sharp enough to impale a falling apple. The beasts, evidently, had sensed our arrival and wandered over to sniff the air and assess the danger level. Their faces were dark, broad, and serious, on the verge of becoming annoyed that someone had interrupted their midday meal, but also curious.

Aurochs.

The herd numbered at least sixty, with a big bull, maybe 1,200 pounds, standing out in front. By the looks of things, they were all competing in a who-can-grow-the-biggest-horns contest, and the big bull was in the lead, his own set being thicker and curving out wider than any of the others. A blond eelstripe ran down his ample back, and he had more muscle hanging from one shoulder than could be harvested off my entire physique. The bull was walking heft. The bull was confidence wrapped in black leather.

Convinced that we represented the same threat level as the flies buzzing around his head, the bull sauntered off to join three smaller cows. Safe, I thought, but not for long, because a younger male with smaller horns—a male with something to prove—caught sight of me and set off my way. His pace was brisk, and as he approached he lowered his head and picked up speed. Horns pointed forward, he thrashed his head from side to side in the manner of a puppy destroying a slipper. I stepped back. The horns did not make contact, but it was hard not to imagine them shredding my skin, catching a loop of intestine and unraveling my insides. If I trip, I thought to myself, he could drop his shoulder on my chest and punch the air out of me.

The aurochs stepped forward and thrashed again. I now believed my life to be in genuine danger of ending. The moment was oddly philosophical. As the distance between my body and the aurochs's head closed, my thoughts turned to my young daughter. She would grow up explaining to people that her father was killed by an extinct species of primitive cattle in the south of France, a story that was equal parts romantic and ridiculous. I would not be the first *Homo sapiens* to perish at the horn of an aurochs, but I would definitely be the most recent. And it was all thanks to the Nazis.

•   •   •

The Nazis are notorious for their repugnant belief in the inferiority of human races other than their own. But the history books have been somewhat narrow in this regard, because the Nazis also applied their unsparing brand of prejudice to the animal world. Some animals, they believed, were better—more mighty, heroic, and noble—than others. While they busied themselves rounding up and killing Jews, homosexuals, and gypsies, they also tried their hand at creation. They invented an authentically pure German hunting dog called a Jagdterrier. They attempted to increase the numbers of Europe's rare yet massive—not to mention mighty, heroic, and noble—forest bison. And when in 1936 the Olympics came to Berlin, they opened an authentically German zoo that displayed wolves, lynx, and other appropriately Teutonic animals.

When it came to cattle, the Nazis knew just what the problem was: domestication. It had "weakened" the bloodline. Just as interbreeding with Jews and gypsies was ruining the Aryan race, so millennia of selecting dairy cattle with big udders and beef cattle with fleshy hindquarters and docile temperaments had brought about a species-wide decline. Modern cattle, in their view, were pallid beasts compared to their mighty forebears.

The Nazis wanted to undo the damage. Their goal: to repopulate *der Vaterland* with the mighty, heroic, and noble—but also extinct—aurochs. Two Nazi brothers believed they knew how to do it.

Heinz and Lutz Heck were zookeepers. Of the two, Lutz was more fully in the grip of the aurochs obsession, imagining herds of the dark, rippling beasts galloping through German forests and dewy meadows. Lutz Heck also happened to be one of history's most well-connected zookeepers, counting among his friends Hitler's second in command, Hermann Göring—who, among his many titles, held that of Reichmaster of the Forest and Hunt. For a man whose job it was to keep animals, Lutz Heck took surprising joy in killing them. A photo shows him hunting alongside Göring on Heck's private estate the year before he joined the Nazi Party.

The Heck brothers were quite aware that aurochs had been extinct for a very long time, but they believed that the species' vital elements existed still. Lutz explained it thus: "No creature is extinct if the elements of its heritable constitution are still to be found in living descendants." Traces of the aurochs, they were convinced, were scattered among the genes of domestic cattle. Just as weakness was bred *into* cattle, so it could be bred *out*: it was a simple matter of putting the right cows together with the right bulls and letting nature—glorious nature—take its course.

Heinz Heck appears to have been the lazier brother, if his aurochs resurrection program is anything to judge by. For genetic stock, he looked no farther than his own herd, a hodgepodge of breeds he inherited from his father (also a zookeeper). Brother Lutz had grander ideas. Believing that the purest, wildest cattle traits would be found among Europe's most ancient breeds, he set off across the continent on a mission to find and bring home primitive-looking cattle.

He happened upon his first specimen by chance in Corsica, where a one-eyed guide from a remote mountain village—"savage-looking but likeable"—was leading him on a search for a rare and wild sheep called a mouflon. They wandered into a river valley, and Heck spotted a reddish brown cow standing near some bushes. As he made a move toward her, the cow lifted her head and eyed him the way a wild African buffalo might. Heck crouched down and began stalking the creature, which silently slipped into the mountain wilderness and vanished. Lutz Heck bought three calves and took them to Berlin.

Next, he set out to procure the genes for enormousness. Aurochs were legendarily large, fast, and agile. A six-foot human would not be able to see over the shoulders of a big male aurochs without a step stool. Heck located the genes he was looking for in the Camargue, a chunk of French terrain between the Rhône delta and the Mediterranean that is home to a strain of cattle that had been saved from extinction by a flamboyant nobleman called Marquis de Baroncelli. For centuries, the French had used Camargue cattle for their bullfights, during which Frenchmen proved themselves by capturing woolen tassels hung from the forehead of a big bull. (Unlike the Spanish, Frenchmen have no need to prove themselves by slowly stabbing a bull to death in front of a paying audience.) Heck tracked down the marquis, and together the two men rode into the wilderness on a pair of small white horses done up in festive tack for the occasion. When they came upon a herd of Camargue cattle, Heck giddily noticed that their horns pointed forward and inward, a characteristic of true aurochs. After an afternoon of wine-aided persuasion, he convinced the marquis to part with a bull, two cows, and one calf.

In Berlin, Heck's Corsican and Camargue cattle were mixed with Spanish fighting cattle, for their angry temperament, a woolly-looking critter from Scotland, and various other breeds. He crossed them and crossed them again. He crossed some bull calves with their mothers, and he kept crossing the most aurochs-looking males with the most aurochs-looking females. And then one day, to Lutz Heck's great surprise and greater joy, an aurochs was born, eelstripe and all. Over in Munich, where brother Heinz was engaged in the same pursuit with his less exotic cattle, the very same miracle happened: a cow likewise gave birth to a calf that looked very much like a wild animal that had been extinct for centuries.

On a crisp, sunny day in the autumn of 1938, the Nazi aurochs fantasy became reality. Several trucks pulled in to one of Hermann Göring's favorite hunting preserves, backed up, and opened their doors. A big bull walked out into the bright autumn light and stood not far from Lutz, its horns glinting in the sharp autumn light. As Lutz wrote, "Its rapid and lively movements and its wildness, heightened by anger and agitation, were fine to see." The aurochs pawed the ground and sniffed the air. After a time, it nibbled tufts of grass and dropped turd. "The huge animal," Lutz Heck later wrote, "was a living picture of primeval strength."

The bull aurochs now thrashing his head back and forth inches from my tender belly was also a living picture of primeval strength, one apparently intent on turning me into a dead picture of modern weakness. More than half a century after the Nazis' demise, it seemed I was about to become their latest victim.

Chanssard intervened. Which is to say he casually extended an arm, grabbed the young bull by the horn, and shoved it away.

Like many in southwestern France, Chanssard lives in the thrall of prehistory. When he was fourteen, he volunteered on an archaeological dig and watched as the skeleton of a woolly mammoth was unearthed. He would be raising mammoth today if it were possible but has settled instead for a herd of aurochs. In the fall of 2003, almost sixty-five years to the day after aurochs were released on Göring's preserve, he bought four females and a single male—all descended from original Heck stock—and released them into his fields. He didn't see them again up close for three years. No matter how carefully he approached, he couldn't get within three hundred meters without the aurochs bolting. With time, they came to know him, and now, if they spot him from across the field, they saunter over for a visit. But Chanssard will not go near them at night, and he doesn't dare approach a mother with a fresh calf, because he is sure she would kill him. There are aurochs in Poland and Estonia, he told me, who get harassed by wolves. When the wolves approach, the aurochs bolt, then form a circle with their horns out, as musk ox do, protecting the little ones in the center.

Chanssard has other fields farther down the road, where he raises traditional beef cattle, a local breed called Limousins that could not be more different from aurochs. During the day, the Limousins will branch off into various groups, but aurochs always maintain the herd. If a single aurochs sits, the whole herd sits, but Limousins make no effort to coordinate their sitting and standing. When a Limousin cow gives birth, she does so in the middle of the field with everyone watching. A pregnant aurochs, on the other hand, disappears into the forest—Chanssard has no idea where they go—and returns several days later, her calf in tow. Aurochs run faster then Limousins, wear a thicker hide, and have a more desperate-sounding moo. Chanssard will not let the aurochs get near the Limousins, because he thinks they would attack and kill their delicate cousins. Compared to aurochs, Limousins are dunces. They don't remember who Chanssard is, even though they see him all the time, while the aurochs come up to him looking for a pat. He remembers them, too, and the memory of certain individuals causes him to tear up.

The male who almost gored me, Chanssard reassured me, was not trying to gore me. He was being playful. The bigger male had by now moved on to the water trough, where he was carousing with three cows nibbling grass. This bull was named Viking, and he was the chief. Just recently, he had dethroned Noel, whom Chanssard pointed out off in the distance. Even from where we were standing, the scrapes made by Viking's horns were visible on Noel's flank. Up until a few months ago, Noel had been number one, but not anymore. Sexually speaking, Noel's greatest days were behind him.

Responding to some silent bovine cue, the aurochs changed direction and drifted across the field and filtered into the forest on the other side. In less than a minute, they were gone, and if it weren't for their scattered droppings, no one would know they had ever been there. Chanssard and I followed them in. It was cool and still in the shade, and the forest floor was dappled with shafts of sunlight shooting down through the leaves. Even though it was possible to see hundreds of feet toward the other side of the forest, only three aurochs were visible. The rest were camouflaged, their eelstripes mimicking shafts of light, making their dark hides all but disappear against the ground. The silence was interrupted only by the occasional Paleolithic moo.

Aurochs will spend at least half of each day in the forest, Chanssard told me. They keep cool and brush up against trees to clear the flies off their hides. Tree trunks were showing blond wood where aurochs had bitten off bark.

We set out back toward the water trough, avoiding the odd pile of droppings. I turned to Chanssard and asked, "When can I taste one?"

"Tomorrow," he said.

Tomorrow was the annual Fêtes de la Ferme. Locals from far and near were coming to Chanssard's farm to eat and drink their fill of organic beef and organic beer. The day arrived tailor-made for an aurochs party, sunny with the odd cottony cloud bobbing in the blue above. Two weeks earlier, Chanssard had lured a three-year-old bull into a livestock trailer with that most non-prehistoric food: grain. Its steaks were about to be cooked on a similarly non-prehistoric contrivance: a Smithfield Pro-Cook. Egg-shaped and green, it was the largest outdoor grill I had ever seen. A metal base was matched to a metal canopy, and sandwiched in between was a circular grill that could be rotated, raised, or lowered by an electric motor, all in the name of heat management. Beneath it sat a layer of hardened lava rocks, and beneath them a colony of gas burners capable of exhaling BTUs in the hundreds of thousands. According to Chanssard, his Smithfield Pro-Cook was one of only ten in existence.

Guests were trickling in by late morning. Some sat at banquet tables underneath a big tent and drank beer while a few stood leafing through a photo album filled with pictures of aurochs. Next to it was a framed photo of an enormous black bull with a massive set of horns, a big neck, and enormous testicles hanging between his legs. The bull was looking into the camera, mean and serious, sporting the ultimate mug-shot pose. His name, Chanssard said, was Siber, and he had been the chief before Noel. His end was as tragic as it was abrupt. He was in the midst of enjoying the great perk of chiefdom—mounting an aurochs cow—when he lost his footing, fell off, broke his back, and died. Chanssard gets emotional just talking about it.

The guests wanted to see live aurochs, so Chanssard took a group over to a field where he found that two guests had already wandered out on their own, without his knowledge. Had he not shown up, there might have been goring and screaming. Aurochs were nowhere to be seen. The field was eerily silent, as though a spaceship had hovered over the farm in the middle of the night and vacuumed up every last beast into its hold. Chanssard cupped his hands to his mouth and let out a loud whooping sound. A second later, aurochs began streaming out of the woods. Chanssard walked over to Noel and slapped his blond eelstripe, sending a burst of dust into the air that smelled of wet, sweet leather. A swarm of flies was buzzing around Noel's head, as flies do in warm weather, and they descended, all at once, onto his steroidal shoulder. Chanssard took aim at the flies and slapped. Noel, however, who was looking the other way, mistook Chanssard's kindly slap for a fly, and jerked his head around, sending his pointed horn into the middle of Chanssard's forehead. The impact sounded not unlike an unshelled hazelnut being hit out of Yankee Stadium. Chanssard stood there, stunned, then steadied himself and announced that he was okay. The point of Noel's horn had left an impression in the skin between his eyebrows. Any more force, and Chanssard's forehead would be referred to in the past tense.

Back at the tent, the Smithfield Pro-Cook was, by now, very hot. Chanssard cut a big rib steak especially for me, and then an equally large rib steak—also for me—from a Limousin cow, the idea being that I would eat both and note the differences. As far as appearance, the two steaks were almost identical, both deep red with hardly any marbling, although the Limousin steak had little wisps of yellow fat on the side that the aurochs steak lacked. The Limousin steak smelled sweet and earthy, and the aurochs steak smelled beefy. I couldn't help but wonder, Was I actually smelling raw aurochs? Was the smell image in my mind identical to one experienced by Magdalenian Woman?

The Heck brothers may have thought so, but they were less than open about their program's imperfections. On Göring's game reserve, calves were often born that did not look sufficiently like aurochs and were shot in the name of purity. Most scientists are skeptical about the genuineness of the Heck brothers' creations, and would consider my referring to Chanssard's animals as "aurochs" to be charitable, if not incorrect. In these circles, they're known as "reconstituted aurochs" or "Heck cattle." In truth, not all Chanssard's aurochs look convincingly aurochslike. Some have dun-colored hides, or horns that point up instead of forward, and eelstripes that are the wrong color. All suffer from short, fat heads that should be longer and more slender; they are not as large as they ought to be—not by a long shot—and many of the females have outsize udders, which, as bovine traits go, is seriously domestic.

The difference in aroma that I had detected among the two steaks, furthermore, may have had more to do with gender than breeding. In America, bulls are almost never eaten because they're considered to have an unpleasant taste. I pressed Chanssard about the apparent phenomenon of unsavory bull beef. He said yes, bulls do taste odd, but only once they get to be about four years old. In France the taste of young bull beef is one that some steak lovers prefer. He took the raw steaks and placed them on the hot grill. They sizzled identically.

With the exception of the Smithfield Pro-Cook—which contained flagrant technological advances like metal forging and the extraction, storage, and transportation of natural gas—the scene was almost prehis-

toric. Male *Homo sapiens* congregated around the cooking aurochs flesh
and assumed the stance of lieutenants, flipping and prodding meat, but
only with Chanssard's permission. Female *Homo sapiens* sat at tables and
talked. To their undoubted disappointment, Chanssard, the prestigious
provider of aurochs meat, is not single.

When the steak was done, which is to say seared on the outside and
raw in the middle, I found myself facing an unusual and difficult moment. Among the Nazis' millions of victims were my father's family. On
July 4, 1941, they knocked on the front door of his home and took his
father, Henryk Schatzker, prisoner, made him dig his own grave, and
later shot him dead. By the end of the war, almost the entire family had
been exterminated. More than half a century later, there I was, sitting at
a table in the south of France, holding a fork in my right hand, on the
end of which was impaled a morsel of Nazi biological engineering.

I started thinking about my father. The Nazis took *his* father away
from him. Eating their racially pure steak seemed like the rudest kind of
affront to the life my father lived, and the life his father was denied.

I thought about the aurochs. Although one of them had almost gored
me, his playfulness, I had to admit, had nothing to do with my partial
Jewishness. Back on Göring's game reserve, the Heck aurochs weren't
exactly respectful of all things Aryan. They trampled some bicycles.
They commandeered a feed trough and gobbled hay and oats intended
for horses. They attacked a hiker, not to mention Göring's forest manager, a man I think we may safely assume was not Jewish. Aurochs are
equal opportunity gorers. So long as I made sure to visit them with their
much-loved keeper Xavier Chanssard next to me and didn't go near the
mothers during calving, they meant me no harm. There was a cube of
cooked aurochs muscle on the end of my fork, so if anything, the opposite was true.

(It also may be worth noting at this point that Göring's boss and the
greatest racist the world has ever known—Adolf Hitler—was a proud
vegetarian.)

I put the steak into my mouth. Aurochs, reconstituted aurochs, Heck
cattle—whatever you call them—make fine eating. The taste was not

gamy but had that quality so absent in the Texas commodity steaks: beefiness. It had other qualities, too, including an herbal note and an almost salty flavor, even though not a grain of salt had touched it.

The Limousin steak presented with a smoother texture, but took as long to chew. It was equally juicy—which is to say juicy, but not memorably juicy—and the flavor was sweeter, less powerful, and faded more quickly on the tongue. In short, it was milder.

The enormity of the two steaks turned out to be a nonissue. After several minutes of chewing and swallowing, I looked down and discovered I was over halfway through both and showing no signs of getting full. Another week of this, I thought, and my stomach would be as distended as an arctic explorer's. I took a sip of beer and ate a few forkfuls of fried potatoes. Then it was back to the steak.

The aurochs was flavorful. The aurochs was juicy. But it was not perfect. Maybe it was because the beast I was eating, having most recently grazed upon the thin spring forage, was lean. Maybe I was channeling Magdalenian Woman. Maybe I'd been eating too much lean protein—a seeming impossibility in France—and was craving kilocalories. Whatever the reason, the aurochs seemed deficient in a single attribute: it could have been a touch more fatty.

No one knows quite how the people of Lascaux cooked their meat, but of one thing we can be certain: French cuisine has come a long way. Over the intervening sixteen thousand years, during which time the French became diverted by wine, cheese, liqueurs, fashion, existentialism, and so on, their love of steak has stayed true. The country famous for pâté, quiche, and untold grand desserts may bring to mind visions of effete, beret-wearing Variety Rotators, but the French happen to be Europe's great Beef Loyals. They eat more beef than the Germans, the Italians, and the Spanish, and almost twice as much as the British. One French steak house chain, the Hippopotamus Restaurant Grill, has 121 locations in France, or one restaurant for every 500,000 French persons, a higher incidence of steak house than is found in the United States with Ruth's Chris Steak House (1 to 2.5 million), Morton's (1 to 3.4 million), and Lone Star Steakhouse (1 to 2 million). It is only slightly less popular than the Outback Steakhouse, which has erected one steak house for every 400,000 Americans. Another French steak house chain, La Boucherie (fifty-eight locations), lists a "Duet of Marrow Bones" on its menu, suggesting that aspects of the Paleolithic remain to this day in French cuisine.

The question is often asked: Of France's great many great dishes, which is the most French? A good argument could be made for *tartiflette*, a potato casserole from the Alps layered with fried bacon, butter, and melted cheese that is, even in France, a courageous celebration of fatty indulgence. *Confit de carnard*, which is French for herbed duck legs simmered for hours in hot fat and crisped under a broiler, makes an equally compelling case. As does *coq au vin*, in which a cut-up rooster is stewed in wine, mushrooms, and, if you can manage to find a butcher who sells it, chicken blood. But the best answer may be steak.

Roland Barthes, a heavy hitter among twentieth-century French intellectuals, was in the steak camp. His book *Mythologies*, one of the few easy reads in the movement known as structuralism, contains an excellent essay on the significance of steak in France. He describes it as "meat in its pure state," and, like wine, "steak is in France a basic element," one that "unites succulence and simplicity." In it, he attributes the "craze for steak tartare" to a belief that it is "a magic spell against the romantic association between sensitiveness and sickliness." Romantic sickliness aside, the relevant point is that I was in a country that has been known to experience crazes over certain forms of steak.

Steak may be the easiest meal to procure in France. It is most commonly served next to a heap of perfectly cooked French fries, a dish known both in and outside France as *steak frites*. You can order *steak frites* at service stops on any *autoroute* or take a walk through a leafy residential enclave and order it at one of the extremely charming bistros you will inevitably come across. Or you can reserve a table at a French steak house, the majority of which are not chain restaurants.

The more important question is, where can you get a *good* steak? France is just the country in which to make this kind of inquiry, being famous not only for food but for rating food. The field's long-reigning champ is the world-famous Michelin guide, published by the same folks that make the tires. No other rating guide carries anywhere near the critical heft of Michelin. The mere listing of a restaurant in the Michelin guide—name, address, phone number—is taken as proof that a competent chef is manning the stove. Better restaurants are awarded a cute little knife-and-fork symbol next to their names. One knife-and-fork symbol is good, two are better, and five indicate a luxurious restaurant of high quality. There is, however, a level of quality that exceeds even the boundaries of the knife-and-fork scale. Such a restaurant receives a more special honor: a star.

Here, you might think, Michelin's rating system would reach its limit. But it does not. Truly superb restaurants—kitchens that approach perfection in every aspect of creativity and execution—can actually earn *two* stars. Such establishments are rare, and if you should happen to find yourself within a one-to-two-hour drive of one, the guide advises that you take the detour and eat. (It is, presumably, acceptable in France to cancel an appointment due to unexpected proximity to an excellent restaurant.) Incredibly, there are restaurants that exceed the two-star rating. Such establishments do not warrant a detour so much as a trip on their own. These fantastic places—there are not many—are known as *three-star* restaurants.

It occurred to me that among all of France's good and great chefs, there was one who had more Michelin stars than anyone else. His name is Alain Ducasse, and the day I contacted his office, he possessed no fewer than fourteen, with two three-star and eight one-star restaurants. Besides operating a restaurant empire, Ducasse has written an encyclopedia of food—currently standing at five volumes—and has helped develop meals for the European Space Agency, so that descendants of Magdalenian Woman may eat "Shredded Chicken Parmentier" or "Swordfish—Riviera Style" as they orbit Earth.

Ducasse, clearly, was the man I needed to talk to. He is a man to whom a lot of people need to talk, however, and getting him on the phone is a tall order. His assistant, it turned out, is not only friendly but wields great power. She made the following suggestion to me: Instead of merely eating a good steak, why not learn to cook one myself? As suggestions go, this was pretty good. Give a man a restaurant recommendation, and he eats steak for a night. Give a man a sauté pan, and he can eat good steak for the rest of his life.

And so my search for steak took me to a bunkerlike edifice in a Paris suburb known as the Alain Ducasse Formation (ADF). Here, Ducasse's international team congregates and, dressed all in white, develops the advanced culinary weaponry—sauces, emulsions, searing techniques, and so forth—used in the battle for Michelin stars. There are four different kitchens at the ADF, all enormous and featuring dark countertops and stainless steel cabinetry. The look and feel is both luxurious and scientific, reminiscent of one of those secret laboratories you see in James Bond movies.

Assigned to me was one of Ducasse's top chefs, a friendly up-and-comer named Christophe Raoux, whom a personal ad might describe thus: "Strapping amateur rugby player who likes farms, abhors pretension, and can whip up legendary demi-glace." This is a man who, some years ago, had gone out for a walk during his break when two mysterious men attacked him and demanded his wallet. The first assailant he bested with a series of hard punches to the head. The second fled. Christophe returned to work with his face and shirt bloodied, but nevertheless ready to pare vegetables, braise meat, melt butter, and reduce sauces. His kitchen mates gave Christophe a round of applause, and the head chef instructed him to take the week off.

It hardly comes as a surprise that Christophe is a man who loves steak. He ate the best steak of his life at the age of twelve, and the experience left an indelible mark in his memory. The meal took place in the city of Vichy, a few hours' drive from Lascaux, where Christophe was visiting his grandparents. He was taken to a restaurant where an old woman who never spent so much as an hour at cooking school or reading about the latest in fusion spicing trends in some glossy magazine prepared traditional dishes in the traditional manner. Christophe ordered a rib eye, and it was served in a wine and mustard sauce. When he put the first bite in his mouth, he was struck dumb by how it tasted. "It had the taste of beef," he told me. "You could taste the hay. You could taste the nuttiness."

That steak had everything to do with the era, he explained. "It was a different time. Farmers still wore wooden shoes. No one raises beef now like they did back then. If you bought a steak, there was no invoice. If you ordered a whole cow, it was a handshake deal. They treated the cows with love. Now it's a business. It has nothing to do with feelings today."

The disappearance of feelings is something Christophe feels strongly about. The old woman from his memory had passed on, and the steaks in her fridge had long ago been cooked and eaten. The breed, on the other hand, is still around. It is called Aubrac, and is one of France's less famous beef breeds. Paris, luckily, is a city of considerable culinary diversity, and among its many steak houses we found one specializing in Aubrac beef. La Maison de l'Aubrac, which can be found on rue Marbeuf (Old French for "Beef Pond Road"), is rustic, woody, and cozy, and on its walls hang large photographic portraits of Aubrac cattle—snapped in a well-lit studio, by the looks of things. A huge and muscular bull stares straight out at diners. A cow, suckling a calf, is less menacing, but looks guarded all the same. After sixteen thousand years, the French still enjoy eating steak next to pictures of big cattle.

We drank half-pints of draft beer and studied the menu. For the main, I ordered an entrecôte, which is what the French call a rib eye, and for a starter chose steak tartare. I was going a bit heavy on the steak, but the waiter assured me that my order—raw steak followed by cooked steak—was not unusual in the slightest. I wanted to understand what the "craze" mentioned by Roland Barthes was all about. In a few minutes I had my answer: texture. The raw, chopped Aubrac beef arrived next to a pile of potatoes—sautéed in beef fat, and among the top five most delicious potatoes I have ever eaten. The steak tartare was cool and smooth to the point of silkiness. My teeth didn't chew the meat so much as massage it. Swallowing proved unexpectedly soothing.

It was tasty, too, but that had to do with the spices, egg, mustard, and other ingredients that had been added to it. Raw steak on its own is bland, tasting gently of blood and not much else. This culinary fact is something Magdalenian Woman could have told you because she did not eat her aurochs raw. Even monkeys—who do not, as a rule, know how to cook—prefer the taste of cooked beef to raw beef. Cooking is what gives steak its flavor. Cooking makes sweet things sweeter and meaty things meatier. We seem to have been designed to prefer cooked food long before we developed the concept of medium rare. When humans discovered fire, their world became more delicious.

Steak tartare, being raw, is not heated. But it is still steak. Better restaurants, Christophe assured me, use the tenderloin, of which there are two on a cow, each running along the underside of the spine. The tenderloin is the tenderest muscle on a cow, and the reason is that it is lazy. Its job consists of supporting the spine—posture, basically. It doesn't do any of the heavy lifting, and that's just what you want in a steak. Do not look for such toothsome muscles on or near the legs, because legs do the work on a cow, and those muscles feature thicker, tougher fibers as well as more connective tissue—the silvery white sheetlike substance that holds everything together and is extremely hard on the jaw.

Arguments about steak always circle around protein and fat, but there is more water in steak than anything else by a country mile. Meat consists of bundles of muscle fibers wrapped in connective tissue with a dappling of fat. All that water is locked inside muscle, and good luck getting it out. The reason the steak tartare tasted silky was because no matter how much pressure my molars exerted—up to 300 pounds per square inch—the water stayed locked in the steak. If you want to get it out, you need heat.

That heat was in the kitchen, being applied to my entrecôte—which comes from a long muscle running along the top of a cow's backbone. As I swallowed forkfuls of tartare and sautéed potatoes, heat was causing that muscle to contract one final time. Proteins were denaturing. Connective tissue was tightening, squeezing out liquid, which dripped onto the hot grill and evaporated instantly, creating the sound we call sizzle. Heat makes meat juicier and easier to chew, but only to a point. Adding more heat does not always equal easier chewing. If you keep a steak on heat too long, its juice will all be squeezed out, and the meat will stiffen and shrink to the point that eating it is like chewing on a muscle cramp. The only remedy is many more hours of heat, which slowly unwinds the proteins and makes the steak chewable again, at which point it isn't steak anymore—it's stew.

While too much heat will eventually ruin every steak, a certain amount is nevertheless necessary if you want the steak to brown. People think the reason you brown a steak is to "seal" the juices inside, but this is a myth: if a steak were perfectly sealed, no water would be released, period, and there wouldn't be any sizzle. The truth is exponentially more exciting. The process of browning—known to food scientists as the Maillard reaction—recombines sugars and amino acids into hundreds of complex chemicals, which later recombine with fats and carbohydrates into yet more chemicals. The brown crust, simply, is delicious.

The French prefer their steak well browned on the outside, but just barely starting to leak on the inside. The word for a steak like this in English is "rare." The French are less squeamish and call it what it is: *saignant,* or bloody. That's what Christophe requested, and that's what he got. You could see the line of red running through the middle. When he cut into it, liquid streamed out onto his plate. Mine was pink verging on gray, and though it had a pleasing beefy taste, the meat was dry and hard on the jaw, having been slightly overcooked. The toughness of this particular entrecôte seemed a bit much for a steak that was, technically, medium well. It was not, evidently, the lost Aubrac steak of Christophe's youth, but I did enjoy it. Unlike the commodity steak in Texas and Oklahoma, the Aubrac steak had flavor. "I'll take flavor over tenderness," I said to Christophe.

"I think one can find perfection," was his reply.

Finding perfection is Christophe's mission. To hear him describe it, good chefs face an ever-worsening scarcity of excellent ingredients. The actual cooking part of cooking, he claims, is easy. Acquiring good ingredients is the big challenge, even in France where supermarkets sell Label Rouge chickens, which are slow-growing varieties raised in smaller flocks and reared for almost twice as long as regular chickens, although an even rarer and more expensive French chicken called *poulet de Bresse* is considered more tender and fine-tasting. Buying seafood, Christophe told me, can be very dicey, unless you know who to talk to—a man named Bataille, apparently, who has a line on extremely fresh turbot, cod, sole, and the like. Beef is a different matter, however. According to Christophe, buying beef in France is like dealing with the Mafia. Even when you pay top euro, you cannot trust what you'll get. A chef friend of

Christophe's was assured he was buying good French beef, but when he began cutting it, he discovered a stamp proclaiming it was of Brazilian origin.

Christophe does have a beef wholesaler he likes, a man named Olivier Metzger, who, if there were ever a competition to determine the world's best-dressed beef wholesaler, would be the odds-on favorite to win. The three of us sat down out front of a little sausage shop called La Maison Pierre Oteiza, eating rounds of Basque salami that Christophe holds in high esteem. Monsieur Metzger's level of chic exceeded the Parisian standard walking by on boulevard Saint-Michel. He wore a red-and-white-checked shirt, a black jean jacket, and, on his wrist, a silver Cartier Pasha Seatimer watch of obvious preciousness. Metzger talked up a breed called Simmental—big red-and-white cows that originated in Switzerland but are now popular all over Europe. The thing to look for, he said, was an old Simmental, and it is here that the French taste in beef diverges from the USDA's. The USDA takes a dim view of mature beef. After marbling, age is the next highest priority on a USDA grader's list. A grader can cut into a loin and find it so marbled as to look like a snowstorm wrapped in fat, but if the carcass shows signs of age, it won't make Prime.

The French, in contrast, consider beef younger than two years old to be insipid. Metzger told me that as cattle mature, they develop more myoglobin in their muscles—redder meat, in other words—and that the flavor is, for this reason, improved. He does not discount marbling, though he estimates that a meager 2 percent of French cattle are finished properly. It wasn't always this bad. "Twenty years ago," he said, "the beef was better because the farms were smaller," sounding the same nostalgic lament as Christophe. "Now they just want to make money." Even more troubling, the decline in quality has gone unnoticed by the latest generation of French chefs. "All they care about is tender meat. They don't know what flavor is anymore."

For Metzger, a flavorful cow could be as old as ten, maybe eleven years old—decrepit by USDA standards. American commodity beef, he believes, is too young. "They produce a standard product," he said. "But not a *gastronomique* product."

•   •   •

The next morning we returned to the ADF, where Christophe wanted me to taste another *gastronomique* product: steak in hay sauce.

It is likely not possible to overstate the importance of sauces in French cuisine. In a French kitchen, the sauce chef—*le saucier*—is the highest-ranking member, performing a task more important even than cooking meat. Of France's many notable contributions to humanity (bicycles, diesel engines, braille, hot-air balloons, stethoscopes), only its great sauces—Hollandaise, Béarnaise, Béchamel, and so on—convey the extent to which the French take their passions seriously. "Anyone can cook," Christophe told me, translating a famous French saying, "but to make a sauce you need to be born with the gift."

The French are not strangers to grilling steak over an open flame, but they are equally enthusiastic about sautéing steak in a pan, and this is what makes a sauce possible. Most of the time, steak is sprinkled with salt and pepper, fried in oil and butter, and served. You can, however, add some other ingredients to the fat, juice, and browned bits left in the pan—wine, cognac, cream—and create a sauce.

Hay is not usually one of those ingredients. Like others around the world, the French think of hay as a food for farm animals, not humans. Not a single French person I asked had ever heard of a hay sauce. Its origin is equally murky for Christophe, who can't remember who taught him the recipe in the first place, or when. It is almost as though Christophe invented it one night while sleepwalking and woke up to find the recipe on his kitchen table.

One evening in 1997, Christophe invited a couple to dinner. Before the meal, he announced that he would be serving steak with a sauce made out of hay, and the wife of his friend jokingly said, "I'm not a cow." Christophe cooked, they ate. Afterward Christophe asked the couple how they had enjoyed the meal, and the wife repeated her little quip. Christophe, who sets the international standard for graciousness, responded with a polite laugh. But as he closed the door behind them that night, he thought, *C'est fini*. It *was* fini. He has not spoken to them since.

Christophe procured the hay for our meal—a brick-sized quantity will more than suffice—from a farmer he knew outside Paris. It was sitting there in a bowl, and he urged me to take a whiff. The hay smelled sweet and nutty. Christophe sprinkled some water on it and told me to smell it again. The interior of the bowl was now a summer afternoon rainstorm on a farm. "You can smell the soil and the sun," he said.

"You can hear birds singing," I said. He looked down at his shoe and pretended to have just stepped in manure.

Hay takes a long time to make. You need to grow grass, cut it, let it dry in the sun, and then bale it. Making hay sauce isn't much faster. It begins with beef trimmings, the little chunks of meat you lop off a cut of beef to make it perfect. Christophe trimmed a tenderloin supplied by M. Metzger. (The cow came from Normandy, but the breed was unknown.) You need a lot of trimmings to make *jus*, eleven pounds for a mere one and a half liters. The tenderloin didn't provide nearly enough, so Christophe grabbed a hunk of ribs and hacked off some meat, handing it over to me to reduce into chunklets. As substances go, Christophe's *jus*, I realized, would be somewhat more refined than the "au jus" ladled on to steak at the Big Texan.

Two-thirds of the trimmings went into a hot casserole pot with some olive oil over medium heat. Just like my entrecôte the day before, the steak released its juice, which formed a thin bubbling layer at the bottom of the pot. "The juice has to darken," Christophe said, "because that's how you get the sugar out." As the volume of juice diminished, Christophe took a basting brush and painted down the residue clinging to the sides of the casserole pot—a signature Ducasse move, he explained—to bring every last bit of flavor into the simmering liquid. This technique, he says, is "extremely important for creating a *jus*."

Registering some development in the pot, Christophe made an announcement: "Soon, the smell will change." Abruptly, the aroma became more pungent, and also sweeter. By this point, the beef was well browned—the Maillard reaction. Christophe monitored the bottom of the casserole pot, inspecting for blackness, as burning would be a disaster, turning everything bitter. Some minutes later, the liquid was gone, rendered into an almost solid layer at the base of the pot. Christophe removed the beef, returned the pot to the heat, and began to melt a stick of Normandy butter in it. To this he added a chopped onion, a chopped shallot, two sprigs of thyme, a few peppercorns, and two cloves of garlic still in their skin. As with the beef, the heat drew the water out of the vegetables, which revived the desertified beef juice. It all bubbled away. The onions caramelized, the thyme pretty much disappeared, and Christophe continued to paint down the sides.

The mixture bubbled for forty minutes, at which point Christophe added several ladles of *fond blanc,* a mild chicken stock that French chefs use so liberally I suspect a few of them wash their cars with it. *Fond blanc* itself takes hours to make, another reason it is best to cook complicated sauces in a well-stocked French kitchen like the one at the ADF, where gallons of *fond blanc* are simmering at all times. (Christophe says it is permissible to use water in place of *fond blanc.*) While the simmering continued, Christophe took the remaining third of beef trimmings and a second casserole pot, and repeated the entire process all over again. But this time, when the second casserole dish reached the stage where it was ready for the *fond blanc,* he poured in the liquid from the first pot, explaining, "This is how you get the concentrated taste." He dipped a spoon into the sauce and handed it to me. The flavor of the onion, thyme, and garlic had vanished. I was tasting beefy nectar.

At long last, it was time to cook a steak. Christophe cut Metzger's tenderloin into thick, round slices, laid each into a hot pan with olive oil and butter, and let them sizzle. Before they were fully cooked, Christophe pulled them off the heat, placed them on a plate, and poured the buttery pan juices over them. He now produced a third casserole pot—there are hundreds at the ADF—and in the bottom formed a nest of hay. Within it, he placed the clutch of steaks. To this he added the *jus,* pouring in the liquid until it reached one-third of the way up the steaks. Placing a final thatch of hay over the steaks, he put the lid on the casserole pot and placed it in a hot oven for ten minutes.

The dish was still a long way from being cooked. Out of the oven, the steaks remained in the casserole pot so they could become infused by hay vapors for another hour. At one point Christophe lifted the lid, and the room suddenly filled with the smell of baking cake. He smiled. "The aroma reminds everyone of their youth," he said, "even people who've never visited a farm." As aromas go, it was as attention-grabbing as the feedlot stench in Texas, but pleasurable instead of painful. It smelled as if a French grandmother was cooking a pecan tart in a wood-beamed hayloft. It smelled like the ventilation exhaust from a German hazelnut cake factory. It smelled as if teddy bears were toasting marsh-mallows roasted in honey and almonds over a crackling fire.

At this advanced stage in the cooking process, the sauce remained coarse and unformed, the culinary equivalent of crude oil. Christophe now poured the hay-infused *jus* from the casserole pot through a fine-mesh sieve into a smaller pot, which already contained an inch of the original *jus*. The pot went on the stove, and the liquids combined and condensed. On another burner, Christophe set a silver pan and tossed in a half pound of butter—the ADF goes through almost as much butter as *fond blanc*—which spread, bubbled, and turned brown, becoming a sub-stance the French call *beurre noisette*. To this the now-condensed hay *jus* was added, synthesizing into a thick liquid as dark and sweet-smelling as melted chocolate. Hours after that first chunk of trimming had been removed from the tenderloin, the sauce was at last finished. Christophe removed the steaks from the low oven where they were kept warm, plated them, and poured the sauce.

Christophe Raoux was born with the sauce-making gift. His hay sauce is a credible version of liquid velvet. The taste was sweet and reso-nantly beefy, the distilled essence of the cow and the fields it lived in, the sun itself concentrated to the point of elixir. After my third bite, I turned to Christophe. "I understand now," I said, pulling a finger through the sauce, which was so thick it parted like the Red Sea. I dabbed it on my tongue. "This," I said, "is why cows eat hay."

A cow had, until somewhat recently, been eating hay in the lower left-hand corner of France in a region called the French Basque Country. The next day, during lunch, I ate a section of its strip loin, and it was the best steak I have ever eaten in France. The strip loin—three-quarters of an inch thick, on the rare side of medium rare—was cooked at a restau-rant called Café Constant. It is not one of Ducasse's many excellent Paris restaurants, but as we walked in, Christophe assured me the food would be good.

The steak at Café Constant was pan-fried in olive oil and butter, and when it was done cooking, the chef fried a diced shallot and chopped parsley in the remaining pan juice, then poured it over the meat. As sauces go, it had nothing on Christophe's hay sauce, but it was in no way an attempt to outdo it—it was just a simple lunch steak, one that was tender and full of flavor that lasted many seconds after swallowing. Did the flavor come from the shallot and parsley? The thought occurred to me. But it was too beefy to have come from a plant.

Alain Ducasse is a remarkable man. He rose from modest beginnings in the south of France—surviving a plane crash in 1984 that killed every passenger but him—and went on to become one of the most successful French chefs of all time. And yet his fourteen Michelin stars have in no way insulated him from the world inhabited by ordinary people, the vast majority of whom, like me, have no Michelin stars. I know this to be true because as I took another bite of that Basque Country steak, Ducasse swept into the room and sat down across from me, next to Christophe. He wanted to talk about steak. "Everyone thinks they have the best beef," Ducasse said. "I've eaten steak all over the world. *Bistecca* in Italy. Kobe beef in Japan. Big, thick steaks in America. It is all good," he said. "The point," he insisted, "is not to say which one is better or worse. Each steak is a different pleasure."

As I sat there chewing one such particular pleasure, it dawned on me that my ambition of seeking out the world's very best, tastiest, most wonderful steak was narrow and single-minded, perhaps even stupid. In France, I had already eaten three good steaks—the aurochs, Christophe's tenderloin in hay sauce, and the partly eaten strip loin in front of me. This last steak was the best of them all, but I wasn't about to say the others should be vanquished from the earth forever. They were good. They deserved places on menus and space in the mouths of humans.

I thought about commodity beef. Ducasse said each steak was a *different* pleasure. Did commodity beef possess any significant or worthy difference to speak of? Compared to the steaks in France—not all of which are good, by the way—the one noteworthy quality of commodity beef seemed to be its absence of qualities. It was like tap water: abundant, dependable, cheap, and uninteresting. So I asked Ducasse, who runs two restaurants in New York City and one in Las Vegas, what he thought of the generic industrial beef. "This is the American way," he said. It was what distinguished American steaks, he said, from French, Japanese, and Italian steaks, but I couldn't tell if Ducasse thought that was a good thing or not. "The challenge we have today," he said, taking a philosophical turn, "is to *celebrate* those differences."

These were the words of a man who'd eaten more, better steak than I had. There was a lot of good, different, unique, and individual steak out there in the big wide world, waiting to be eaten. That's hardly a bad thing. And yet I couldn't help but think of what Christophe Raoux had said a few days earlier, about that Aubrac steak: *One can find perfection.*

CHAPTER THREE

SCOTLAND

The window of time in which to place an artificial vagina on the erect penis of a pedigree bull is narrow. When the penis emerges from the bull's furry sheath, no more than two or three seconds pass—four, tops—before the bull ejaculates or loses interest and dismounts. That gives Jim Cameron somewhere between one and two seconds to crouch underneath the two-thousand-pound animal and then another second to take the artificial vagina he is holding in his right hand—which, minutes earlier, he filled with warm tap water to make it feel more, how to put it, *vaginesque*—and aim the open end onto the penis, which is thrusting, and intercept the spurt of semen. That's the difficult part. Once the penis is inside the artificial vagina, it all goes quickly. There is one thrust, maybe two, and the work is complete.

It is dangerous work. During collections, a bull can lose his footing and fall on the man crouching beneath him. In more than thirty years of semen collecting, this has happened to Cameron once, in 1985, when he was collecting from a dairy bull. "He fell right across me legs," Cameron remembers, "and I tore cartilage in both knees." The injury required two operations, and now when Cameron flexes his stiff knees, the bones scrape against one another. The bull was fine.

It is, therefore, the stoicism of the Scots talking when Jim Cameron tells you, "Semen collecting is easier than it looks." On a cool and overcast summer morning at Spylaw Stud Farm, in southern Scotland, just next to a handsome little town called Kelso, Cameron took me inside a barn and demonstrated. Tied to one railing was the "teaser steer," Big Al, staring at the wall, presenting his rump for all the world to admire. Tied to a railing on the opposite wall stood two big bulls, shifting their weight from hoof to hoof and casting the occasional glance back at Big Al and his big rump. Haltcliffe Braveheart was thick and rippled with muscle, but not as tall as the bull next to him, Roundhill Cramses, who was also longer, but not as muscular, though superbly built nevertheless.

A farmhand walked over and untied Roundhill Cramses. It was time. The big bull lumbered over to Big Al, sniffed the apex of his rump, jumped up on his hind legs, and grasped Big Al's ampleness with his front legs. He held the position for a tension-filled second but did not thrust, and just as the act teetered on the verge of resolution, Roundhill Cramses slid off, his hooves clacking on the concrete floor as he walked away. This is called a false mount, and it was all part of the plan. "It helps to get the sperm livened up," Cameron explained.

The benefit of using a teaser steer—a castrated male who gets humped an awful lot—is that the bull cannot accidentally impregnate it and, in so doing, contract VD. With heifers and cows, this is a legitimate risk. But since bulls are not, generally, in the habit of mounting steers, they need to learn how. When a pedigree bull attends his first semen collection, he just stands there and watches. Veteran donors have the know-how, but they still need to be put in the mood. That is why bulls are tied up next to one another: it gets them excited.

The farmhand walked Roundhill Cramses toward the opposite wall, then circled back to Big Al's rump. The bull mounted again, and this time Cameron crouched down. When Roundhill Cramses' penis emerged from its hide-covered sheath, Cameron popped the artificial vagina on top of it and held it there. Intercourse, if it can be called that, lasted three seconds—there was a weak thrust, then a more pronounced one, and it was over. Roundhill Cramses dismounted, and Cameron slapped his flank and said, "Good lad." Big Al just stood there.

Cameron turned his attention to the artificial vagina. It consists of two parts: a hard outer shell, which looks like a one-foot length of black PVC pipe, and a disposable latex inner lining, which is skin-colored and wrinkly and oddly reminiscent of a human scrotum. At the opposite end of the opening, a long section of latex dangled, with a lump in the very end of it formed by a torpedo-shaped piece of plastic called the collection tube. The enthusiasm behind a bull's ejaculation is such that the semen made it all the way into the collection tube, which was now filled.

Had Jim Cameron not captured it, ejaculate could have sailed through the air past Big Al's head.

We walked over to the stud farm's small office, where a microscope stood on a table scattered with plastic vials. Cameron dipped a glass straw into the collection tube and smeared some semen on a glass slide. Not wanting to waste a drop, he put his lips around the dry end of the straw and gently blew the remaining semen back into the collection tube. Such is its preciousness. The glass slide was placed beneath a microscope, and he peered into the lens at swimming sperm. Motility scored a three-plus—the highest rating is five. The quantity, 4 milliliters, was similarly judged to be good, as was the color: rich and creamy, which is the most desired hue. Rich and creamy indicates lots of swimming sperm. Some bulls produce yellow semen. There is nothing wrong with yellow semen, but it is not prized the way rich, creamy semen is.

Pedigree semen comes from bulls that are considered exemplary specimens of their breed. The total number of cattle breeds in the world today is around a thousand, but at the early dawn of civilization—in the Middle East, about ten thousand years ago—the only cattle were the formerly wild aurochs that had recently been turned docile and obedient. As crop-growing, steak-eating humans spread over the globe and began dressing differently, talking differently, praying differently, and singing differently, their cattle, too, started to become different. Just as cultures became defined by geography—big rivers, tall mountains, deep seas—agriculture did, too. In northern Italy, the cattle were bright white with black noses. The ones farther east, toward the Adriatic Sea, were shorter and gray. In Switzerland, cattle were brown, medium sized, and such good milkers that the Swiss became famed cheesemakers. In southeastern England, they were red and furry. In southern France, some of them still looked like aurochs. As the land changed shape and color, the cattle changed shape and color, too.

For ten thousand years, nobody particularly cared. Like politics, all cattle were local. Then, about 250 years ago, an Englishman named Robert Bakewell started paying attention. Bakewell was a walking agricultural revolution, the kind of man who spent his waking moments thinking about better ways to irrigate fields, rotate crops, or deploy manure. One day, he took a considered look at the local cows and noticed that those with particularly long horns seemed to produce more meat than the others, even though they ate less grass. Bakewell picked out the meatiest ones he could find and separated them by sex. Rather than let mating occur randomly out in the fields, as humans had been doing for roughly ten millennia, Bakewell took the fattest bulls and put them with the fattest cows. Their fat, meaty offspring were bred—and inbred—with one another, until Bakewell one day found himself with truly fat, truly meaty cattle. His cows looked so different from all the others, in fact, that they seemed like a different animal altogether.

What Bakewell had created was the first distinct cattle *breed*. His cows eventually got their own name, and are still known as Dishley longhorns. Anyone hoping to eat a Dishley longhorn steak, unfortunately, is more than two centuries late, as one of Bakewell's students—empowered by the techniques of his master—wasted no time in creating a newer, better, fatter, meatier breed than the Dishley longhorn. This one had shorter horns, so they called it the shorthorn, and thanks to it the Dishley longhorn went out of fashion almost as quickly as it came in.

For as long as is historically known, there have been cows in northeastern Scotland that are black and hornless, and so sleek in summer as to appear brushed with pomade. These animals were not raised to pull plows or carts or to turn the grass they grazed into butter and cheese that could be sold. They were raised to be eaten. Local Scots gave them endearing names, some calling them doddies—"dodded" meaning that they had no horns—while farther north, they were known as hummlies. Since Roman times, the cattle have been grazed on the marginal pastures that grow on the thin layer of soil draped over the immovable Highland rock. They were raised by herders who, like the American cowboys their descendants would become, drove big herds to better pastures where they became fat, then herded them south to market. Centuries before the railways laid their web of parallel iron over Britain, sleek black cattle born on the North Sea were eaten as far away as London.

In time, Bakewell's breeding techniques made it to Scotland. Farmers began picking out the fattest doddies and breeding them and inbreeding them. Eventually, they found themselves with cattle that were walking monuments to beefiness, with thick shoulders, ample rumps, and meaty loins. They came from the neighboring shires of Aberdeen and Angus, and they became known as the Aberdeen-Angus breed.

The cattle formerly known as doddies are today Scotland's most famous export. More than any Scottish export—haggis, bagpipes, tartan, shortbread—the world loves Angus steak. Only Scotch whisky has achieved a similar level of transcultural penetration, though it is not consumed in the same quantity—most of the time, anyway—or by as many people. Steak bearing the Angus brand is for sale in more than sixty countries, including Egypt, Singapore, Thailand, Peru, Panama, Lebanon, Haiti, Azerbaijan, Cambodia, Oman, Spain, the Marshall Islands, Guam, Russia, and China, and there is at least one brand of dog food that contains Angus beef: Alpo Chop House Filet Mignon Flavor. Angus steak is, by reputation, the best going. The worldwide faith in a single true breed sprang from the green and rain-soaked earth of Scotland. In the world of steak, Scotland is Jerusalem.

There I was, standing in a barn in steak's Jerusalem, watching as semen was collected from a pedigree bull, noting to self that the locals indeed take their cattle seriously. Jim Cameron's intimacy with cattle is not merely a professional occupation. His favorite food is steak, and he reckons he eats beef once a day, at the very least. When he goes out for dinner with his wife, he orders steak without so much as looking at the menu. He used to eat more steak than he does now, but Cameron, like other Scottish steak lovers, feels the quality isn't what it used to be.

Cameron has crouched under an aroused bull to intercept semen more than sixty thousand times, which amounts to more than ninety-five gallons of bull semen—enough to fill two claw-foot bathtubs. Each batch is put on ice and sent by Royal Mail special delivery to a sperm bank in Devon, where it is stored in liquid nitrogen for up to forty years inside tiny glass straws. The straws are sent all over the world to customers who inject the contents into the uteruses of cows in heat. Cameron's first-ever semen collection took place in 1974 on a bull named Horoscope of Upsall—a shorthorn. Since then, he has amassed twenty-five artificial vaginas. Some he pumps up with air, to create a tighter and, presumably, more pleasurable fit. Others have soft sides, allowing him to modulate tightness with his grip. Some artificial vaginas are made in Britain, but Cameron says the best come from France, and if a Scot says this, it must be true. The very first artificial vagina he bought was French, and it is still in rotation.

It was still morning when Roundhill Cramses and Haltcliffe Brave-heart had given up all the semen they would that day, an amount exceeding 20 milliliters. Cameron and I stepped outside the office and chatted. I asked him if he could remember the best steak of his life. Cameron, whose Scottish pride is more durable than Highland granite, wishes he could tell me that the steak came from an Angus cow. The steak was eaten in the mid-1990s. It was summer, and Cameron was in Wales, collecting semen. "The steak was always good at the Old Oak Hotel in Ruthin," he told me, his eyes fixed on some distant point on the horizon, "but this one, well, your knife just fell through it."

The Old Oak Hotel had a peculiar habit of not trimming any of the fat off its steak, and Cameron's strip loin arrived surrounded by a thick frame of it. It was better than any previous steak Cameron had ever eaten, and better than any subsequent steak he would eat. It did not come from a doddie, however, but from a shorter, curlier breed called a Welsh Black.

If what you want is Angus semen of the highest quality, Jim Cameron is the man to know. For Angus steak of the highest quality, he doesn't have much in the way of recommendations. I got back in my car and drove, on the left side of the road, north, past Dalkeith, past Edinburgh, over a foggy and very cold-looking Firth of Forth, and arrived, finally, in the picturesque town of Perth. Perth is not famously associated with doddies. It is miles from Angus, and even farther from Aberdeen. But on a majes-tically named street called Kings Place, across from a big park near the train station, stands a stately sandstone edifice called Pedigree House, which is the home of the Aberdeen-Angus Cattle Society.

Inside, you can stand face-to-face with Old Jock, the first bull ever entered into the Aberdeen-Angus herd book. He lives eternally in an antique painting, and his midsection is so beefy it calls to mind the images at Lascaux. Standing watch over a winding staircase is the mounted head of a bull named Paris, still soft to the touch after more than a hundred years. He was the grand champion at the Exposition Universelle held in Paris in 1878, which caused quite the stir. French farmers had never before seen a bull with no horns and claimed that Paris (the bull) was not, in fact, bovine at all but some other kind of furry creature. When the trophy, a large and ornate silver bowl, was nevertheless awarded to the Scottish contingent, the French got their revenge. Ringing the prize were several busts of Paris, but unlike the real champion bull, the likenesses on the trophy all had horns.

The trophy had been missing for decades, but recently it turned up in the garage of an elderly lady who'd passed away, and now it sits on the walnut table in the society's boardroom, which is festooned with other adoring images of famous doddies, including paintings of the Angus bull that was presented to Napoleon Bonaparte; the oldest ever Angus cow, Old Grannie, who lived to the ripe old age of thirty-six, and was finally killed—and partially cooked—by a bolt of lightning; and a cow named Erica, considered by many to be the finest specimen in the history of the breed. At the head of the table, a walnut bookcase holds the Aberdeen-Angus herd books, the early editions so old as to look biblical. Erica's entry, like all the very old ones, is handwritten. The nineteenth-century script is looping and strikingly elegant, but nearly illegible. I studied an entry for a female born on January 4, 1854: Blossom, daughter of Dewdrop and Rob Roy, bred by the trustees of the late Robert Scott Balywillo. How did Blossom taste? I wondered. Even if she'd lived as long as Old Grannie—at which point she probably wouldn't have tasted good at all—there would still be more than a hundred years standing between myself and Blossom's potentially excellent steak.

The president of the Aberdeen-Angus Cattle Society is a wiry Scot named Ron McHattie. We sat down at the walnut table, surrounded by no fewer than eleven bronze statuettes of doddies and next to a painting of an Angus cow so extravagantly fat that she would have had difficulty walking. We talked steak. Or we attempted to, at least, but McHattie confirmed that there wasn't much to talk about. Scotland may be home to the world's most famous beef breed, but Scottish steak is in a period of decline. I walked in expecting McHattie to furnish me with a long list of restaurants and hotels serving legendary steaks from Angus cattle so pure as to moo with a Highland accent. McHattie couldn't name a single one.

What I could do, McHattie told me, was visit a Scottish supermarket and buy a certified Aberdeen-Angus steak. But that in itself was no guarantee of breed purity. Genetically speaking, it was required to be merely half Angus. Still, that is a far cry better than what gets sold in the United States (and Canada) as Certified Angus Beef, whose specifications require *nothing* in the way of genetics or heredity. For an American cow to qualify as Certified Angus Beef, it must possess certain carcass characteristics— fine and ample marbling, a well-shaped rib eye, not too much back fat, and so forth. The cow must also have been—here it comes—at least 51 *percent black.* The thinking is that since Angus cattle are black, a cow that is mostly black is mostly Angus—the logical equivalent of proclaiming that since cats have fur, any animal that is at least half fur-covered must therefore be a cat. Angus cattle, it so happens, do not enjoy a monopoly on blackness. Black Simmentals are black. Welsh Blacks are black. Black Charolais are black, and so are Galloways, Salers, and black Limousins. A lot of Holsteins, the famous black-and-white dairy cows, possess blackness in excess of 51 percent. (More than one cattle industry type has told me that thousands of Holstein steers—which, being male, can't be milked—are fed flaked corn and sold as Certified Angus Beef.) Some Angus cattle, furthermore, *are not black.* There is a gene for redness in Angus DNA, and it is recessive, which means that two flagrantly pure black Angus cattle can produce a calf that will be as red as the morning sun. If you drive by a herd of black doddies grazing the electric green Scottish countryside, look hard enough, and you will see red ones. Some believe red Angus represent the very purest strain, because a red Angus bull with a red Angus cow will only produce red calves, whereas with black parents you don't know what you're getting. And yet in the United States, a pedigree, award-winning red Angus steer—so devoutly Angus as to bring to mind visions of bagpipers marching over heather—would nevertheless fail to qualify as Certified Angus Beef.

The problem in Scotland, McHattie explained, is that no one has any idea what constitutes good beef anymore. There is historical precedent. Three hundred years ago, most Scots couldn't afford to eat meat. What little they did consume was likely from a deer someone poached. Butcher shops didn't appear until the 1700s, when they were called flesh mongers. The Scots kept sheep for milk and wool—not meat—and cattle were either milked or driven to market and sold. Religion didn't help; Presbyterianism does not favor indulgent forms of eating. All too often, their prized doddies ended up being eaten by the hated English.

Among the very few Scots who did eat steak were the drovers. During cattle drives that would rival those yet to come in America, they cooked steaks on shovels held over a wood fire. But for most Scots, the only beef they ever ate was in the form of blood. During the bone-chilling damp of the Scottish winter, they would draw blood from their cattle, mix it with milk and oats, and boil it into a pudding. (The nearest thing to it today is a British breakfast sausage called black pudding, which is in itself tasty enough to warrant a trip to Scotland.)

Three hundred years ago, those who toiled outdoors or worked in poorly heated stone buildings—the entire population of Scotland, in other words—prized fat. The Scottish feel very differently about fat nowadays, McHattie told me, and that's another big problem. For decades, the government has been concerned over the legendary unhealthiness of the Scottish diet and has been telling the people their steak should be lean and red. The carcasses that grade the best—and therefore pay the farmer the most money—are lean. While a USDA beef grader is on the lookout for white, his British counterpart wants to see red.

Gray-haired Scots can remember a time when every main street in every Scottish city and village had its own butcher shop. The butchers knew their customers by name, and they knew quality meat. Those days are gone. Scottish foodies now speak of the few remaining butchers as if they were a species on the verge of extinction. A good butcher does not flog meat on Styrofoam trays. A good butcher, McHattie told me, will explain that an Angus cow will give you marbled flesh and a thick layer of back fat—the same fat surrounding that legendary strip loin Jim Cameron ate in Wales—which insulates the steak inside from bacteria-ridden air and allows it to hang in a cold room and dry-age for a month, maybe longer, which makes the meat more tender and more delicious. (Supermarket steaks in Scotland age for as few as four days.) But if you run the meat department at a big British supermarket and want bright red four-day-old steaks to sell on Styrofoam trays to fat-phobic customers— customers who will nevertheless consume raging numbers of calories in the form of French fries, potato chips, chocolate bars, and soft drinks— you do not want steaks from an Aberdeen-Angus cow. You want anything but. Not surprisingly, though it sure struck me as a surprise, Angus cattle now make up a mere 14 percent of the Scottish herd.

Even that number represents an improvement. Back in the 1960s, cattle from France, Germany, and Italy—which are bigger, leaner, and grow faster than British cattle—became trendy with Scottish farmers. In no time, these "continentals" dominated the Scottish beef herd, and the Angus breed entered a long, lean winter, its popularity declining so precipitously that it nearly qualified as a rare breed. The society's walnut bookcase tells the sad story. From the end of the nineteenth century, the herd books get progressively fatter, but then abruptly begin to grow thin until they reach the point of emaciation, as though stricken by some exotic disease.

Today, the most popular cattle breed in Scotland hails from the same country as the most popular artificial vaginas in Scotland: France. The breed is Limousin, and they are big and brown and have rear ends so plump that from behind you could mistake one for a hippopotamus. Roundhill Cramses, it so happens, is a Limousin, as are Haltcliffe Braveheart and Big Al. Despite numerous phone calls, during the week I spent in Scotland I wasn't able to find anyone who was harvesting semen from an Angus bull.

I left Pedigree House full of questions. What did a real, 100 percent Angus steak taste like? Was it even possible to find such a steak any longer in Scotland? And if not, would the airline be willing to refund my ticket?

Then again, what was I actually missing? McHattie handed me a stack of brochures to read along with a journal called the *Aberdeen-Angus Review*. The cover featured a big Angus bull exhaling smoke and a cover line that said, "The King of Cattle Continues to Reign Supreme" (best said in that slow ultra-deep voice that announces motorcycle shows and pro wrestling matches on classic rock radio stations). Between its glossy covers, I expected to find story after story proclaiming the superior deliciousness of the breed, backed by scientific proof, celebrity chef testimonials, and maybe a quote or two from Prince Charles, who has his own herd of doddies.

Not a one. There were stories of prizewinning bulls and heifers, updates on the breed's economic progress ("Angus Females in Demand"; "Bavarians Keen to Buy Aberdeen-Angus"; "New DVD Will Drive Home the Aberdeen-Angus Message to Suckler Herd Owners"), and a lot of ads, a high percentage of which promoted semen from bulls who have shown unsurpassed growth rates. One raved about a bull that was among the heaviest ever at four hundred days. The brochures extolled this "low-cost" breed that "demands a premium." So far as I could tell, there wasn't so much as a word about flavor or tenderness or juiciness.

McHattie suggested I contact an organization called Quality Meat Scotland. When I did, the woman who answered—the very definition of a Scottish lass, by the sounds of things—connected me to a man who may well be the most experienced and knowledgeable meat eater in all the British Isles. He is also, curiously, a man who has much in common with Roundhill Cramses and Haltcliffe Braveheart and Jim Cameron's favorite artificial vaginas. His name is Laurent Vernet, and he comes from France.

Scottish weather notwithstanding, Vernet is living the meat lover's dream. He is, technically, the head of marketing for Quality Meat Scotland, but Vernet does not consider himself a marketer so much as "a man of passion." Here is an individual paid a salary to find good meat, eat that meat, and then talk about it. He studied economics—"a fascinating subject filled with boring people"—wrote his thesis on lamb, then pursued his lifelong dream to live in Scotland, which he describes as "a rough land with uncomplicated food." After he graduated, he drove from France to Scotland and took a job in a slaughterhouse, gutting sheep and harvesting the meat off their heads.

One morning Vernet was reading the newspaper when he spotted an employment posting from the Northern Ireland Meat Board. He applied and a short time later was offered a job traveling around the world to see how different people and cultures eat and enjoy meat. The idea was that by visiting Japan, South Korea, Malaysia, Argentina, Mongolia, and a few other countries to eat meat, watch the locals eat, visit their butcher shops, and so forth, Vernet could help the Northern Irish understand how to sell meat to those very foreigners. Vernet accepted, of course.

He described this rather too nonchalantly as we drove from his office outside Edinburgh an hour east to a pretty town called Aberfoyle, which has one of the few remaining classic Scottish butcher shops, one that smells like a butcher shop should: of bone meal, sausage, dried blood, haggis, and aging meat. Vernet deems the Aberfoyle Butcher the best in Scotland. It is run by Jonathan Honeyman, a reedy man with a thin mustache and combed-down hair who looks as if he just stepped out of a black-and-white film and speaks with such a thick burr that the word "farm," when uttered by him, can have as many as three syllables. Honeyman trained as an engineer, but his love of meat was such that he gave up the stability and comfort of a professional career to deal in meat for a living. His wife is a shepherd, and they have six border collies.

Honeyman has definite ideas about how the craft of butchery ought to be practiced. He dry-ages sides of beef for around twenty-one days, but rather than hang sides of beef from the hind leg, which is how it's normally done, he prefers to hang his from the hipbone, believing this stretches the muscles in a way that improves the texture of the meat. He sells Shetland sheep from a herd whose bloodline can be traced back to the 1800s, when it changed hands as part of a wedding dowry, and which are, to this day, plunked down on various tiny islands in the North Sea to fatten during the summer, then picked up by boat and sent to market.

If a customer walks into the Aberfoyle Butcher on a typical day and asks for steak, he will be presented with three different breeds from which to choose. Some of Honeyman's customers prefer the White Park breed. Others prefer Scottish Highlands—though Honeyman will tell you that Highlands haven't tasted the same since the European Union, panicked over mad cow disease, decreed that they be slaughtered at too young an age. And some prefer Angus. "When you buy red wine," Honeyman says, "you don't just pick a dark bottle." He thinks the same ought to be true of beef. The different breeds, he says, have different textures. "It's the feel in the mouth, basically," he explains. "I have noticed that on Charolais cattle, the texture is more open and grainy." Some customers have no stated preference. They walk in the door, ask to have a look at whatever loins are aging in his fridge, and only then will they make a decision, at which point the knives come out and the steaks are cut and wrapped in butcher paper.

When I asked Honeyman to recommend a cut, he stopped me. He first had to determine if we were even speaking the same language. A sirloin in America, he cautioned, is not called a sirloin in Scotland, where requesting such will get you a rectangular-shaped steak that Americans call a strip loin (technically, part of the longissimus, whereas the American "sirloin" is usually cut off the glutius medius). He warned against the dangers of ordering a particular muscle in the rump, sometimes called the round, sometimes called the thick flank, but which goes by no fewer than twenty-nine different names in Britain. Honeyman could—and well might—write an ode to every cut of beef, but when asked to choose the greatest steak cut qua steak cut, his choice is the rib eye. "There is a lot of flavor there," he explained. "There's a lot of fat there, too. But texturally, it's more open. It's not as tightly grained." The question of cut, nevertheless, is the last thing a steak buyer should worry about, according to Honeyman. "You'd be better off knowing what breed it came from," he says, "and how it was raised."

He disappeared into the fridge and emerged carrying four packages of steak, which he handed over to Vernet. We had the makings of what wine types call a horizontal tasting. During a horizontal tasting, wine lovers sit down with wines that are all from the same year (and often the same grape variety) but come from different wineries. As the wines are tasted and compared with one another, differences in geography and the wine-making art become more apparent. Our plan was to do the same thing with some Scottish steaks. (In a vertical tasting, wines from the same winery, but from different years, are sampled, so a person can see how a

wine from, say, 2004 compares with one from 1968. Doing the equivalent
with steak is not advisable.)

As we drove back to Edinburgh, Vernet and I discussed flavor. Vernet
does not worship at the altar of marbling. He considers any steak with a
USDA grade of mid-Choice and higher to be too fatty. *Some* marbling,
he agrees, is necessary for a good steak. "But when a steak has too much
fat," he warned, "the only taste you register is neutral cooked oil."

For Vernet, fat alone does not equal flavor. Science does not disagree.
It is primarily amino acids and sugars—not fat—that are the constituents
of Maillard reactions. But fat deserves some share of the credit, although
it is incorrect to think of there being a single kind of fat in steak. There
are at least twenty-five different fats, and more may yet be discovered.
Technically, they are fatty acids and range from the highly unsaturated
DHA—which is liquid at room temperature, found in abundance within
the flesh of coldwater fish, and considered so healthy as to be sold as
little gel pills in health food stores—all the way up to palmitic acid, whose
every molecule has so many hydrogen atoms connected to it that scientists call it "saturated." Palmitic acid is firm at room temperature and
won't melt until the thermometer reaches 63°C (145°F), whereas the
fabulously unsaturated DHA melts at –45°C (–49°F).

The fourth most prevalent fatty acid in beef is called linoleic acid, and
the heat of a grill or pan turns it into a substance called hexanal, which
tastes "green," "fatty," and "oily" and, despite these less than appetizing asso-
ciations, is considered delicious by food scientists. Hexanal is one of steak's
many "flavor compounds." According to the food science database Volatile
Compounds in Food, 340 such substances have been identified in grilled
or roasted beef. Consider for a moment that red wine—a substance that has
launched an entire genre of magazines, Web sites, and books devoted to
printing descriptions of its flavor—has 386 flavor compounds, a mere 46
more than steak. (White wine, which most wine connoisseurs consider to
be less sophisticated than red wine, has, unexpectedly, 687.) Many of the
flavor compounds in steak do come from fat, but many come from other
things—sugars, amino acids, peptides, proteins, even ammonia—that com-
bine and recombine into the kind of substances it takes years of graduate-
level chemistry to comprehend.

There may be more than a hundred hydrocarbons in steak, to say nothing of the alcohols, aldehydes, ketones, esters, ethers, and amines. Oxazols and oxazolines are found in steak, and so are thiazols and thiazolenes. Butanoic acid, a rancid-tasting ester, lives in steak as well as in vomit, body odor, and Parmesan cheese. Too much butanoic acid in a steak is not good, nor is too much hexanoic acid, for that matter, which tastes sweaty and like barnyard animals. One-octen-3-ol, on the other hand, tastes mushroomy, and delta-nonalactone gives notes of sweet, dairy, and, oddly, waxiness. Decan-2-one tastes musty and fruity. Two-methyl-3-[methylthio]furan tastes meaty, sweet, and sulfurous. Acetaldehyde, methylpropalan, and 3-methylbutanal are formed by amino acids. They taste meaty.

The juice that flows out of a steak is rich in umami, the savory tonic that quenches the craving for meat. While it is heat that releases the juice from steak, too much exposure to heat can release too much juice: a well-done steak has 80 percent less umami than one cooked to medium rare. (This might be taken as scientific proof that steak should not be cooked to well done.) Where a steak meets intense heat it turns brown—Maillard reactions—and here the chemistry of steak gives rise to a dizzying number of complex, and often delicious, chemicals: furanoids, for instance, carbonyl compounds, benzenoids, lactones, and sulfides. Certain substances—a few alkylpyrazines and some meaty-tasting hydroxyfuranones and thiamenes—are found in grilled or roasted beef and nothing else.

Scientists refer to these compounds as "volatile," and for good reason. They don't last very long. They are created by heat, and when heat is removed, many of the flavor compounds are, existentially speaking, on the brink. When a red wine is poured into a glass, oxygen begins reacting with its tannins and other chemicals, and the beverage is often considered to improve after being exposed to a little air. Wine "breathes." Wine "opens up." When a steak is taken off the grill and placed next to that wine, the rising steam announces its half-life. Flavor compounds are degrading, and unless it is eaten shortly, it is on its way to becoming cold steak. Heat cannot undo the damage, as reheated steak gives rise to a new class of flavor compounds that taste "warmed over."

.   .   .

There is a big stainless steel vent in the middle of Laurent Vernet's kitchen that rises up to the ceiling like a church steeple and evacuates the considerable quantity of evaporated grease and meat odor generated on his stovetop, sending it out into the Edinburgh air. The kitchen is big and bright, with windows that look out onto the Port of Leith and the police station where Inspector Rebus, hero of the Ian Rankin crime novels, solves mysteries. Occasionally, fans of the detective series ring Vernet's doorbell and ask him if he has seen the fictional inspector lately. To date, he has not.

Vernet laid the steaks out on the counter so that they could reach room temperature before cooking. He considers this important for tenderness. "What you don't want is a thermic shock," he instructed, "which can cause a small bit of blood vessels to explode. Also, at cold temperatures, you block the enzyme that makes the meat tender."

A disquisition on the texture of steak had commenced.

"There are two kinds of juiciness," he continued. "You have volume of juiciness, and you have length of juiciness. If you take meat from South America that is hot boned"—sliced into cuts while the carcass is still warm—"it's often very juicy, but after the second or third chew it's dead dry. When that happens, you can be sure that there was a problem at the maturation level." By this, he meant that the steak hadn't been aged properly. "Nine times out of ten," he said, "it will be imported beef. A normal steak should go up to five and six chews and remain juicy."

Related to juiciness is tenderness, for which Vernet has an elegant definition: "A steak is not tender enough if you want to swallow but find that you still need to chew." Tenderness, however, should not be confused with springiness, which is not always a bad thing. The cut Vernet calls the *bavette*, which goes by the name of flank steak in America, is springy. But springiness, in turn, is not to be confused with squeakiness, which is never, ever desirable. "Imagine chewing on polystyrene," is how Vernet describes it. He has tasted steak that spared his imagination the task, and he believes the phenomenon is related to animal welfare. "If an animal has suffered and been slaughtered in extreme pain," he says, "its meat will have the squeaking feeling."

Steak can also cause a metallic taste in the mouth, though he classi-
fies this as a *feeling* rather than a *flavor*. "It's like in the morning, when
you take a spoon and touch it to your teeth. There is no scientific expla-
nation why this happens, but it does. In my experience," he went on, "it
is related to the age and sex of the animal. You find it with males who
have not been properly castrated, or a very young heifer or a young bull.
You do not get it from a steer. It's also related to beef that has been vacuum packed.

"I only use iron pans," Vernet said as he reached for one and then
repeated, "*Only.*" This was a griddle pan with ridges running across its
bottom. "A flat pan is okay," he conceded, "but if the steak is going to
give a lot of juice—a skirt steak or rump steak that has been vacuum
packed, for instance—then the water will come between the meat and
the pan and cause boiled flavors."

Vernet puts no oil or butter in his pan. He says that even a lean steak
possesses enough fat to lubricate the cooking process. During a tasting,
he will not salt his steaks, either before or after cooking, nor will he allow
any other form of flavoring to be added. He considers steak sauce and
"au jus" to be egregious sins. In order to keep the palate clean, he says,
it is inadvisable to eat meat for twenty-four hours before a tasting. Between steaks, he clears his palate with warm filtered tap water. He set a
glass down in front of me. Cold water, he said, "anesthetizes" the tongue,
and mineral water is too sweet.

When the pan was hot, Vernet laid the first steak across the ridges. It
was one of three leaner steaks, a lighter red than the others, from a cow
that was half Charolais. I expected it to stick to the pan and burn, but it
called upon some invisible reserve of fat, and when Vernet flipped it, the
steak was a gorgeous, even brown. "There is fat in the muscle, even if
you can't see it," he said. He cooked it to medium rare—about 60°C
(140°F)—which Vernet believes to be the ideal doneness. "If it's rare,
you don't get enough flavor. If it's well done, it's too dry."

The moment of tasting was approaching. I cleansed my mouth with
warm filtered water, cut a triangular morsel of Charolais steak, put it in
my mouth, and crushed it between two molars. Juices were released.
Texture was experienced. Sugars, peptides, acids, and salts landed on my

taste buds. Esters, ketones, aldehydes, benzenoids, lactones drifted into my nose. Neurons fired. A flavor image appeared in my brain. I now had to describe it.

Vernet told me to go with my first impression. "Don't think about it too much," he said. I thought about it too much. Sitting in the kitchen of a professional meat taster makes it difficult to know just what to say about the meat that is in your mouth. The temptation is to just stick with tap water.

At the best of times, language is ill equipped to describe experiences of the senses. How, for example, would you describe what an orange looks like to a blind person? How would you describe the way an orange tastes to someone who'd never eaten one? You might say it's sweet and juicy and just a little sour, but this description applies to almost any fruit, and there's nothing distinctively orangey about it. Someone once quipped that writing about music is like dancing about architecture, and the sentiment applies equally to using words to describe food.

This has not stopped wine writers, who take two approaches. There is the old, and now dying, British tradition of describing wines the way you might describe the character of a person. A wine could be impetuous, callow, and immature, or it could be elegant, refined, and noble. The problem with this method is that too often wines became victims of the British class system. A fine wine typically sounded as if it went on pheasant shoots with its chums from Oxford and knew what fork to use at dinner, while a bad wine sounded like a foul-tempered dockworker.

In the 1970s a newer American system took hold, one that endeavored to be both more precise and more agricultural. Wines, which were products of the earth, were now described with reference to fruits, vegetables, and flowers—call it the pastoral language school of flavor description. Instead of saying a wine was callow and hot-tempered, you would instead observe that it had intense but fleeting notes of strawberries, black currants, and eucalyptus. And with good reason. Wines do taste and smell of fruits, vegetables, and flowers. The smell of roses, for example, is considered a telltale sign of red wines grown on a particular patch of soil in Burgundy, France, called La Tache. Malic acid, which you find in white wines, smells like green apples.

Even the most florid of pastoral descriptions, however, is usually followed by the thing everyone cares about most: the score. Most of the time, a wine is scored out of 100, though scores don't tend to go below 50, so really they're out of 50, although in a sense they're only out of 30, because a score below 70 is extraordinarily rare—not to mention bad. Anything above 90 is considered very good. A score above 95 is excellent.

Vernet has applied the pastoral language approach to steak. He believes that, like wine, the flavor of steak is something like a symphony, and that individual notes can be distinguished and appreciated. How many notes? At least fifty-eight, judging by his scoring sheets. He uses these to assess each steak he tastes and keep a record of his findings. He handed me a stack, so that I could do the same.

The first table included the general category of "Smell," which was, in turn, subdivided into "Fresh," "Pleasant," "Off," and "Others," all graded on a scale from 0 to 5. There followed "Juiciness," "Tenderness," and finally "Texture & feelings," which judged "fibrousness," "uniformity," "Gristle," "Connective tissues," "pleasant," "grain," "Squeak," "metallic," and "Others." And that was just the first table. There were three.

The second tracked flavor and was quite a bit more complicated. It started with the five basic tastes—sweet, salt, sour, bitter, and umami—which were followed by a long list of general flavor categories, themselves broken into more specific individual flavors. For example, "Green" ranged from "Cucumber" to "swamp," "Green shoots," "Green woods," "forest," and "Fresh cut tree." There were, all together, thirteen broad flavor categories within which I could track a steak's flavor. And finally, there was "Length," which ranged from "None" to "flash," "short," "average," "long," and, last, "persistent." A steak, presumably, could taste of cucumber and furniture, with a hint of hazelnuts, caramel, and clotted cream, but that flavor could last for no more than a flash.

A steak does not end at flavor for Vernet. The flavor box is repeated (more blood, more green, more earth)—this time, however, for "Aftertastes." Wine lovers call this the finish, and a longer finish, so long as it is pleasant, is considered a good thing.

Sample: _____

		0	1	2	3	4	5	Notes
Smell	Fresh	none	fresh	acceptable	good	appetising	Matured	
	Pleasant	none	not acceptable				dribble	
	Off	none	acceptable			Not acceptable		
	Others							Fishy, gamy, onion
Juiciness	Moisture release	Cloying	wet	juicy	succulent	luscious	damp	
	Length (chews)	Very short	short	average		long	too long	
	First bite	hard	firm	resistant	easy	tender	melting	
Tenderness	Length (chews)	Very short	short			Long	too long	
	Springy	not					very	
	Other							
Texture & feelings	fibrousness	thin	silk	string		cord	coarse	
	uniformity	messy	irregular			uneven	homogeneous	
	Gristle	None		Some		Some and unacceptable (mess of gristle)		
	Connective tissues	None		Some		Some and unacceptable (mess of gristle)		
	pleasant	Rough (see grain)		pleasing	velvety	silky	Over-oily	
	grain	smooth	toothpaste	rough	grainy	cardboard	Leather bowls	
	Squeak	None	Present			Unacceptable		
	metallic	none	discreet		present		iron	
	Others							Specify: sour or sweet

"Round" is a good term to give a good overall "texture & feeling"

Basic Tastes / Flavours		0	1	2	3	4	5	Notes
Basic Tastes	Sweet	No	Little				Strong	Too strong	
	Salt	No	Little				Strong	Too strong	
	Sour	No	Little				Strong	Too strong	
	Bitter	No	Little				Strong	Too strong	
	Umami	No	Little				Strong	Too strong	
Flavours	Green	Cucumber	swamp	Green shoots*	Green woods*	forest	Fresh cut tree	* depends on association with sweetness or sourness
	Brown	Dry straw	silage	Timber	Timber +	furniture	Waxed wood	
	Earth	dust	earth	Wet earth	humus	mushroom	rotten	
	Liver	No	Liver discreet	Liver	Liver strong	Too strong		
	Gamy	No	matured		venison	Gamy	Too strong	
	Nuts	No	Light/hazelnuts		Chestnuts*	Strong/Walnut		* Chestnuts: grilled, boiled or raw
	Blood	No	Fresh blood					
	Fat	No	Neutral		Flavoured oil (see dairy)			
	Cooked beef	No	Roast −	Roast +	Burnt (level of bitterness)			
	Caramel	No	Light caramel	caramel		Toffee*	Treacle**	* associated with dairy ** associated with bitterness
	Sweet	No	Neutral	candy	Flower −	Flower +	honey	
	Dairy	No	Semi-skim	Whole	Cream*	Clotted cream	butter	* "crème fraîche" if associated with sourness
	Off flavours	No			Invasive			Not expected flavours such as fish, onion, garlic . . .
	Others							
	Length	None	flash	short	average	long	persistent	

(continues)

	0	1	2	3	4	5	Notes
Green	Cucumber	swamp	Green shoots*	Green woods*	forest	Fresh cut tree	* depends on association with sweetness or sourness
Brown	Dry straw	silage	Timber	Timber +	furniture	Waxed wood	
Earth	dust	earth	Wet earth	humus	mushroom	rotten	
Liver	No	Liver discreet	Liver	Liver strong	Too strong		
Gamy	No	matured		venison		Too strong	
Nuts	No	Light/hazelnuts		Chestnuts*	Strong/Walnut		* Chestnuts: grilled, boiled or raw
Blood	No	Fresh blood		Gamy			
Fat	No	Neutral		Flavoured oil (see dairy)			
Cooked beef	No	Roast –	Roast +	Burnt (level of bitterness)			
Caramel	No	Light caramel	caramel		Toffee*	Treacle**	* associated with dairy ** associated with bitterness
Sweet	No	Neutral	candy	Flower –	Flower +	honey	
Dairy	No	Semi-skim	Whole	Cream*/clotted cream	Butter/young cheese	matured cheese	* "crème fraîche" if associated with sourness
Off flavours	No	Invasive					Not expected flavours such as fish, onion, parmesan, garlic . . .
Other flavours							
Length	None	flash	short	average	long	persistent	
Other comments							

Aftertastes

Last update: 21 August 2008

A second morsel of the Charolais cross was now in my mouth. I endeavored to distinguish the various notes and chart them in pencil. Under "Juiciness," I noted the steak as being "juicy," though the length of the juiciness was "short." Fibrousness I put down as "string"—which isn't as bad as it sounds—and uniformity as "irregular." But when it came to flavor, I was stumped. I was tasting steak, and that steak tasted nice, perhaps very slightly sour. That was all I could say. I registered no timber, no wet earth, no venison, chestnuts, or honey. I could taste the symphony, but no individual notes.

Vernet was not stumped. He was tasting plenty. For well over a minute, he just sat there chewing and concentrating, making the occasional notation with his pencil. Finally, he spoke: "For me it's a nice steak, it's a pleasing steak. It's honest. It has a nice smell. It's not fresh, but slightly mature. I find it quite short on the juiciness. It's a steak in a hurry—you have to swallow it quickly to enjoy it." He kept going. "The tenderness, I find it easy, though not specifically tender. The chew is short, and there was no springiness. Fibrousness was stringy"—we agreed on something—"the grain, I found it a little bit grainy."

He paused for a breath, then addressed the subject I could not: flavor. "I found it sweet and salty, and sourness on the finish, but a short sourness. It was slightly more salty than sweet. Within the green, a slight what we call 'forest,' not a green vegetal flavor, but if I had to say it was a fruit or vegetable, I would say a dry flower. No earthy flavor, no liver flavor, no gamy flavor whatsoever. On the nuts I would say hazelnuts—dry hazelnuts, not the green ones. No blood flavor. Roast was very discreet, despite the nice browning. There's a light caramel. On the sweetness, very discreet, so flower-minus. And dairy I would say semi-skim. You can feel a little bit of dairy flavor, but it's not overly powerful. And I didn't put anything for aftertaste, because I think it's quite short. But I would not put it as flash, I would put it as short."

In stark and alarming contrast, I found the steak merely uninteresting. I detected precisely none of the flavors that Vernet had. Was I merely inexperienced? Was his tongue a more sensitive tasting instrument than my own? Do two people taste steak the same way?

Steak number two came from a Limousin heifer and sizzled in much the same manner as its predecessor. But it did not taste the same. It was, comparatively, dry and tough. Vernet found the smell "fresh," and the taste moved from salty to sour and then bitterness. "I would put it as green woods and silage. I found a slight liver flavor, but it didn't stay long. I didn't find any other flavor, not even dairy flavor. I think it finished on a very green shoot flavor."

Under flavor, I circled "Green woods" and "silage," but only because Vernet had cited them. I doubt that I would have come to them on my own, in part because silage—fermented grass—is not a smell I'm familiar with.

That is one of the great pitfalls of the pastoral language approach: obedient mimicry. Flavor descriptions uttered by people with renowned palates have a funny way of becoming self-fulfilling prophecies. If a big, important critic pronounces that a particular wine has a bouquet of honey, toasted oak, and cherry blossoms, then all over the world, aspirational types who live in big cities—people who spend almost no time in the country smelling things like honey, toasted oak, or cherry blossoms—drink that particular wine and all end up detecting the same aromas and notes.

The third steak was an Angus-Limousin cross—Scottish father, French mother. It didn't perform as well as the others, though it didn't embarrass itself, either. Vernet found an initial sourness that gave way to the aroma of honey, though not the *taste* of honey, and it finished quite strongly, he thought, on raw fresh mushrooms. "I would say that it's a ladies' steak," he pronounced. "It's discreet, and not my favorite, but similar to the filet." Women, he informed me, prefer the tender, milder tenderloin, while men prefer fattier, more robust-tasting rib eyes. This rib eye, hence, was mild enough to suit the tastes of a lady.

All the steaks, thus far, had come from cows that had been fattened on grain. The last of the bunch was the reason I had traveled to Scotland. It was pure Angus. It had been finished in the true Scottish manner: on grass. It was also, somewhat unexpectedly, the most marbled of the lot, and this was a surprise because grain-fed steaks almost always outmarble grass-fed ones, yet this one carried enough specks of fat to qualify for the upper end of USDA Choice.

How does purebred Aberdeen-Angus steak taste? Sour, almost to the point of ammonia. It began with the smell, which Vernet placed as "vinegar and cold sweat." He registered lilac and jasmine, milk, and a gamy venison taste. I registered dank. It reminded me of sweaty blue cheese. And that was a big shame, because in every way other than flavor, it was excellent: tender, popping with juice, and silky.

I asked Vernet why he refuses salt during a tasting, given that almost everybody puts it on steak. Why not replicate real-world conditions in the lab? Vernet explained that he didn't want to adulterate the taste in any way. He wanted to keep it pure. This is a man, after all, who won't add so much as a teaspoon of butter to his steak pan.

Unlike Vernet, I am a Salt Loyal. Salt makes steak taste better, plain and simple. More to the point, salt adds more than saltiness to food. It is an amplifier of flavor. Salt brings out character. It has what science calls a synergizing effect. When salt is added to a solution of umami-flavored water, the umami flavor becomes magnified. (Umami, likewise, magnifies the flavor of salt, which is why you often find MSG in low-sodium canned soups.) There is also scientific evidence suggesting that salt amplifies other flavors, including sweet. Sprinkled judiciously, salt turns up flavor's volume knob.

Now that the official portion of the tasting had concluded, I was free to adulterate. As Vernet cooked another Charolais rib eye and another purebred Angus rib eye, I broke out the salt. It did nothing to help the Angus rib eye. If anything, the sourness was more extreme. The steak now tasted like bad wine.

The Charolais was another story. As if to prove Vernet's earlier directive to let steaks rest at room temperature before cooking, the now well-rested Charolais steak displayed a markedly different character than it had an hour earlier, even before so much as a grain of salt had been sprinkled on. It now smelled of almonds. Vernet registered it. More important, I registered it. The smell of almonds was unmistakable. The taste, too, was somewhat sweeter than before.

Then I sprinkled some salt, and the smell of almonds graduated from aroma to a faint but discernible flavor. The steak was sweeter, tangier, beefier, and deeper. The steak was delicious.

It would be a mistake, however, to say that the steak *tasted* like almonds. It tasted a lot more like a steak than like a nut, which brings us to what is, perhaps, the most serious problem with the pastoral language approach: Does it actually communicate anything? To those who never ate that Charolais cross, I can tell you that a pack of almonds is no substitute, and neither is "forest" or dry hazelnuts, just as eating wet leather rubbed with cherry blossoms and vanilla beans would tell you very little about a wine that is said to evoke those very notes. Wines don't taste exactly like vanilla, cherry, wet leather, or whatever. They possess notes that gesture, sometimes quite forcefully, in that direction.

But all these notes—however powerful—don't tell the whole story, and the reason is all the flavor notes we don't have names for, the tastes and aromas in steak and wine that don't resemble nuts, green shoots, liver, vanilla, forest berries, and so forth. What about them?

This may be why so much wine writing sounds ridiculous. Consider the following flavor description I once read in a magazine: "Herbaceous notes of cut grass and fruity undertones of stewed apple and overripe banana." This was not, in fact, a description of a wine. It was not a description of a steak, either, or a fruit salad, or some blended health beverage meant to be consumed following yoga. It was a description of *tap water*. For those who have never tasted Toronto tap water but are curious about its flavor, I would say that putting cut grass, stewed apple, and overripe banana through a juicer will not result in a similar-tasting substance at all. This is the problem with all flavor descriptions: they sound pretty but run a serious risk of being useless. At best, the information they contain resonates only with those who have tasted the thing that's being described.

The problem, of course, is that you have to say *something*. You can't consume something as delicious as steak or wine and just sit there in silence.

Steak, it seems to me, tastes more like steak than any plant, fruit, or mineral. Steak is its own flavor note. If someone gave you a grilled mushroom that tasted like steak, you would say, "It tastes like steak." You would not say, "This mushroom tastes like silage, cream, liver, and fresh cut tree." Whatever else is going on with steak—340 volatile compounds, at last count—the main attraction is the taste of meat.

I raised the issue, somewhat warily, with Vernet. He agreed. He said flavor is, primarily, a personal experience that is very difficult to communicate. He did not create his tasting sheets so that the whole world could start talking about steak as though it were wine. He drafted them for himself, so he could keep track of all the steak he was eating. He only began handing them out to others because people asked him to. As for all the various shades of beefiness and meatiness that make steak *steak*, he acknowledged there was a lot of work to be done in this area. "Beef is something we've been eating for millennia," he said, "and yet we have no good way of talking about the way it tastes. It's actually a cultural disaster."

That is why everyone loves wine scores. They may be crass. They may take a rich sensory experience and boil it down into a number. But they sure are precise. It may be impossible, in the end, to verbally communicate exactly how a thing tastes, but the whole world understands a score out of a hundred.

While Vernet does not give steaks numerical scores, he has an easier time with assigning letter grades. I asked him to name the best steak among the four we'd just tasted, and he chose the Charolais cross. This was not a case of patriotic bias. If anything, Vernet was inclined to prefer the Angus steak, because he prefers grass-fed beef over grain-fed beef, believing it to be more "interesting." "It's like wine," he says. "There are hundreds of flavors. You never know what the next one is going to bring, and that makes steak exciting. It makes me wonder what I'm going to have tonight."

I agreed with Vernet's choice, despite my inability to register the same notes as him. The Charolais cross won the day.

"How would you rate it?" I asked.

"A solid B-plus," he said. "It was a good, honest steak."

"Have you ever tasted an A-plus?"

Here, Vernet paused. "If you're a naive steak lover," he told me, "you eat A-plus steaks all the time. But once you become an expert, you are never satisfied."

This was not good news. Here I was, a pilgrim in the Holy Land of steak, reeling from the religious epiphany that the most famous beef breed in the world tastes like bad homemade wine. Worse, according to Vernet, A-plus steak would forever be out of reach, and all because I'd set out to find A-plus steak in the first place. I felt like a character in some absurd Greek tragedy, doomed to walk the earth hungering for a food that did not exist.

Scotland is a pretty country. The roads are so winding that they seem designed to ensure a maximally scenic experience, and the fields are greener than in most other places by orders of magnitude. They are also pleasantly irregular, having been parceled off in an age before right angles, and are separated by fences hewed out of rock or long and commendably trim hedges. A knight in armor on horseback would look less out of place on a Scottish road than a car does. But what would look most natural of all is a golf cart. The entire country is a vision of the golfing afterlife, with epic stretches of fairway and rough, and the odd clump of forest for texture. Fields stretch out to the horizon, covering the rises in the land the way a taut blanket covers an uprise of toes. Looking skyward, you have the feeling that the hand of God might plunge through the cloud cover to stroke all that dewy pasture like an old woman patting a cat.

I crested a hill and beheld yet another panorama in green. It is impossible, I said to myself, that such a fine chunk of geography could not produce an excellent piece of beef. I was willing to concede artificial vaginas to the French. But not steak. I had to keep looking.

I drove back south to Kelso, the little town next to the stud farm where I met Jim Cameron. As luck would have it, I know someone who lives there. PJ—short for Peter John, though no one calls him that—and I had spent a lot of time together back in our university years, most of it inebriated. I found him living in a cute house in a cute town with his wife, Charlotte, and two daughters, whose cuteness surpassed their surroundings. He was fairly shocked to hear what Big Al and company were up to just down the road. We went out for steak, as I felt I needed to get out of the lab, so to speak, where the bright light of scientific inquiry was ruining the experience. In the fresh air of the real world, I thought, steak would be satisfying again. We hit a local pub, and the steaks were awful— dry, burned, and cardboardlike. I could almost hear Laurent Vernet saying, "I told you so." We salvaged the outing by draining many pints of beer and glasses of wine, the exact number of which remains uncertain.

The next morning, PJ showed me the fat he'd been stockpiling. In a jar in his fridge was an off-white blob of goo that looked like a home-made lava lamp. I picked it up, contemplating the oleaginous substance inside. "Fine work, PJ," I said.

For the last several months, every time meat had been roasted in the oven, PJ and Charlotte retained the fat and poured it into a jar. This was at my request. The name for this substance is pan drippings, and in this day and age the vast majority of them are thrown out. But it was not always thus. In the age when fat had value—an era stretching from at least the Paleolithic to roughly fifty years ago—people stored pan drippings in jars so that the fat would live to fry again. They used pan drippings to fry potatoes or as the base for a gravy. Some people, bless them, would even spread the stuff on toast.

I learned the value of pan drippings years earlier, when my wife—at the time, still just my girlfriend—and I were living in London. I was working at a magazine called *Group Travel Organiser*, which was, as its name suggests, a publication best avoided. I would spend each eternal workday writing soul-destroying stories about, say, what happens when a group of retirees from rural Birmingham plans a trip to Madame Tussauds wax museum and the bus breaks down on the motorway. I was given an hour for lunch every day, and a few blocks up the road was a butcher shop. The beef was Scottish, and if you phoned ahead, the butcher would make you a rib eye sandwich. That sandwich was the only aspect of life at *Group Travel Organiser* that I did not detest. I so relished those rib eye sandwiches that I forced myself to consume them sparingly, not wanting to exhaust a resource so precious. I would spend a day or two anticipating the next rib eye sandwich, wishing it could come sooner, and the day after it was eaten, I would buy a grease-stained paper cone of fish and chips and lament the rib eye's passing. Eventually I started eating them more often, and soon I was phoning in orders whenever the craving struck, as often as three or four times a week. This in no way diminished the cravings.

I was not the sandwich's only fan—by noon a line typically stretched out the butcher's door. But one day, I got there as the lunch rush was tapering, so I took the opportunity to ask the butcher his secret. "The drippings stay in the pan," he said, which was a nice way of saying that the black iron pan behind the cash register never got washed. The drippings stayed put, congealing, coagulating, and maturing, becoming more replete with beefiness with each successive sandwich. I went home and described the technique to my wife. Her verdict: disgusting. But the taste was such that the process could not be questioned.

That butcher shop is gone now, I am sad to report, a victim of a new mega-supermarket that opened down the road, which sells lean steak aged for four days on Styrofoam trays.

Pan drippings are another of modernity's victims. Several months before leaving on my trip, I attempted to track down some Scottish pan drippings by phone, thinking that in the land of deep-fried Mars Bars my chances might be good. To no avail. Everyone could remember an aunt or a grandmother who kept a greasy pan on the stove, or a jar of fat on the windowsill. But no one said, "Yes, I can get you drippings." So I asked PJ, a Canadian transplant, to collect some. What he'd produced so far was indeed impressive. All I needed now were delicious Scottish rib eyes.

Two days later, I had them. Acquiring these steaks required a considerable amount of time on the phone, and a good deal more in the car, but there they were, sitting on PJ's kitchen table, waiting to be laid in hot, aged fat. I had amassed four rib eyes altogether, and four pope's eyes, too—"pope's eye" being the local, not to mention baffling and unappetizing, name for rump steak. (Farther south, over the border in Dorset, a pope's eye refers to a cut the Scots call a salmon-cut silverside, which is called bottom round in America. Go figure.) Charlotte handed me two pans. I put them on burners turned up to high, then spooned a gob of fat into each, which oozed across the hot metal.

The steaks came from two farms, the first of which, in another stroke of geographic good fortune, was just outside Kelso. Hardiesmill was recommended by Laurent Vernet for the simple reason that it is one of the few farms that sells 100 percent pure Angus beef that is fed on grass. Steak doesn't get more Scottish than that.

As though being paid to market their own farm, black doddies (and a few red ones) were out in the fields munching grass when I pulled in to Hardiesmill. The farm is run by Alison and Robin Tuke, and the herd originally belonged to Alison's father, who was the kind of man who walked into a restaurant and asked what breed the steak was from, and would then walk out if the waiter didn't know the answer. Alison is a trained florist and Robin is a former telecom executive, but they now raise beef that they like to think of as *premier cru*—a term the French use to denote top-drawer wine.

We walked out into the field to have a look at all those doddies. Cows grazed next to calves, eating around the manure patties, where the grass grew in tall tufts. Over in the far corner was the bull, a rippling immensity, with muscles so numerous and defined he looked as if he'd just lumbered off a photo shoot for the front cover of *MuscleMag*.

We drank tea and talked steak in the Tukes' kitchen. From the beginning, their goal has been to raise the kind of traditional Scottish beef you don't find anymore. They once gave some to an old butcher who works down the road, who said, "I haven't tasted beef like this in thirty years." Their doddies are fed hardly any grain, just a pound of barley a day during winter, to help the vitamins go down. We visited their beef fridge, which is in their barn, and I was handed several steaks descended from Erica, the most famous cow in the history of the breed, whose painting I had seen at the Aberdeen-Angus Cattle Society's boardroom. Alison later handed me a sheaf of papers to prove it.

I was nevertheless apprehensive. The grass-fed steak in Texas tasted like river bottom. The grass-fed steak in Vernet's flat tasted like bad homemade wine. What would this stuff taste like? Sour milk? Vinegar? Rancid anchovies?

The steak *looked* okay: bright red and marbled with yellowy wisps of fat. When raw, it had a mild beefy smell.

Lineage, apparently, matters. That steak was outstanding—fabulous, a eureka moment, an Aberdeen-Angus tour de force. It was tender, juicy—both initial and sustained—and hugely flavorful, a flavor that was smoky at first, then resonantly beefy, bursting with juice on each chew. There were other notes present, perhaps hundreds, but I was too excited to pick them out. The pleasure of Erica's distant progeny rendered me near speechless. If the Charolais cross Vernet and I tasted was a solid B-plus, then this was easily an A. Nine out of ten. A 93. In short, it was the best Scottish steak I've eaten in my life.

Then we tried the steak from the second farm, and it was better.

My late uncle Chuck, a steak lover through and through who breathed his last breath while eating prime rib, told me that if I was going to Scotland, I had to find Highland beef. Not one to dishonor the memory of one of the better joke-tellers I have known, I phoned the Highland Cattle Society and managed to get my hands on a copy of the *Highland Breeders' Journal*. In the back, I found a long list of farmers raising a breed known as Highland cattle, and I began phoning at random. Most didn't have any steak. One who did—thousands of pounds, by the sounds of it—assured me that it tasted no different from the shorthorns and Galloways he also kept, and he explained at length how good he had become at fattening Highlands—which are notoriously slow-growing—quickly and getting them onto refrigerated shelf space by the time they were just over a year old. Laurent Vernet warned me about people like that.

One farmer sounded quite promising until he mentioned where he and his Highland cows lived: on the Isle of Mull, a rainy, wind-battered chunk of rock off the west coast of Scotland, which was three hours and a ferry ride away by car. Such a trip, I decided, was best saved for retirement, when I could take my time and collect bottles of Scotch and jars of marmalade along the way. At length, I found myself scanning the *Highland Breeders' Journal*, looking for the most Scottish-sounding names. There were some good ones: Mr. Iain McKenzie, Mr. Archie McIntyre, Mr. Donald McDonald.

I settled upon one A. R. Mackay and dialed the number. A man with a deep voice picked up the phone, and I asked him if he sold Highland beef. "Aye." The following exchange ensued:

Me: "Would you say your beef is any better, or different, than the beef other people sell in Scotland?"

Angus Ruadh Mackay: "I think beef can be every bit as distinctive as a glass of single-malt Scotch, depending on where it's made and who makes it. My beef is the most intense I know. If you like a rich flavor, then this is the beef for you."

Jackpot.

Some take the view that Scotland gets progressively more Scottish the deeper into the Highlands you go. The whiskies become peatier, as do the accents. Clinging to that tundralike landscape is a breed of cattle that is fittingly called the Highland. They graze the rocky slopes and somehow thrive on land that would kill ordinary cattle. Centuries ago, their meat was so loved by Londoners that Highland beef fetched two cents a pound more than the meat of other breeds. Angus Mackay represents the continuation of a long tradition. He travels to far reaches to find cattle: the Isle of Islay, the Isle of Mull, and the Isle of South Uist, where he once bought cattle from a woman who shared her home with her Highlands, one of which provided the family with milk. One door led to the kitchen, another to the bedroom, and another to the byre, which is Scottish for cow barn. The lady saw nothing wrong with that.

Rather than walk his cattle hundreds of miles south or southeast, Mackay loads them onto a trailer. He doesn't cook steak on a shovel over an open fire, either, though he has heard of the technique and would like to try it. His Highlands fatten on a shaggy mane of grass that grows next to the river Earn, near the town called Bridge of Earn. (When Mackay says the words "Bridge of Earn," he rolls his r's in a manner that brings to mind a drumroll.) They eat clover and ryegrass, a diet that won't get them fat for two years, an eternity compared to the five-month turnaround achieved with steamed, flaked corn. At that age, a steer or heifer has a poorer kill percentage than a younger animal. There is more bone, more guts, less meat. But it is Mackay's belief that they taste more like beef when they are more mature, which is not what the USDA thinks. The secret to good steak, he says, is time. He likens supermarket beef—in either Scotland or the United States—to three-year-old whisky, a substance "you simply wouldn't want to eat." "All the modern technology in the world," he told me, "hasn't sped up the whisky-making process. The same is true with beef."

Every day, Mackay steps into the fields and visits his cattle. At no time will his speed exceed a walk, because even a light jog will worry them. "They become very suspicious," he says. "A lion can walk through a herd of wildebeest and not disturb them because it's moving at the same speed they are. You move at their pace and you can do anything you want." The cattle know Mackay and respond to his voice. When the time comes for his cattle to become steak, roasts, and mince, he rounds them up and drives them to the slaughterhouse personally, to keep their worry down. Anxiety equals stress, which Mackay forbids, because it can affect the quality of the meat. He has found that when Highlands suffer through a hard winter and don't get enough to eat, they will have a line of gristle in their flesh, like a stunted growth ring in tundra spruce. He does not buy these Highlands.

I tried to find Mackay's farm and got lost. He told me to drive north out of Bridge of Earn on Highway A912 and look for the farmers' market on the left in front of a field of grazing cattle. There was indeed a farmers' market, but no cattle, only the largest, shaggiest sheep I'd ever seen, reddish blond, with long, pointy horns and big eyes. They moved like goats—one of them practically hopped—but the woolly coats assured me of their sheepness. They looked resoundingly Scottish. The tourist board, I thought to myself, must put them in fields next to the winding roads to add to the overall effect.

At the farmers' market I found a fridge full of local meats and another full of cheeses. The woman behind the cash turned out to be Mackay's sister. She took me outside to have a look at the sheep, which turned out to be cattle—Highland cattle. The cows had little calves next to them, and since it's not a good idea to get between them, we walked slowly and fought the urge to wrap the littlest ones in hugs. Up close, Highlands do not resemble cattle any more than they do from a distance, but they do seem less sheeplike. Their hide brings to mind a prehistoric shag rug, and the horns could pass for tusks.

Behind us loomed a bench of quartz called Moncrieff Hill. A bull was grazing not far from the cows. He was another tough customer, as compact as a car battery, his horns sharp, curved, and pointed forward. He wasn't as big and muscled as the Angus bull at Hardiesmill, but I might still put my money on him—size is an advantage, but it does not always win. The bull finished eating and hunkered down. With every movement, his body language broadcast a disdain for the cows around him, none of which were in heat. He did nothing to acknowledge our presence, either, but being ignored was its own kind of acknowledgment, and it felt like an honor.

Mackay wasn't around, unfortunately, having traveled up to the Highlands for his summer vacation. While the rest of the country was suntanning in the south of France or on some beach in Spain, he'd headed north to where the land was colder, rockier, and harder. But he'd left me some papers detailing the provenance of the steak that was for sale in the well-lit modern display fridge. The lineage could be traced all the way back to a cow born in 1861 whose name was Magan, and whose father was called Dun Bull. Magan was mated to a fellow named Duntuilm Riabach, and their progeny would include, almost 150 years later, a steer with the sadly non-Gaelic name of 502552/600084, a steer who was nonetheless not the product of artificial insemination or embryo transfer, but who was conceived the old-fashioned way.

I will venture a guess and say that Angus Mackay's Highland rib eye steak is not the first of its kind to be cooked in aged pan fat. The flesh was darker than that of the Angus steak, the fat equally yellow, though brighter. It caused audible groaning. PJ put a piece in his mouth and on his second chew paused and declared the Highland steak to be "phenomenal." On his third and final chew—only three were necessary—he said, "I've never had a better steak."

The juiciness begged credulity. It seemed impossible that a piece of meat so small could contain such a volume of liquid. A man lost for days in the desert, it seemed, could be rehydrated with a single Angus Mackay Highland steak. Its tenderness was equally astonishing. I was able to cut my rib eye with the side of my fork. I discarded my knife and sliced into it as though I was eating cheesecake.

Did it all come down, finally, to breed? Perhaps. Mackay takes the subject seriously. Once upon a time, he raised Charolais cattle—a big, high-yield breed—but he was so put off by the amount of grain they needed that he set out to stock his farm with cattle that had not been "improved" by the hand of man. He settled on Highlands, because during the nineteenth-century boom in breed refinement, they were never tinkered with the way Dishley longhorns, shorthorns, Angus, and all the rest were. And for all the inside breeder talk of "purity" and "full-bloods," almost every breed has been mixed with other breeds, at some point. Angus, the story goes, were crossed with red longhorns in an effort to bulk them up, and they forever carry this taint. Highlands, however, remain pure. They look and taste, Mackay says, like they did three hundred years ago.

Highlands remain pure in part because they are hard to sell in today's yield-obsessed world. They're small, they grow slowly, they're too shaggy for the hot Texas sun, and their long horns would cause untold laceration in the close confines of a feedlot. Beef today is about selling as many pounds as possible, and Highlands give fewer pounds than a fast-growing Angus or a big Charolais. Highlands may be delicious, but they don't make money.

There may be a scientific basis for the way a Highland steak tastes. About three hundred miles southeast of Mackay's farm lives a professor of veterinary molecular medicine at the University of Nottingham named Kin-Chow Chang who has spent a great deal of time studying how muscles grow. The muscles that grow quickly, he told me over the phone, tend to be of the "fast-twitch" type, which are better for sudden and intense bursts of movement, such as sprinting. Unfortunately, they don't taste very good, as they are thick and tough and their cells contain less myoglobin—the substance that makes red meat red. Slow-twitch muscles, on the other hand, are designed for sustained exertion. Unlike fast-twitch muscles, which use sugar as an energy source, slow-twitch muscles contain fat, and their fibers are smaller and finer than their fast-twitch cousins'. According to Chang, all those big, high-yielding continental breeds—Charolais, Limousins, and others—which were used for centuries to pull plows and haul enormous carts and have, more recently, been bred to grow astoundingly fast, contain lots of fast-twitch muscle fibers. Their steaks, therefore, are tougher and less flavorful than the steaks from smaller, finer-grained British cattle. It also means that all those high-performing muscle-bound Angus bulls pictured in the *Aberdeen-Angus Review*—with their high-priced semen that will produce similarly fast-growing progeny—will also produce tougher, less flavorful meat.

Angus Mackay's Highland steak did have an undeniably fine grain to it. Of all the breeds I'd sampled, it possessed a distinctive mouthfeel. Was its superiority simply a matter of fiber size? What about Angus Mackay's ryegrass and clover pastures? Did this combination of alluvial soil—the fertile muck left behind by millennia of spring floodings—and those particular grasses make for sublime beef? Or did I just happen to luck out with 502552/600084? Maybe he was an exemplary representative of the Highland breed, and I was comparing him to a merely average doddie?

It hardly mattered. Outstanding meat is the enemy of thought. It causes a single-minded focus on the pleasures of the mouth. We tore through the rib eyes, and then through the pope's eyes, communicating via groans and the odd squeal, pausing only to make exclamations about juiciness, or philistine assertions like "I never want it to end." To someone standing and listening just outside the door, the meal would have sounded rather like an orgy.

Minutes later, the three of us sat there in the satisfied quiet that follows bouts of extreme physical pleasure. PJ leaned back in his chair and sipped his wine. Charlotte lit a cigarette. After a time, I broke the silence and made a pronouncement that Laurent Vernet had told me was impossible.

"That steak," I said, "was an A-plus."

CHAPTER FOUR

ITALY

I f we were looking for reasons to turn back, we did not have to look hard. The road leading out of Agropoli, for instance, did not remain a road for very long. As it climbed up Monte Tresino, it became a bouncing strip of rocks and dirt. To our left, the well-vegetated mountainside tumbled down and then plunged into the Mediterranean, which is just what a car would do if it bounced the wrong way and veered off course. After one particularly higher-than-average bounce, I buckled my seat belt, and Mario—the driver, and probably the world's best-looking cattleman—openly laughed at me. He had dark curly hair down to his shoulders, a goatee, and was wearing a collared shirt, black Calvin Klein jeans, and a belt with a big, shiny buckle. He took both hands off the wheel—the car was still moving—punched his chest with both fists, gestured at the magnificent view in front of us, and laughed again at the idea of a man so cowardly as to deny himself the thrill of life unbelted.

Next we spotted the ax-wielding Italian cowherd. He came sauntering unconcernedly down the mountainside, but when he saw Mario, a playboy in the fullness of life driving along *his* road, he walked toward the car, took the ax off his belt, and began sharpening it. The Italian cowherd, it quickly became apparent, knew Mario. This was potentially very bad because the Italian cowherd might have had a sister. Earlier, at an espresso bar in Agropoli, Mario told me, more in hand gestures than words, that before settling down with his wife he was something of a legend among the local ladies. Fortunately, the cowherd smiled at Mario and continued on his way. If he had a sister, she was good at keeping secrets.

Not long after that, we discovered the church of devil worship, and a few minutes later were picking our way down an overgrown hillside infested with snakes. But we pressed on—surrounded by snakes, under the shadow of Satan—because we were searching for something important: the quintessential Italian dish of all time, if not the greatest European dish of all time. And all because years ago, during a honeymoon in Italy, I ate an uncommonly delicious steak, a steak so enjoyable that within a short time of finishing it I began subscribing to an obscure Italian magazine called *Taurus International*, which led, eventually, to my phoning up strangers in Italy and asking them what the local cows looked like.

One of those strangers was now standing next to me. Clotilde Vecchio—everyone calls her Tilde—is, by training, a PhD archaeologist and, by practice, a working schoolteacher who also runs a food-themed bed-and-breakfast (which also serves terrific dinners) called Iscairia, and who spends whatever idle hours she has left combing the local hillsides in search of exalted food and recipes. A year or so earlier, I found her phone number on the Internet and dialed. There was a particular kind of Italian cow called Podolica I had read about in the pages of *Taurus International*, and what I wanted to know was, were there any near her? "Yes," she said, "they live in the valleys in winter and move into the mountains during the summer." She said they were rare. She said that if you just went to a local butcher shop and bought steak, it would not be from a Podolica, and by her tone I could tell she regarded this as something local butchers ought to be ashamed of. You had to know someone. You had to meet him at an espresso bar in Agropoli, drive up a mountain where an ax-wielding cowherd lived, and look for the cattle yourself.

The road out of Agropoli ended at the church of devil worship, which was formerly a monastery of considerable magnificence but had been abandoned long ago. Judging by the freshness of the graffiti, the devil worship was a recent development, but decline had been setting in for decades, if not centuries. The stone walls were ensnared by roots so gnarled as to look arthritic, and the building had been half digested by the slow-moving earth. You could count the remaining roof tiles, but crossbeams still spanned the distance between the walls, holdouts against the forces of rot. We peeked inside long-disused rooms that smelled sweet with decay and floated theories as to why the monks had left. Walking inside anyone's home, inhabited or abandoned, creates an immediate and sometimes uncomfortable intimacy. To me it felt as if we were rummaging through the affairs of the dead. Tilde, who does this sort of thing all the time—she is an archaeologist in a country speckled with abandoned buildings—saw things on the bright side. She pointed out the wild roses in bloom. She picked mulberries off a tree, and I ate the same sweet fruit that had been enjoyed, presumably, by monks. She found wild fennel growing, then a bush with yellow flowers she called *ginestra*. None of this surprised Mario, who seemed to know his way around. Podolica cows, he said, eat all the wild herbs, flowers, and berries.

"The flavors are present in their meat," he said.

"Of course," Tilde said.

Snakes were probably everywhere, but the infestation was most extreme, according to Mario, on a series of grown-over rock terraces that led from the monastery toward the sea. As long as I stuck to the dirt path, I was told, I would not be bitten. We saw patties of Podolica manure, and it was evident by their placement that the cows did not stick to the dirt path. It led us to a couple of superbly old stone houses in the same sort of condition as the monastery. One was used for smoking and aging a traditional cheese called *caciocavallo*, which is made from Podolica milk. The fireplace was blackened from years of cheese-smoking. In a yard outside, a mother Podolica had been corralled. Her name was Badessa, and standing next to her was her little calf, Giacomino, so fresh to this world that his umbilical cord was still attached and dangling almost to the ground. The ax-wielding cowherd was back. His name was Nicola, he turned out to be Mario's brother, and he was now going to demonstrate how a human gets milk from a semi-wild cow. Nicola tied Badessa's head to one tree and her hind legs to another. He then invited Giacomino, who was all too willing, in for a suckle, a trick I would guess is roughly ten thousand years old. This settled Badessa down, and Nicola crouched down next to Giacomino, grabbed two teats, and began firing squirts of milk into a red pail. None of this was new to Tilde, who told me that when she was a little girl her father would milk the family Podolica and aim little blasts of warm cow's milk into her open mouth.

Badessa, tied to two different trees, looked helpless but resigned to the situation. I watched Nicola's pail fill and was struck by a thought: the supermarket dairy aisle is filled with stolen property. When Badessa was released, she didn't charge us, or attempt to gore Nicola, who stood there casually pouring her milk from the bucket into an empty Coke bottle. She simply walked away, and Giacomino followed. She did what an aurochs would not do: she let us get away with it, which is why there is such a thing as a modern dairy aisle.

Farther down the hillside, we found Podolicas. A big herd, mostly females and young males milling about. The bull was in rough shape. He looked timid and tired, and had long scrapes on his flank and rump. Someone, evidently, had beaten the crap out of him. That someone was standing on top of a rise of land, sniffing the rump of a female and looking mighty. This usurper, Mario told us, had loped in from the forest some months ago and imposed his hugeness first on the bull and then on the bull's cows. It hadn't been much of a contest, as he had more brawn and bigger horns than Mario's bull. For Mario, he was a problem. He was of unknown genetic heritage, and Mario wanted him out. Asking politely did not work. Neither did chasing, because the interloper ran too fast. And neither did Mario's tranquilizer gun. He aimed and fired at the interloper, but the dart bounced off his hide. For now, all Mario could do was stand there with us and watch as the bull ate Italian herbs and sniffed Italian rear end. The look on the interloper's face was one of self-satisfaction. The look on Mario's was one of respect.

For Tilde, this trip was just a typical day at the grocery store. On one mountain foray a few years back, she found a seventy-six-year-old grandmother living in a one-room cabin that had been connected only ten years earlier to Italy's electricity grid for the first time. While the old woman's husband played the accordion and sang dirty Italian folk songs, the old woman peeled the top off a bucket of lard and pulled out cured pork sausages that were nestled deep inside. On another adventure, Tilde visited a small seaside village near the Amalfi Coast to find a woman who knew an ancient Roman recipe for making sauce out of rotten fish. In the village where Tilde grew up, another old woman—103, on her deathbed—was the last living person who knew an ancient recipe for stuffed cuttlefish. Tilde begged her sister, who still lives there, to ask the woman for the recipe, but her sister considered it unseemly to make such a demand of someone so near passing. Tilde begged again, and eventually the sister complied. Now Tilde—and no one other than Tilde, so far as Tilde knew—possessed the ancient recipe for stuffed cuttlefish. Or so she thought. A few years after writing it down, she was reading a two-thousand-year-old Greek poem, and in it she found the very same preparation.

Back at Iscairia, Tilde poured the Podolica milk out of the old Coke bottle and into a pot. Milk is traditionally associated with whiteness, but this stuff was yellow, so much so that there are sunsets that aspire to less. Tilde spooned a sip. This is a woman, it is worth pointing out, who knows milk, who makes fresh cheese—out of local cow's or goat's milk—almost every day of every year. This particular milk educed a state of awe. Tilde spooned another sip and said, almost matter-of-factly, "This is the best milk I have ever used."

The milk was warmed on the stove to roughly body temperature, and then Tilde added rennet, an enzyme found in the intestines of calves that causes milk to separate into liquid whey and solid curds—which is what you make cheese out of. (All cheese is half-digested stolen milk.) She let it sit for four hours, strained the curds from the whey, and poured the curds into little round forms, which is what gives the Italians their word for cheese: *formaggio*. Now we had little disks of the freshest, purest cheese in all of Italy.

It was eaten as a first course at dinner, accompanied by nothing more than a fork, and it registered a blast of milkiness so intense as to make all other milk taste like bathwater. It left a trail of herbal sweetness in its wake—*ginestra* whispering, fennel talking—and tasted almost as rich and sweet as custard. Eating it put everyone in mind of Monte Tresino, even Tilde's husband, Nello Fariello, who spent the afternoon at the office. (He operates Fariello Mattresses, which holds the Guinness record for the world's largest mattress.) The cheese was a distillation of the hillside we'd walked, a summer breeze expressed as protein and fat. Here was a food that could be reduced to a simple equation: cows + mountain = cheese. In that sense, it was a profoundly Italian experience. No other mountain has quite the same soil, rain, and pasture as Monte Tresino.

But the recipe was also profoundly Italian, and in a broader sense, profoundly European. And the reason is that, a thousand years earlier, Europeans were crazy about Indian food.

There is a strong sense in Europe that all the food is as old as hills like Monte Tresino. (If you spend any time with Tilde Vecchio, it is almost literally true—she once made me a bean salad that is said to pre-date even the Greeks.) This is the reason why so many French and Italian wine or olive oil bottles have labels whose script appears to be older than the discovery of the New World, and why the packaging on fine cheeses and expensive butters habitually depicts bucolic landscapes or peasant maidens at the butter churn. In Europe, culinary heritage runs deep.

Most of the time, however, it's a myth—Tilde Vecchio the food-obsessed archaeologist notwithstanding. What people think of as typical European cuisine—especially the fancy stuff known as haute cuisine—is roughly three hundred years old, if not younger. Look back in time much further than that, and the fancy dishes served at fancy occasions become increasingly unrecognizable. If you go back all the way to the medieval era—that long, dark hangover that followed the collapse of the Roman Empire—the food eaten by wealthy Europeans is so unusual as to seem verging on ethnic.

When a medieval king or lord invited important guests over for dinner, he didn't serve veal in a wine and cream sauce, or plate seared tuna on a bed of kiwi and arugula with a perfect oval of red pepper–pomegranate coulis filling the white space. He likewise didn't serve freshly curdled cow's milk, however exquisite it may seem to the modern-day visitor to Italy, because that was what peasants ate.

The rich and powerful of the medieval period—like the rich and powerful in every other period—were out to impress their rich and powerful friends. The host of a big feast set dishes in front of his guests that were exotic, rarefied, colorful, richly spiced, unusually textured, massively flavored, and as unlike ordinary food as possible. Spices were extremely expensive—having arrived from far-off lands by way of long, often perilous, sea voyages—and so the more a chef used, the greater the display of his lord's wealth.

Medieval chefs practiced what is known as a cuisine of mixture. Flavorings were blended together to create new flavors. A dish of chicken wasn't about the taste or character of chicken so much as the sauce that accompanied it. Meats were stewed in thick and intense sauces and mixed with ingredients like ginger, sugar, vinegar, wine, raisins, mace, cloves, cumin, cardamom, cinnamon, pepper, and honey. A typical dish of the era was called "mawmenny," and to make it a chef would take ground beef, pork, or mutton, boil it in wine, and serve it in a wine-based sauce thickened with pounded chicken and pounded almonds, flavored with cloves, sugar, and fried almonds, and finally colored with an indigo or red dye. Dinner guests were smacked in the mouth with fantastic, never-before-tasted flavors, an assault of gustatory shock and awe.

Feasts were multicourse events, and a single one could feature five such dishes, a mode of service known as *service à la française*. In Europe a thousand years ago, a big feast wasn't all that different from a meal at an Indian or Chinese restaurant today: lots of different highly flavored dishes all served at the same time.

Around the eighteenth century, for reasons that don't appear altogether clear, food changed. Instead of carpet bombing guests with flavor, quantity, and variety, chefs began to worship at the throne of subtlety, their dishes taking a turn toward the delicate. The medieval cuisine of mixture was replaced by a new cuisine of *essence*. When preparing, for example, beef, the intention was now to celebrate the flavor of beef, not mask it. If steak was served in a sauce, the sauce was meant to complement the flavor of steak, perhaps even amplify it, but not cover it up. Food now tasted of what it was, and for the first time in European cuisine, less was more. Chefs reduced the number of ingredients and began using more herbs. There was a renaissance in vegetables. Gone was the practice of serving an armada of dishes simultaneously at banquets. Instead, each one arrived in a predetermined order, a mode of eating called *service à la russe*. The buffet was out; à la carte was in. Bold was out; refined was in. Every guest would set out on the same gustatory journey, beginning, say, with caviar, followed by soup, then building to vegetables, seafood, and meat, and gliding, at the end, to a pleasant finish with sweets, cheeses, fruits, and finally a liqueur.

Less hasn't stopped being more. This is not to say, of course, that European cuisine is devoid of mixture. Italians continue to relish one of the world's most famous mixtures of all time: pesto (pine nuts, aged cheese, basil, garlic, and olive oil, the combination of which creates a flavor greater than the sum of its parts). But in matters of food, no country reveres simplicity the way the Italians do. When Tilde makes a pizza sauce, the only herb she adds is basil, because any others would cover up the taste of tomato. When she makes cured sausage from pork, she doesn't add a single herb or spice—only salt and pepper—because she wants to taste the character of her pork, which is raised deep in the hills of Cilento on chestnuts and acorns. While the continent of Asia continues to smother its meats in ginger, garlic, scallions, and fermented sauces like soy sauce, hoisin sauce, fish sauce, oyster sauce, and black bean sauce, Europeans, by comparison, prefer their food more simple.

You might say, then, that the cheese made from Badessa's unpasteurized milk represents the apotheosis of Italian culinary simplicity, the end point of European culinary evolution since the Middle Ages. But that honor may be better suited to the dish we followed it with: grilled Podolica steak. The portion, after all, was quite a bit bigger.

The night I ordered steak on my honeymoon in Florence, it was served with nothing more than a glass of red wine and was flavored with nothing other than salt and pepper. I expected garlic. I expected sauce. I expected other things on the plate—potatoes, perhaps, green beans or a salad. But *service à la russe,* as I'd learned that night, is at its most extreme in Italy. The waiter informed me that the steak came from a local breed called Chianina, an ancient line of pure white cattle named after the Chiana Valley. That knowledge led me, eventually, to *Taurus International.* Every few months, a new issue would arrive and offer me some connection to the delicious steak of memory. I would gaze at the pictures of big white cattle grazing or big white cattle winning awards at Italian cattle shows. The Chianina was the most celebrated breed, but there were others, like the Marchigiana, Romagnola, and Piedmontese. There was also one breed from the south that received scarcely any mention: the Podolica. One day, I phoned up the editors of *Taurus International* and asked them about this mystery cow. No one had anything bad to say about the Podolica, but no one had anything good to say about it, either. All they would acknowledge was that the Podolica was "from the south," as though the south were a strange and unknown country. On the famous boot that is Italy, anything from the ankle on down is viewed with some degree of suspicion from the people above it: the south is unindustrialized and underdeveloped, southerners do not work hard or long, and everyone knows someone in organized crime. The people who say this sort of thing are northerners, whom the southerners believe to be uptight and lacking in passion. Given that *Taurus International* was published well north of Rome, were their views on the Podolica cow—or lack thereof—free from bias?

My attempt to answer that question led me to Tilde, the snake-infested slopes of Monte Tresino, and, one breezy evening in southern Italy, the gazebo that stands next to Tilde's olive orchard, where a bag of pre-charred wood known to Italians as *carbone* was being dumped into her outdoor grill. Earlier that day, after spending half an hour gazing at the interloper and his stolen harem, Mario drove us down into the valley to a barn just outside of Agropoli, where the *finissagio* takes place. This is the Italian word for "finishing," and it means the same thing in Italy as it does in America. Mario takes the cows to his barn to get them fat. (He leaves his bulls intact because if you castrate them, he told me, they get *too* fat.) The herbal diet on Monte Tresino, he told me, makes the meat taste too strong, so in his barn they eat grain that has been ground down into a powder, along with hay from a nearby farm. They eat about twelve pounds a day of the grain—about half the amount Bill O'Brien feeds his feedlot cattle.

Mario's Podolica steaks feature close to zero marbling. We bought them at the family butcher shop in Agropoli called U' Ruscignuolo, where the butcher is none other than Mario and Nicola's mother. She hung the side of beef for three days, then cut steaks off the rib eye as we waited. (We did not specifically request rib eyes, incidentally; we asked for the best *bisteccas* she had, and rib eyes are what we got.)

As the cheese was curdling that afternoon, Tilde's daughter, Wanda, asked a question of her mother—"Mama, are we going to marinate the steaks?"—that was met by a sharp "No!" in the kind of spontaneous spike of emotion that Italians, particularly southern ones, are famous for. Echoing Allen Williams, the disillusioned meat scientist, and Jim Cameron, the Scottish semen collector, Tilde insisted the Podolica steaks from Monte Tresino would take only salt. "I use sauce only if I know the beef is no good," she explained. No salt may touch her steaks until they are done cooking, however, because to apply it earlier would, in Tilde's words, "draw out the blood."

For reasons I am unable to fathom, Tilde does not take due pride in her grill. "It is nothing," she said, "compared to the grills of America." The truth is that it's much better than the grills of America. Its singular feature is the cooking grate itself, whose height can be adjusted by turning a crank. If the *carbone* is producing a thermal intensity appropriate to blacksmithing, it can be raised so that a large steak, or perhaps a leg of lamb, won't itself be turned into *carbone*. If, on the other hand, the steak has been sliced thin and the idea is to sear both sides while leaving the middle rare, then the space between the grill and the coals can be made appropriately intimate. The Podolica steaks were sliced at two centimeters—just under an inch—and Tilde turned the crank until there was a space of three inches between the meat and the glowing coals beneath.

After having tasted a Podolica steak of Monte Tresino, I have this to say to the editors of *Taurus International*: it could have been a lot more tender. It failed Laurent Vernet's test, which is to say that once you reached the point where you felt like swallowing, you still had a fair bit of chewing ahead of you. But I would also say this: Podolica steak from Monte Tresino is darn tasty. It possesses a gentle and sweet, even floral, flavor, with the same caramel note that's evident in the milk. (It is likely strange to read that a steak tastes of caramel, but the effect is much better than you might imagine.) It didn't have anything close to the intensity or sustain of Angus Mackay's Highland—the flavor curve dropped off the table, comparatively speaking. But it was good. In order to compare, Tilde also cooked a generic butcher-shop T-bone, and it tasted like water, only a lot drier. The T-bone was more tender. But what is tenderness without flavor? The answer: a steak that needs sauce.

Despite the weeks the Podolicas had spent in the barn eating hay and grain, something of Monte Tresino remained in the steak. This excited Tilde greatly. When she put the first bite in her mouth, she had a look of disbelief that melted into a smile. She had found what she is always looking for. She pointed at the steak and said, "Mark, this is a pure savor."

Pure savor means pure flavor. Pure savors are what Tilde has spent her life searching for. The seventy-six-year-old grandmother's sausages are a pure savor. The tomato sauce she makes for her pizza—tomatoes, garlic, and basil—is a pure savor. A roast potato drizzled in olive oil—so long as it is a good potato, grown in good soil, and drizzled with good olive oil—is a pure savor. And Mario's Podolica steak—not to mention the Podolica milk—is a pure savor.

The bigger question was this: How would a Chianina steak hold up against the Podolica? Would it still taste as good as it had on my honeymoon? Or was I cherishing steak memories from a more gustatorily naive time?

To find out, Tilde, Nello, and I set out to visit the greatest celebration of steak in all of Italy, and possibly the whole world: the Sagra della Bistecca. It takes place every August in the medieval town of Cortona, which, as medieval towns go, is quite the archetype. Cortona is a maze of narrow, winding streets with stone steps that have been worn smooth by the geologic action of tourists. A step in any direction presents a postcard snap of a perfect cobbled alleyway or a glimpse of the Val di Chiana—the Chiana Valley—which has a habit of appearing both suddenly and magnificently between two ancient buildings. The valley itself is a sprawl of tilled fields, cyprus trees, and olive groves that induces a sizable percentage of foreigners to buy a vacation home in rural Tuscany. Almost every view in Cortona is breathtaking, so much so that if you keep your eyes open for too long, you will run short of breath.

It was evening at the peak of the Italian summer when we arrived, and strolling conditions could not have been better. A person could walk with no more than a Kleenex draped over his shoulder and feel neither too warm nor too cold. In a town made for strolling, during an evening made for strolling, we strolled over to the cathedral, which has looked out over the Val di Chiana since the eleventh century. The nearest field was at least a few miles away, and if Chianina were grazing, it wasn't possible to see them. Outside the cathedral, a crowd had formed around a parked ambulance. Robed priests and nuns were carrying a statue of the Virgin Mary from the cathedral in a slow procession, and they placed her into the ambulance's interior, which had been decorated with sheer pink curtains, flower garlands, and silver and pink ribbons. The three of us strolled into the cathedral and were met by the cool, damp embrace of thousand-year-old stone. As with all ancient European cathedrals, it was filled with the tombs of important people who'd been dead for centuries. One of the very biggest was in the middle of the central aisle and featured as its insignia the horned head of a cow. A good sign.

Back outside, a priest closed the ambulance doors. It drove off, and the crowd broke into a prolonged round of waving and clapping. The Virgin Mary, apparently, was going to make it.

Strolling back to the central square—Piazza della Repubblica—we passed a trattoria, and next to its entrance was a little blackboard on which was written a single word in chalk: "Bistecca." Two attractive female customers—shapely, stylishly dressed, cell phones at the ready— were carving hunks off a steak so large it would not have looked out of place on *The Flintstones*. A very good sign.

The Sagra della Bistecca, which was celebrated for the first time in 1959, may be the newest thing about Cortona. At various strategic points around town, promotional posters—one of which I stole—displayed a still life of an earthenware jug filled with wine standing next to a big steak fabulously branded with grill marks. When we arrived at the *sagra*, it looked like a summer fun fair that had caught fire. There were festive lights, the din of voices, outbursts of laughter and music—and massive clouds of smoke. We headed straight for the grill, which, though not height-adjustable, was huge—six feet wide by twenty feet long. It had been made especially for the *sagra* by a local ironworker and appeared to be brand-new. But in a few years, another grill would be commissioned because this grill, like all that have preceded it, would eventually become bent and ruined by combustion.

A field of embers glowed yellow and white beneath the grill. Surrounding it stood eleven men, eight of whom were wearing white hairnets and aprons, dodging billows of smoke, and turning steaks with pitchforks. Another man wheeled over cartfuls of *carbone* and added them to the inferno. (He shovels five hundred pounds an hour.) Another collected cooked steaks. Another Frisbeed raw steaks on the grill, tossing them with the grace and accuracy of a professional card dealer, ensuring maximal grill coverage at all times.

Over the three days of the *sagra*, some eight thousand people come to Cortona to eat *bistecca*. It is considered an important part of the local economy, according to Andrea Vignini, Cortona's mayor, whom I found myself sitting next to. The Chianina cow, he explained, is deemed sacred. It was first raised by the Etruscans—the people who lived in Italy before the Romans—though it is unclear if they ate *bistecca*, which we know for certain has been enjoyed since the nineteenth century, but likely much longer. Spiritual ownership of the Chianina cow is a contentious matter. Cortona counts the cow as its own, but so do three other cities in the Val di Chiana. "In Cortona," the mayor said, "the belief that the Chianina originates here is the only thing that unifies the left and the right."

Before the *bistecca* arrived, we were served beans, sliced tomatoes, and bread, all on separate plates, the implication being that each should be enjoyed as a separate course. *Service à la russe*. Tilde tasted the beans and announced, "My recipe is completely different." The Tuscan recipe, she diplomatically conceded, was good, but she disagreed with the use of tomatoes in the sauce. "We would only use oil, vinegar, and garlic," she said, as always preferring her food as unencumbered as possible.

A heap of *bisteccas* arrived at the table, a teetering pile of one-and-a-quarter-inch T-bones sitting in a lake of juice deep enough to float a toy sailboat. By Tilde's salt-only standards, they were seasoned liberally with salt and pepper and a few drops of olive oil, too. The steak had a crispy and delicious crust that protected a juicy and rare interior, and the charring was at its most pleasant on the perimeter of the steak, where, underneath, rested a soft layer of creamy white fat.

I have eaten more tender steaks in my life, but that didn't bother me.

At the time, I scrawled down the following notation in a juice-spattered notebook: "It's nice to have a bit of chew, so long as it doesn't dry out." The Chianina *bistecca* did not dry out. It went down a whole lot easier than the Podolica steak, which was due in large part to a long *frolatura*— the Italian word for suspending a side of beef in a refrigerated room and leaving it for a while. The Scots call the process "hanging," and North Americans call it dry aging. (You can also age beef by sealing whole cuts in plastic. This is called wet aging, and though purists don't like it, some studies have found it to be superior to dry-aged beef.) The Podolica beef dry-aged for three days and the Chianina for three weeks. The process of aging is often likened to a controlled rot, but this is not true. The meat does not turn rancid—if it does, it's ruined—and the tenderizing agent involved is not bacteria but a family of complex proteins called calpain enzymes. In living muscle, calpain enzymes break down proteins, so that they may be synthesized into newer proteins. When proteins are synthesized faster than they are broken down, a cow is gaining weight. In living muscle, calpain enzymes are controlled, but after death, they are free to break down proteins as they like. The longer meat sits, the more time calpain enzymes have to go around busting strands of muscle fiber, and the more tender the meat becomes. The more tasty it becomes, too, because as proteins are broken into amino acids, levels of umami rise. (Beef aged for seven days has been found to have more than double the glutamic acid of beef aged three days.) There are more sugars, too, which react with amino acids during Maillard reactions. In the Chianina *bisteccas*, calpain enzymes had a lot more time to unzip proteins and loosen fibers than they had with the Podolica *bisteccas*. You could feel the difference. You could taste it, too.

Tilde seemed to know this without having ever heard the words "calpain enzymes." She finished her steak and said, "The *frolatura* was perfect, and the cooking was perfect." But she then added: "It did not have the flavor of the Podolica." This could be taken as yet another instance of Italian tribalism. Every region, town, and household in Italy, after all, thinks its foods and recipes are superior. But I am not from Italy, and I say Tilde had it right.

We ate peaches for dessert. Everyone peeled his, but I ate mine skin on, and so did Tilde. The flesh was a little firm, and not as sweet or juicy as peaches are supposed to be. Tilde took a bite and observed, "The *frolatura* was not long enough."

Chianina beef, despite its excellence, won't win any admirers at the USDA any time soon. It's too lean. The breed marbles as poorly as any, resulting in a steak that is an uninterrupted stretch of red. Most would grade it Select, or worse, Standard, though Select is nothing to rave about. Chianina *bistecas* come from cows that are comparatively old, and the USDA does not look favorably on age. Americans prefer to kill their beef cattle at around fourteen to sixteen months, but in Italy, Chianinas are grown to twenty-two months, often much older.

According to a local *bistecca* enthusiast named Giancarlo Pretotto, this is precisely the reason they taste so good. "If you ate a Charolais or Limousin at twenty-two months old," he told me, "they would taste good, too." Pretotto is a Chianina farmer who lives on a two-thousand-acre property on the other side of the Val di Chiana, not far from a pretty and absurdly ancient village—though almost all Italian villages are absurdly ancient—called Gubbio. His barn could not be more different from the one near Agropoli. It is newer, wider, longer, taller, tidier, brighter, better organized, and mechanized. Where Mario feeds his cows with a bucket, Giancarlo Pretotto dispenses feed from a small tractor that runs up and down a central alley. His barn, in other words, is a northern Italian barn. About 300 cows and their calves live inside it, and 150 more, pregnant, wander his hills and graze.

Like Tilde and every other Italian, Pretotto takes enormous pride in all that is local, and very little in all that is not. We met at a restaurant on the outskirts of Gubbio and ate lasagne with truffles and mushrooms, a preparation called *lasagne funghi e tartufo* that he made a point of telling me you only find in places where white truffles are found—places like Gubbio. Pretotto's cows enjoy a diet that is similarly regional: a mix of alfalfa, hay, corn, and barley, every stem and grain of which is harvested right on the farm, and soybeans, which are never genetically modified and, when possible, are grown in Italy. When his cows reach six months, they begin the *finissagio*, a drawn-out, eighteen-month-long session of fattening—almost four times as long as a standard American feedlot stint. The lengthy *finissagio* is due partly to the fact that Chianina are the world's largest breed of cattle and need a long time to grow, and partly to the fact that Europe forbids the feeding of antibiotics to cattle and the injection of growth hormone pellets into their ears, but mainly because Italians like doing things the slow way—highway driving notwithstanding. A long, slow weight gain, Pretotto believes, makes the meat taste better.

Considering there are three hundred cattle defecating and farting under one roof, Pretotto's barn smells surprisingly pleasant. You could stand next to a pen of Chianinas and eat a bowl of *lasagne funghi e tartufo* and not feel the slightest bit queasy, though you'd be a fool to do so, given that right outside the barn, which is perched on the side of a hill, a superb view awaits. The cattle share their barn with a very rare breed of horse—also local—called TPR, which stands for *tiro, pesante, rapido*, which means something like "strong, hardy, fast." Like the white cows next to them, they are raised for meat. The residents of the city of Piacenza love horsemeat, which is tender, dark, and sweet. Pretotto hopes the TPR will become the Chianina of horsemeat. "Horse *bistecca* is delicious," he said. "Italians consider it good for pregnant women." I looked at one of his horses and remarked to myself how refreshing it was to be in a country that prefers prenatal horsemeat to prenatal yoga.

A few decades ago, the Chianina was almost as rare as the TPR, displaced like the Angus in Scotland by fast-growing, high-yielding Charolais and Limousins, languishing the way the Podolica is now languishing. But as Tuscany became a trendy place for tourists, the Tuscan breed of cattle achieved a status verging on celebrity. Tourists from distant continents now include the words "Chianina *bistecca*" in their fragmented Italian and can be found sitting in Italian restaurants and asking for the steak by name, which was unthinkable a few decades ago. They never ask to eat Maremmana *bistecca*, incidentally, which is Tuscany's other native cattle breed and remains as unpopular as ever. The Maremmana, Pretotto told me, is more marbled than the Chianina and has a more pronounced flavor. "When the meat is grilled," he said, "it is soft and tasty." The problem is that it doesn't fill out like a Chianina, resulting in a poorer yield.

A few stalls down from the horses lives a bull. His name is Nano, and the name is intended ironically because he is one of the world's largest bovine creatures, standing at six feet and ten inches at the shoulders and, from rump to nose, measuring almost twelve feet. The majority of Italian cars weigh less than Nano. Julius Caesar once observed that aurochs were "a little less than elephants in size," and he would have said the same thing about Nano. If Nano were black, he would look something like an aurochs. But, like all big Chianina cattle, he is pure white. He is also so docile that you can pose next to him for a picture.

When Nano's progeny graduate from the *finissagio*, many of them will do their *frolatura* at Antica Macelleria Falorni, the oldest butcher shop in the world. It is in the Tuscan town of Greve in Chianti, and locals first walked through its doors to buy Chianina beef in the year 1729—two years before Charles Darwin's *grandfather* was born. Back then, it was just Macelleria Falorni. (The word *antica*, which means "ancient," first appeared on a sign erected in 1840 that still hangs.) The founding patriarch was a butcher named Gio Batta, and the shop is today helmed by his great-great-great-great-great-grandsons, Lorenzo and Stefano Falorni, who met me there a few days after the *sagra*. Stefano Falorni has the bearing of an accountant on a yachting holiday— mustachioed, wearing tan pants and sailing shoes, and very much in control. Antica Macelleria Falorni is as much a busy butcher shop as a living ode to its butchering past. Out front, facing the town square, stands the butcher block—the most magnificent butcher block I have ever seen—that served as the primary meat-hacking surface from 1820 to 1956. The interior is festooned with butcherana. Hanging on the wall are ancient cleavers that look like small medieval axes and, in their day, cut untold *bisteccas*. There is a stuffed wild boar, old copper scales big enough to weigh two babies, old black-and-white photos of Chianinas (including one of a prizewinning bull from 1934), a bright red meat grinder from 1957, and a sausage-stuffing machine from 1930. From the ceiling are suspended 1,600 Italian hams, undergoing their *frolatura* (though, in the case of hams, the technical term is *stagionatura*), while customers search out and purchase meat beneath.

The hams come from a local variety of swine, extremely rare, called Cinta Senese, which are black with a white band around their midsection. You can see them in Tuscan frescoes dating to the 1300s, but they are not nearly so abundant nowadays, having been pushed to the edge of extinction by high-yield commercial pig breeds. The most famous pig breed in Europe is Spain's black-hoofed *pata negra*, which is fed acorns and said to produce uncommonly excellent hams. Stefano Falorni, another raging localist, insists that the Cinta Senese are better. When grilling, he is so particular about his wood that if someone invites him to a barbecue, he brings his own oak, which he fells and chops personally.

The best *bistecca* Falorni ever ate was in the mid-1990s. It was one of his own, aged in the family fridges and consumed at an extremely expensive winery and hotel called Borgo San Felice. (He brought the oak.) Falorni ages his beef loins for up to fifteen or twenty days—sometimes up to a month—and Borgo San Felice extends the period of *frolatura* for up to another three weeks. The hotel is, in fact, an ancient farming hamlet of small stone buildings that has been refurbished to a state of high luxury. You find it in the heart of Chianti, which is world-famous wine country, within which the wines of Borgo San Felice command a great deal of respect. Wealthy people from all over visit so that they may drink wine they adore while surrounded by the hillsides that produced the grapes. Invariably, they eat *bistecca*.

Borgo San Felice seems to have been created with the intention of proving that money can buy happiness outright. It would take the average working person a week's earnings to spend a single night there, but a single night offers considerably more pleasure than a week of work does in pain. The views of classic Tuscan countryside—vine-covered hills, stone houses, olive groves, cypress trees—set the standard for what would be a visual cliché if it weren't all so lovely. But the very best view at Borgo San Felice is the one that unfolds when you enter the dining room: a wood fire burning under an iron grill—height adjustable—in front of which sit, on a platter bedded with fresh herbs, several of the thickest T-bones you ever did see. To call these pieces of meat "slabs" is to be generous to the term *slab*. These are not standard *bisteccas*. In Tuscany, a T-bone of such stellar thickness has its own name: *bistecca alla fiorentina*—a Florentine steak. To qualify, the chop must be the width of two ribs, which, in the case of the world's largest beef breed, works out to at least two and a half inches. The steaks are so big you could use one as a plate on which to eat a normal-sized steak. Although most guests end up sharing one with a like-minded partner, some do opt to keep an entire *bistecca alla fiorentina* all to themselves. Unlike at the Big Texan, there is no countdown clock, no vomit pail, and no one gets it free.

The general manager at Borgo San Felice is an attractive and elegant woman named Cinzia Fanciulli who is friendly to the point of disarming. (Attractive Italian women do not generally suffer from haughtiness or inflated egos, as in other countries, which is yet another factor contributing to Italy's greatness.) She offered to share a *bistecca alla fiorentina* with me—but not immediately, as the fire under the grill had just been ignited, she pointed out, and the bed of coals would not be thick enough, white enough, or hot enough for two hours, minimum.

When two hours had passed, there was the small matter of first courses. Dinners at Borgo San Felice are a grand exercise in *service à la russe*, a procession of pure savors as ordered as a Catholic mass and just as long. They build from subtlety to grandeur, climaxing with the *bistecca*.

We began with a tasting of olive oil, a blend of four olive varieties that looked like liquid amber, smelled of chopped fresh herbs, and possessed undeniable notes of toasted nuts, so much so that anyone with a nut allergy should probably have an EpiPen handy. The olives were grown on the same land that produced the tomatoes featured in the next course, an old peasant soup called *pappa al pomodoro*, which was the most incredibly tomatoey substance I have ever put in my mouth. This was followed by *panzanella*—bread with tomatoes, cucumber, onion, and garlic, all from the garden, splashed with a vinaigrette consisting of homemade wine vinegar mixed with homemade olive oil and perfumed with tarragon, also from the garden. The dish that followed was called *nudi*, a playful term for a pasta filling without the pasta, and it consisted of garden-grown spinach with ricotta cheese and shavings of pecorino cheese that were not—gasp—from the hotel's garden, but did come from within walking distance.

The theme, obviously, and not surprisingly, was locality, and it was perhaps stated best by the wine, which was made out of a special grape called *pugnitello*, which means "little fist" (it has the same Latin root as *pugnacious*), so named because the grapes grow in clenched little clusters. Like the Cinta Senese and the Chianina, the *pugnitello* was pushed to the edge of extinction, again because of poor yield—other grapevines simply produced more juice. It was thought to have vanished, until in 1981 a researcher discovered some vines. The master vintner at Borgo San Felice took an interest in *pugnitello* precisely because of its low yield. High yield may be the friend of the grape farmer's balance sheet, but it is the enemy of good wine. Fine wine makers do not want a lot of juice. They want very good juice, and they will cut as much as half the grapes off a vine mid-season so that the remaining fruit becomes more concentrated. In 1987, twenty-five acres of *pugnitello* were planted, and after years of experimentation, a new—and yet very old—wine was born. (*Wine Spectator* gave it the following pastoral description: "Lovely nose that reminds me of Zinfandel, with plum and flowers. Full-bodied, with jammy character, yet fresh, silky and long.")

If you spend enough time eating in Italy, it begins to feel less like a country than like a collection of Italian-speaking tribes who happen to live on the same peninsula and eat similar food, though they themselves believe their foods are distinctly different. They cling to local food not to reduce carbon emissions or in the name of maximum freshness, but out of pride: Italians are the world's proudest regionalists. Culinarily speaking, they cling to their dialects.

The *bistecca alla fiorentina*, originating all the way over in Perugia, was verging on alien. Everything else was grown on land that I could see. In the same way that Tuscany pleasures the eyes with its cypress trees and olive groves and farmhouses and hills crowned by walled cities that rise from fertile valleys, it pleases the tongue with dishes like *pappa al pomodoro* and Chianina steak. The region has a distinctive look, but it also has a distinctive taste.

There is a term that describes this phenomenon. It is a foreign word—from France—and one that is often bandied about by pretentious people who stifle the atmosphere at dinner parties. It is, nevertheless, a good word: *terroir.* Describing what *terroir* means is not easy. An advertisement for a wine I once found in a magazine does a good job: "The location, soil and climate of a given vineyard site directly affect the flavor and characteristics of the wine produced from that vineyard." But Tilde has an even better definition. I once asked her to tell me what a pure savor is, and she said: "Any food where you can taste the nature that produced it." A Podolica steak raised on Monte Tresino is a pure savor, but a feed-lot steak from Texas, fed Nebraskan corn, coated with Montreal steak rub, and swimming in a puddle of canned broth produced in some unknown factory, is not. (It is, rather, a prime example of *cuisine of mixture.*) It was this very idea that Angus Mackay had in mind when he said that beef can be every bit as distinctive as single-malt Scotch. *Terroir,* simply, is the idea that you can taste geography. And in Tuscany, the geography tastes very good.

Every night, Borgo San Felice removes its steaks from the fridge four hours before dinner and places them near the fire, so that they may slowly rise to room temperature. After we swallowed the last bites of *nudi,* Cinzia and I visited the grill so that we could watch and listen to beef sizzling over an open flame. This is something Magdalenian Woman, no doubt, did a lot, and as forms of entertainment go, watching steak cook is one of the oldest, and still one of the best.

The chef laid the steak on the grill and flipped it after seven and a half minutes. (I was the one timing the steak; the chef "sensed" when it was ready.) He sprinkled salt and pepper on the cooked side and, after several more minutes, pressed his finger into the crust to assess doneness. The *bistecca* was showing signs of becoming firmer, so the chef flipped it on its back, the rib pointing straight up, so that the steak could absorb heat through its broad bony base and send it radiating through to the meat above. Juice began to trickle out the bottom, flowing over the hot bone and hissing as it landed in the coals. The fire was so hot I couldn't stand closer than four feet, and even then spent the rest of the night with my face radiating heat as though it was sunburned.

Being the elegant sort of place it is, Borgo San Felice saves its guests the labor of cutting *bistecca*. A waiter wheels over a table with a big cutting board on top and does it for you, using a long, curved butcher knife that would not look out of place on the wall at Antica Macelleria Falorni. Each strip of meat was a textbook example of the spectrum of beef doneness. The center was red and barely above room temperature, the exterior was nearly black, and infinite points lay in between.

When Cinzia bit into the *bistecca*, she said something that caught me by surprise: "It is not so perfect." She had just swallowed a morsel that was not the embodiment of tenderness. "But it is authentic," she said, and I had to agree. The problem was that I couldn't stop thinking of Italy's neglected authentic food. The Podolica, barely loved, grazed in obscurity in the south on a hillside on which even the monks have given up. While Chianinas enjoyed their unexpected rise to celebrity, the Maremmana languished. Would they, like the *pugnitello* grapes, one day flirt with extinction?

I took another sip of wine. "The *bistecca* is indeed authentic," I said, turning to Cinzia. "But I think since we're drinking *pugnitello* wine, it would be even more authentic to eat a Maremmana *bistecca*."

Cinzia swallowed a bite of imperfect but still damned good steak, followed it with a sip of wine, and said, "I agree."

CHAPTER FIVE

JAPAN

The Japanese are famous for their acutely overdeveloped sense of specialization. They are the world's foremost perfectionists, even more so than Germans, and it took me all of one hour on Japanese soil to witness this singular cultural trait.

The event took place at one in the morning on the shuttle bus journey from Narita International Airport into downtown Tokyo. Like shuttle buses the world over, the one I was riding was equipped with a transponder allowing it to cruise through tollgates without waiting in line to pay. As we approached the first tollgate, the driver gave no indication of decelerating. It seemed, at first, like nothing more than exuberant driving, but as the gate got closer and the speed remained constant, the driver crossed an invisible line where collision went from unlikely to inevitable. Even if he had wanted to slow down, there wasn't enough time to do so. I gripped the armrests and braced for impact. There wasn't time to scream. In less than a second, the windshield would shatter and the tollgate would snap like a twig, helicoptering through the air in slow motion until it struck a toll collector handing out change, perhaps breaking the man's collarbone. In that endless instant before impact, I pictured myself watching Japanese police push the shamed bus driver into the back of a Toyota squad car as I waited for a replacement shuttle bus to arrive. And then at the last moment, with at best inches to spare, the gate flipped up, lifting with a speed and robotic nonchalance that seemed exquisitely Japanese. The driver zoomed through and continued on toward Tokyo, having shaved seconds off the journey. Every subsequent tollgate—there were several—proved equally exhilarating. After each one, I would notice myself breathing again, and watch as color returned to my knuckles. It was, by several orders of magnitude, the most thrilling trip from an airport into a city I have ever taken.

By five that morning, I was standing in a large room surrounded by the frozen carcasses of many dead, extremely expensive tuna, a can of hot coffee in my hand. There had never been, until that moment, a hot can of anything in my hand. After less than four hours of sleep, coffee was what I needed, and a guide I had hired to show me around took me into a convenience store where, next to the cash register, I found a hot display case filled with hot cans of coffee.

The problem with hot canned Japanese coffee isn't the taste—the stuff is genuinely good—but that you need oven mitts to drink it. As we walked toward the fish market, I juggled it like a baked potato, and it wasn't until several blocks later that it was cool enough to grasp, open, and gingerly sip. Later that day, I bought another.

The frozen tuna were so cold, they appeared harder than the concrete floor on which they were lying. They were laid out in long rows, and their eyes were covered with yellow or red stickers indicating their weight. In a few minutes' time, each one would be carted off by its new owner in the course of the famous tuna auction at Tokyo's Tsukiji fish market, the largest wholesale fish and seafood market in the world. But what was being sold to the highest bidder was not so much tuna itself as the fat that happens to come wrapped in the skin, tail, and fins of a tuna. All around the room, Japanese fish buyers in tall rubber boots were taking tiny pickaxes and hacking into the tails of the frozen fish. They looked like geologists prospecting for indicator minerals, but the riches they were after were fat. The fattier the tail, the more fat would be present in the tuna's precious belly.

At precisely 5:30 a.m., the Japanese fat prospectors turned away from the frozen tuna and faced an auctioneer wearing a red hat. The auction commenced. Fish buyers began raising their arms in a throwing motion. There was grunting and shouting. Somewhere, a bell would not stop ringing, and men kept yelling the same word in unison, holding it like a long note, so that it was impossible to hear the auctioneer. The din of commerce would rise and fall and rise again, like the roar of a crowd at a soccer game. Another man holding a black crayon scurried from fish to fish, marking each one with the name of its new owner.

"How do they know which fish is being sold?" I asked my guide.

"I have no idea," he said. "I can't understand what they are saying. Sometimes, he says some numbers."

The largest fish on the auction floor was 122 kilograms, but large fish do not necessarily get the highest bids. Fresh tuna, a buyer told us, sell for ten times more than frozen tuna. And flesh that is a deep red is more desirable than pale flesh. But more than anything, the fish buyers are looking for fat. The more fat, the higher the price the tuna will fetch.

The most expensive fish to sell that morning went for 2 million yen, which is about as much as a brand-new four-door Volkswagen. Like all the fish that had been auctioned, over the next few days it would be diced into thin rectangles by sushi chefs wielding extraordinarily sharp knives and transferred by chopsticks to the open mouths of thousands of sushi and sashimi aficionados, where, apparently, the mere heat of their tongues would make it melt.

Like the dead frozen tuna on the floor next to me, fat was the reason I had come to Japan. The country may be the most technologically advanced in the world, the spiritual heartland of futuristic consumer electronics, but when it comes to fat, the Japanese remain hunter-gatherers at heart. They revere it.

I was here to sample a different kind of fat, one that is also said to melt in the mouth. It is found in Kobe beef, from cattle that are fed beer and massaged with sake to make them succulent. Tuna fat was just the warm-up.

When the auction was over, my guide led the way out toward the perimeter of the market. We passed a knife shop, in front of which stood a man honing a large silver blade on a whetstone with an air of religious seriousness. Nearby was a seaweed shop that stocked more than one hundred different varieties, at least ninety of which come from the island of Hokkaido, which is itself divided into five different seaweed-producing regions. In a single three-hundred-foot stretch of market—which I would estimate to hold no more than 1 percent of Tsukiji's biodiversity—I cataloged the following: piles of dried fish that were just thicker than yarn and shorter than a baby's pinkie; clams as large as a dinner plate; stacked cans of corned beef; wooden bins filled with dried tuna shavings piled into huge fluffy mounds; stacked cans of Spam; trays of salmon steaks marinating in yellow miso; boxes of whole dead salmon resting in crushed ice; whole mackerel; various dried fruits; grilled scallops, ready to be eaten; raw fish eggs; pickled fish eggs; large dried fish; frozen Alaska king crab legs; boxes of strange root vegetables as long as a man's arm; and aquariums full of puffer fish that have to be expertly sliced so their poisonous organs will not taint their flesh and make it deadly.

We arrived at a sushi shop called Sushisay. Sushi isn't generally a breakfast food in Japan, but the reputation of Sushisay is such that if you want to eat lunch there, you'd better show up at breakfast. Even at eight thirty in the morning, the lineup to get in was twenty minutes. Inside, three sushi chefs cut and assembled raw fish and hand-shaped mounds of rice at a clip reminiscent of a bus hurtling through a Japanese tollgate. When they talked, which was not often, they sounded ferocious and constipated, as sushi chefs are supposed to.

The fattiest cut of tuna is called *otoro*, which comes from the belly of a bluefin tuna. A slightly leaner cut is known as *chutoro*. We ordered both, bypassing the even leaner *akami*. Raw tuna is usually a deep red, but the *otoro* was so fatty as to be mild pink. It had a thick grain of white fat running diagonally across it, along with thinner veins of fat woven like lacework into its flesh. As promised, it melted in my mouth, but not the way chocolate melts. It simply gave way under pressure from my tongue with the ease of a bowling ball falling through wet tissue paper. It may have been cut from a big ocean-dwelling fish, but it didn't taste of the sea. If anything, it had a pleasing sweetness, but I don't think the Japanese eat *otoro* so much for the taste as for the texture, which is un-like anything my mouth had ever experienced. The *chutoro* was firmer and possessed a mild briny tang. I liked both, but of the two, the *otoro* tasted much more expensive.

Otoro tastes so expensive that single bluefin tunas occasionally go for as much as a top-of-the-line sports car. But only in Japan. Like their bullet trains and shuttle buses that push the tollgate envelope, *otoro* is another case of far-reaching specialization. I mentioned this to my guide, whose name is Seichi Chada and who is the owner of Michi Travel, which specializes in culinary tourism. He was puzzled by what I said and asked me for an example. The one I supplied is not what you would call judicious, considering I had known Chada-san for all of three hours. Perhaps it was the fog of jet lag or the caffeine-induced effects of two hot cans of coffee, but the example I raised to illustrate my point was the notoriously deranged and fetishistic sexual tendencies of Japanese businessmen.

Chada-san is himself a Japanese businessman, a fact I would have done well to note. He asked me, once again, politely, what I was talking about. I pointed out the well-known fact that there are vending machines on subway platforms all over Japan that dispense underwear that has been worn by teenage girls, which isn't all that surprising for a country that massages its cattle with wine.

Chada-san was now more puzzled. The phenomenon of the teen-underwear vending machine, he said, was not, technically speaking, a fact. As I finished a piece of barbecued sea eel, he said, "I have heard there are some stores where you can buy underwear that has been worn. These are for crazy people. I don't know where they are."

Still buzzing on *otoro*, we continued exploring the market and soon found ourselves staring at a display fridge full of meat, though it was so fatty that "meat" may no longer have been the correct term for it. We were gazing at a loin of beef ornamented with wisps of fat that looked like crochet work, a pervasive filigree that reached into every nook of red muscle. It was the most marbled steak I had ever seen.

"Kobe beef," I said, nodding my head, appraising the effects of hand massages and beer finishing. I had seen any number of photographs of Kobe beef on the Internet, but they had in no way prepared me for the sight of the real thing. It seemed unbelievable—and in a technical sense, it was, because the store owner informed me that I wasn't looking at Kobe beef at all. It was Iwate beef.

Chada-san explained. Iwate beef, he said, is a different *brand* of beef from Kobe beef. In Japan, the word "brand" more closely corresponds to the way it's used by American ranchers, who sear brands into the rumps of their cattle. A brand in Japan tells you where your food has come from. Kobe beef comes from Kobe. Iwate beef comes from Iwate. As the Japanese see it, every part of their country has its own distinctive climate, geology, water, traditions, and so forth. Each region, therefore, produces its own equally distinctive foods, and they all compete with one another to produce the very best. Branding, you might say, is the Japanese version of *terroir*.

Some of that Japanese *terroir* is better than other *terroir*, which means that products from some regions are more expensive than products from others—Kagoshima pork and Koshihikari rice, to name two. Unscrupulous restaurants have even been known to lie about the brand of food they are serving. Every now and then, Chada-san said, the police would bust a restaurant for selling, say, Nagoya chicken—which is considered excellent—that is, in truth, a lesser brand of chicken.

As brands of beef go, Iwate is no Kobe. The most marbled beef I'd ever seen wasn't actually all that well marbled, at least not as the Japanese view it. They have an elaborate grading system to rate marbling and beef quality. The most marbled beef is rated A5. The Iwate loin scored A3, which made it firmly middle-of-the-road beef. The Iwate beef may have been so marbled as to look like a doily, but in Japan a steak that looks like a doily is merely average, apparently.

Ten hours later, I encountered A5 beef, though A5 fat would be a more accurate way of putting it. Chada-san invited me to join his family for dinner at a place called Fuku Buku. It was a *yakiniku* restaurant, which means you sit in booths around a table with a grill at its center and a waitress ferries platters of raw, thinly sliced beef from the kitchen that you cook yourself while drinking successive glasses of ice-cold Japanese draft beer. It sounds like a scheme hatched by a restaurant accountant as a means of moving chef salaries off the balance sheet, but the spectacle of beef cooking provides unending entertainment.

The A5 steaks were at most 3 millimeters thick and cut into perfect rectangles the size of business cards. They looked like right-angled snowflakes. They were not Kobe beef but A5 Saga (the loin) and A5 Kagoshima (the shoulder), and both brought to mind a gum I chewed in my youth called Freshen-up, which came in cube-shaped pieces that

JAPAN   151

featured a gel center that detonated between two molars to the great
thrill of its chewer. The burst of beefy deliciousness from the steak, however, was exponentially grander, and I had to restrain myself from verbal
exclamation, which would have sent out a spray of beef fat—every drop
of which I wanted to keep in my mouth. In terms of tenderness, the beef
was about as tough as overripe banana. It was not soggy or mushy—there
was structure—but it did not put up a fight. I think thinness had something to do with it. The steaks were so thin, in fact, that they push the
very definition of steak. The grill was hot enough to forge high-carbon
steel. I couldn't so much as lean my head in Chada-san's direction
while talking to him without getting scorched, but the culinary result—
maximum Maillard—was worth the risk of a first-degree burn. My chopsticks delivered glistening morsels of fatty crust onto my tongue, one
after another, interrupted by sips of cold beer and exclamations like "Son
of a bitch" and "Damn."

The best beef I ate at Fuku Buku that night was not A5. That honor
goes to a cut it had never before occurred to me to eat: beef tongue. The
tongue was, technically, A3 Gumma tongue, sliced across the grain and
as mouth-poppingly luscious as the A5 meat. In one department, however, it had the A5 beat: flavor. It didn't taste like liver or kidney or any
other body part that fulfills some essential biological role. It tasted like
steak, just more so than the others.

I woke up the next day feeling like an eight-year-old on Christmas morning. The world teemed with wonder and possibility. My heart was filled
with hope. It was A5 Kobe beef day. Chada-san had already made the
reservation. That night, we would dine at a famous and expensive steak
house called Seryna.

Chada-san, it turned out, was a fellow Kobe beef virgin. In an effort
to boil off some of the mounting anticipation, we explored Tokyo. Ever
since the *otoro* at Sushisay, our dialogue, which was constant, oscillated
between two different subjects: Japanese beef and Japanese eccentricity.
Chada-san insisted that Japan was no more peculiar than any other
place. It sounded to him like I'd been fed exaggerated stories of some of
the more extreme aspects of the culture. Chada-san himself, it must be

said, seemed the embodiment of the habitual and conventional—a creature from the middle of the bell curve. He is not consumed by a passion
for karaoke. He does not wear jeans sewn from Japanese hand-dyed
denim, a single pair of which costs more than an Italian suit. He does
not have a vast collection of sexually perverted Japanese cartoons known
as *hentai*. (All of which is not to suggest Chada-san is boring, because he
is not.) The Japanese, he pointed out, may produce beef that is exponentially more marbled and expensive than any beef in the world, but I was
the one who flew halfway around that world to taste it.

He would have had me convinced, but Japan kept on serving up example after example of eccentricity taken to the point of fetish. Consider
Sembikiya, a store that sells the most expensive fruit in the world, where
every specimen is perfect and without blemish. I beheld pears, tanger-
ines, and apples so flawless as to look almost fake. There were Shizuoka
muskmelons for sale, a pair of which cost more than two nights at my
hotel. The fruitcakes were more affordable—a single one was going for
the same price as a designer cocktail dress. I bought the cheapest fruit
in the store: a three-dollar mandarin, an exquisite specimen snatched off
the digitally retouched cover of a food magazine. (Later, my hotel room
became instantly misted with mandarin perfume as I punctured the
peel. I placed the segments in my mouth, one after another, and they
were a perfect balance of sweet and tart, but also explosively juicy.)

At a soba restaurant called Kikouchitei, I met a chef who had abandoned a safe and respectable office job so that he could study the art of
making soba dough for three years and become a soba master. He grinds
his soba—buckwheat, in English—on a custom-made granite millstone
that sits behind glass as though it were some kind of shrine. The flour is
mixed with water from Mount Fuji, which must be cold, because hot
water makes the dough easier to roll, but it also ruins the taste. Not a
grain of wheat flour is permitted, even though wheat flour makes the
dough more pliable, because it, too, will alter the taste. The result is soba
dough more fragile than antique butterfly wings. An apprentice, who'd
been studying for a year, attempted to demonstrate, but he failed grandly,
lacerating a sheet of dough so badly that the soba master burst into
laughter. After painstaking rolling, the dough is cut into noodles, cooked,

and dipped in a broth made from macrobiotic tuna shavings, *wasambo* sugar (which costs twenty times as much as regular sugar), rice vinegar that has been aged for two and a half years, and the most expensive dried shiitake mushrooms money can buy.

The soba obsession in Japan is pervasive. Some of the customers at Kikouchitei actually follow the Japanese buckwheat harvest, so that they may be the first to determine which region has the very best. "This year," the soba master told me, "Yamagata and Fukui have particularly good batches." The very best soba, apparently, comes from mountain villages just beneath the fog line, where there are large daily temperature differentials.

(Tilde Vecchio has never visited Japan, but if she did, I am confident she would proclaim soba to be a pure savor.)

The soba master mentioned that Canada produces a tremendous amount of buckwheat, an achievement he seemed to respect. Flushed with pride, I asked him what he thought of Canadian soba. He said something in Japanese that was clearly not complimentary, and yet he somehow retained an aura of extreme respectfulness. I was not humiliated, but I did feel shame.

Chada-san and I spent several hours at the Takashimaya department store in a part of town called Shinjuku, home to the world's busiest train station. The bottom floor is the food market, called Kinokuniya, and a person could pass the better part of week there in rapt awe. No food on earth looks quite so spectacular. Aisle after aisle housed museum-quality culinary creations that were more pleasing to look at than a Zen rock garden. A row of salads sat in large bowls, shaped into precise, tapering piles that appeared to have been assembled leaf by leaf. At the end of the aisle, we saw a salad as it was being composed. A woman was dressed as though for surgery in a white coat, a surgical mask, a bouffant cap, and latex gloves. In front of her was a spinach salad, half complete, being erected one leaf at a time.

Chada-san interrupted the salad sculptress and asked her how long she had trained. From behind the surgical mask came the answer: "Three years."

In a display fridge a few aisles over was pound cake that had been crisply sliced with an extraordinarily sharp blade into perfectly rectangular slices, the corners of which appeared sharp enough to take out a person's eye. A slice of cake, I noted, can please not only one's sense of taste but also one's sense of geometry. But only in Japan.

If a USDA meat inspector ever walked into the meat section at Kinokuniya, he would think he was in heaven. The display fridges all glow brightly, their gleaming glass fronts are free of finger smudges, and their interiors boast a plenitude of A5 Yamagata beef that costs more than *otoro*. Raging in those fridges is a celestial festival of marbling red meat pointillated and swirled with so much white fat that it looks like steak painted by Van Gogh.

The greatest example of the degree to which the Japanese are obsessed with marbling is not to be found at the beef counter, however, but on the eleventh floor, in electronics. Chada-san and I began at a wall of washlets, which have nothing to do with marbled beef but are nonetheless notable from the point of view of cultural observation. A washlet is a toilet seat fitted with fans and water jets designed to keep a person's posterior hospital-clean. Some have settings for oscillation and pulsation, and the better models offer charcoal-filter deodorization and blow-drying. Of all the toilets in Japan, more than half include washlets. There is one in almost every Japanese home, and my hotel room, which was one of the cheapest in Tokyo, had one, too. Beneath the knob controlling pressure was a button that depicted the human buttocks with equal parts cuteness and accuracy. Near it was another symbol: a woman with long hair sitting, with a fountain of water coming up to meet her backside. Her body language, it seemed to me, was one of delight, as though she were being tickled. As the two of us stared, I asked Chada-san to explain the Japanese obsession with cleanliness. He could not. He said that the Japanese have an advanced standard of hygiene. This is something hard to find fault with.

Not far from the washlets was an aisle full of brand-new fridges. A fridge of medium quality—it didn't include ice making or rapid freezing, as better models do—featured a sticker depicting ridiculously marbled steak on its door. "At least A4," Chada-san remarked. The sticker suggested a tier of steak eating totally out of line with the fridge's price point. Next to it was a more expensive model whose meat drawer featured four stickers—steak, fish, fruit, and raw tuna—so that its new owner would know what food goes where. The tuna was lean *akami*, but the steak was A4. It was becoming clear to me that in Japan, the very *concept* of beef is highly marbled. While marbled beef is prized in America, the generic image of a standard American steak is red, not white. In Tom and Jerry cartoons, when a bulldog is thrown a big steak, the only white is in the trim and the bone; the meat is a model specimen USDA Standard. In Japan, on the other hand, all steak is at least half white.

Inside one of the better fridges at Takashimaya, I found a steak—a slice of rib eye, by the looks of things, A4 or A5—made out of plastic, though you had to reach out and touch it to know for sure. A lot of the food in Japan is fake. You see it displayed in restaurant windows or sitting on tables outside, so that potential patrons have an idea of the creations being served inside. If you avoid places like Tsukiji fish market, the likelihood is you will probably see more fake food in Japan than real food.

Chada-san explained that high-quality plastic food is an art, and the people who make it are respected and well paid. Over in the frying pan aisle, we found an entire plastic dinner sitting atop an electric Sanyo fryer: a fake crab claw, three fake scallops, three fake matsutake mushrooms, two fake whole green peppers, and a fake A3 strip loin. For a customer who couldn't afford to buy an actual stove, it was quite the meal.

The next floor down, Chada-san and I spotted a bottle of Kobe water and it was very fancy. The bottle appeared to be inset with fake diamonds, and it cost more than lunch at a fine restaurant. Chada-san now seemed embarrassed. He acknowledged that Kobe wasn't actually famous for its water. "No one I know," he said, "drinks Kobe water."

A young and fashionably dressed Japanese couple was standing in front of the Kobe water display, holding hands. The woman, gazing at the bottle with a misty-eyed look that seemed almost a parody of rapture, whispered, "It's so beautiful." We did not stay to see if they bought one. The Kobe water had put us both in the mood for Kobe beef.

Outside Seryna, a squad of dignified-looking middle-aged parking attendants stood on the sidewalk, wearing gray tuxedos with blue lapels and white gloves, waiting for cars to pull up. Inside Seryna, it was wall-to-wall carpet and silence. The lighting was dim, and the staff moved noiselessly in dress that harkened to a more formal era, with waiters in black tuxedos and waitresses in kimonos. The manager, also in a tuxedo, beckoned us to sit. He assured us that Seryna sold true A5 Kobe beef. It sold other brands of beef, too, he said, but many of his customers preferred beef from Kobe. More important, he confided, some restaurants lied about their beef, claiming it to be Kobe when it was not. Seryna was not one of them. He got up from the table and returned with a plaque that certified that Seryna sold beef from cattle that were born, fed, and slaughtered in Hyogo Prefecture, of which Kobe is the capital. The cattle also drink Kobe water, but not out of fancy bottles. The manager handed me a piece of paper that listed the specific cows whose meat had been sold to Seryna that day. In minutes, he said, I would be eating a steak from a cow formerly known as 1208354834.

A major perk of working at Seryna, it seemed to me, was access to all that A5 Kobe beef. I asked the manager how much of it he ate, expecting him to say something like "Twice a day. More on weekends." With a straight face he said, "I prefer fish."

Among those in Tokyo who do not prefer fish, Seryna is famous for pioneering a form of cookery upon rocks originating from the sacred Buddhist town of Nikko, which are heated in a kiln for eight hours until they reach 300°C (almost 600°F), whereupon they are placed in front of a hungry diner, whose nose immediately begins running due to the intense heat. On such rocks, the cooking time of a steak can be measured in seconds.

Westerners don't ordinarily go for hot-stone cuisine but prefer their steak *teppanyaki* style, that is, cooked on a hot flat metal grill right in front of customers by a chef. (In Japan, *teppanyaki* does not include the culinary acrobatics—slicing a lemon in midair or creating a "volcano" out of sliced onion that spews flame—for which it has become famous in America. Where *teppanyaki* is concerned, Americans are clearly weirder than Japanese.) Asians, however, generally prefer the hot-stone method. The Chinese kung fu superstar Jackie Chan came to Seryna to eat A5 Kobe beef cooked on a hot stone, which he enjoyed, according to the manager. But when Tom Cruise visits Seryna to eat A5 Kobe beef, he always chooses *teppanyaki*.

Chada-san and I were now escorted into to the womblike dining room. Behind the bar sat a large aquarium that looked like the cover of a fantasy novel. Inside it was a landscape of ancient undersea ruins with blue fish swimming around in circles. (The fish were fake, controlled by a mechanical arm.) Muzak emanated softly from hidden speakers.

A waitress in a kimono—young, demure, and beautiful—introduced herself and took my order: A5 Kobe beef strip loin. A short time later, she returned with a brown apron that she tied around my neck, her smooth fingernails and soft hands gently tickling my skin. Minutes later, she reappeared, this time with the rock. It was set inside a silver dish encased in a thick and ancient-looking wooden box that looked like a prop from a samurai movie. The rock looked generic, rounded and oval-shaped, perhaps eight inches in diameter, and it gave off a fantastic heat, more intense even than the Smithfield Pro-Cook or the gas-powered grill at Fuku Buku. I blew my nose. Chada-san and I moved a little farther down the table so as not to bake in its presence. The waitress returned with the steak, which was at most half an inch thick and pre-sliced into wedge-shaped strips. I considered putting one in my pocket and taking a direct flight to Lubbock, Texas, so I could flabbergast the marbling-obsessed meat science faculty at Texas Tech.

A Muzak version of John Lennon's "Imagine"—arranged for flute—began wafting out of the ceiling as the waitress sprinkled Himalayan sea salt on my Kobe beef. Using two very long chopsticks, she daintily laid three slices across the rock, and they roared to an immediate sizzle. The air became thick with the aroma of grilled beef, and little droplets of melted fat began sliding down the side of the stone like rainwater trickling on a window during a downpour. In less than a minute, the first side was browned. The second side went even faster. The stone was smoking when I bit into my first-ever piece of Kobe beef, which reached the sensory peak of richness. The flavor was beefy, sweet, and nutty, but flavor seemed like almost an afterthought to the texture, which was smoother than hot buttered silk. Chada-san took a bite and said, "Very nice. Delicious." He closed his eyes, chewed more, and said, his eyes still closed, "Artistic."

We ate our way through the three little strips of steak, and my notepad, camera, and digital recorder became spattered with fat. The stone had lost none of its intensity, and as the flute gave way to saxophone, the tempo of "Imagine" started to build. The waitress was onto the last two pieces of the A5 Kobe strip loin now, the fattiest of the lot, and she kept them on the stone longer to make them even crispier. When I put the final piece of A5 Kobe beef in my mouth, I had to seal my lips to keep fat from dripping down my chin. The stone was dark and glistening, as though it had just been dredged after a thousand years at the bottom of a river of hot beef fat.

I was, by this point, struggling to overcome fatigue, lethargy, and a feeling of intense stupidity, a state I tend to reach when I eat too much fat. It had happened most acutely a few years earlier in Quebec, where I was researching a story for a travel magazine that involved eating foie gras twice a day for six consecutive days. I now felt as if liquid fat were running through my arteries and gumming up the synapses in my brain. I was experiencing the opposite of meat hunger: vegetable hunger. I wanted raw cucumber. I craved undressed salad. As the saxophone segued into a blistering guitar solo, I stared dumbly at the still-sweltering rock.

The Japanese love their *otoro* and their marbled beef, but they rarely OD on fat. Fat is considered an occasional treat in Japan, even for the well-off. It is the leanness of the Japanese diet that makes fat a gustatory thrill. It is a land of grilled fish and pickled vegetables, where people snack on rice balls, not potato chips. No Japanese person would ever eat beef ranging from A3 to A5 twice in less than twenty-four hours, as I had just done.

It is ironic, in fact, that Japan is famous for steak, because the Japanese are not Beef Loyals. They eat only twenty pounds a year—a third as much as a typical American (or Canadian). They have only been eating steak since 1868, when a thousand-year-old ban on eating four-legged animals was lifted by Emperor Meiji. They eat it in little pieces, as though one and a half centuries later, they're trying it for the first time.

By the 1950s, they had mastered the technique of producing beef that, in terms of marbling, had no equal anywhere in the world. They perfected beef just as they perfected the art of deep-frying (which they were taught by Portuguese traders in the sixteenth century); jeans (Japanese selvage denim is without peer); French pastry (many consider the French desserts in Tokyo to be superior to those for sale in Paris); the art of folding paper (origami's roots are Chinese); the grill-your-own restaurant (*yakiniku* is from Korea, originally); martial arts (karate's roots are in China); and cameras, cars, knives, and toilet hygiene technology.

The Japanese are not famous for inventing things. They are famous for perfecting the inventions of others. They take foreign things and improve them to a point where they become nearly unrecognizable from the original. In Portuguese deep-fried fish, they saw a diamond in the rough, and by the time it was carved and polished it wasn't Portuguese anymore, it was Japanese *tempura*. It became, like the bonsai tree (another foreign import), almost a caricature of perfection, though with an unmistakably Japanese soul.

In the case of Kobe beef, the Japanese soul is the breed of cattle. The Japanese call it *kuroge wagyu*, "black-haired Japanese cow," and to foreigners it is the black Wagyu. Imports from mainland Asia, these cattle first appeared on Japanese soil around two thousand years ago and spent the subsequent centuries as beasts of burden, plowing rice paddies, dragging logs out of forests, or hauling ore out of underground mines.

Black Wagyu have more slow-twitch muscle fibers than other breeds and marble to a degree an Angus rancher could only dream of. Like all cattle—all mammals, actually—they possess a gene called SCD, but in black Wagyu, it is particularly well expressed. SCD produces an enzyme called delta-9-desaturase, which grabs hold of a stearic acid molecule, which is saturated, and sticks a double bond in its long chain of carbon atoms, converting it into the monounsaturated oleic acid. Thanks to delta-9-desaturase, the fat in a Wagyu steak is so soft it melts in your hands when raw and washes off with warm tap water. On the grill, it produces its own distinct flourish of volatile compounds. It tastes and feels Japanese.

I wanted to see a black Wagyu. I wanted to hold the bucket as he drank beer, and watch as his keeper poured rice wine over his back and massaged it into his muscled flesh, each finger pushing the marbled fat into ever more tiny flecks.

The next morning, Chada-san and I were seated on a train headed into Wagyu country. Next to us, a young child was sitting in a stroller, munching a rice ball while his mother read a magazine. Outside, Japan's unbroken urban sprawl was giving way to plowed fields, slow-moving rivers, and geometrically arranged rice paddies. In the distance, a ridge of mountains crinkled up and down on the horizon.

We were nowhere near Kobe. We were traveling south out of the city of Nagoya—famous for its chicken—to seek out a brand of Japanese beef that many consider to be superior even to Kobe. The brand is called Matsusaka, and the reason foreigners seldom discuss Matsusaka beef is that there isn't much of it, and what little is produced, the Japanese keep to themselves. No beef exceeds the price of Matsusaka beef.

By this point in the tour, I was pointing out examples of Japanese peculiarity at random—a man riding a bike wearing a doctor's mask; yet another grown woman wearing a Hello Kitty backpack—and Chada-san would attempt to place it in context. On the train, seated directly across from us, was a middle-aged man who looked in every way average but who was reading a book with a large drawing of a friendly cat on the cover called *Have a Nice Time*. The man put it in his bag and retrieved a different book, *The Ukulele Chord Book*. Chada-san was not blind to the humor. He said, "I cannot believe that of all the trains for this strange man to sit on, he would have to sit across from you."

Small-town Japan strikes an almost Zen-like contrast with the backlit bustle of Tokyo. The streets in downtown Matsusaka were quiet, and the houses were well kept and fronted by prim lines of hedges as superbly rectangular as the pound cake back at Kinokuniya. Cars were parked in neat long lines by the side of the road, evoking a sense of serenity. Going out for steak in Matsusaka could not be easier, because there are signs on the street pointing out the steak houses. The first one we visited was a near shocking disappointment: the chef did not sell Matsusaka beef, explaining that it was too expensive. And then he dropped a bombshell: "People can't tell the difference, anyway." We did not eat there. We sat down at a refreshingly down-market *yakiniku* spot and ordered some A3 steak of unknown origin, and also a plate of A3 Matsusaka steak that cost double. Despite having received the same quality grade, the Matsusaka meat was more marbled, tasted sweeter, and was undeniably more tender. Its behavior was also exotic and unsteaklike: unlike the generic A3 beef, the edges of the Matsusaka A3 did not curl when cooking, and the meat didn't stick to the grill. The generic steak, however, did something that the Matsusaka steak did not do, something I had not, as yet, seen any steak do in Japan: it *beaded*. This is a word I have coined to describe the little droplets of meat juice that form on top of steak as it grills. Heat causes a steak's connective tissue to squeeze, forcing liquid to the surface where it sits in tiny puddles. The brand-unknown steak, in other words, was juicy.

The Matsusaka steak was juicy, too, but in a different way. Juiciness comes down to two different kinds of liquid. There is melted fat, which feels luscious and smooth in the mouth and induces salivation, creating the illusion of what sensory panels call "sustained juiciness." But there is another kind of liquid that constitutes *juicy*, namely juice, the blood-tinged, umami-rich, water-based savory nectar that reddens a plate after a steak is cut. The steak world affords juice no respect. Everyone talks about marbling and tenderness, but juice must not be underestimated. The only ones who discuss juice seriously are meat scientists, who refer to it clinically and unsexily as "water-holding capacity." The factors that influence it are beyond my technical understanding, but one aspect of its existence is clear and simple: juice lives in muscle fibers. If a steak has more fat than muscle, there won't be much juice, because there aren't the fibers to hold that juice.

All of which explains the lack of beading in the Matsusaka beef. The generic steak delivered a meaty punch that the Matsusaka steak did not. But the best meat of all, again, was not, technically, steak: it was Matsusaka beef tongue.

If there is a secret ingredient that makes Matsusaka beef taste the way it does, the local government is unaware of it. Chada-san and I dropped by Matsusaka city hall, where we sat in a boardroom with two officials whose business cards displayed photographs of A5 beef. The younger one preferred A5 beef. The older one was an A3 man, explaining that "only the very young like A5." Both men ate beef less than once a week—which, in Japan, still makes you a beef lover. To qualify as Matsusaka beef, they told me, a cow must be female, it must be a virgin—"Virgin females have better quality meat"—it must be finished in Matsusaka, it must live in Matsusaka longer than it has lived anywhere else, and it must be of the black Wagyu breed. There was nothing special about the local feed, apparently, because Matsusaka farmers may feed their cattle whatever they like. The single variable that unites all Matsusaka beef, according to the government officials, is that they drink the local water, which comes from one of two clear mountain streams, and which should probably be bottled and sold at Takashimaya at an absurd margin.

The Japanese secret to growing beef, it turns out, is the same as the Italian one: time. Cattle in Japan are finished for thirty months, a glacially drawn-out period of fattening compared with the five-month turnaround at a U.S. feedlot. In Matsusaka, inspectors bestow a grade even higher than A5 for cattle that are finished for thirty-five months. This beef is called Matsusaka Special Beef, and according to the officials, it is incomparably marbled and tender. But no matter how marbled and tender, Matsusaka Special Beef would never qualify for USDA Prime, because a USDA meat grader would deem the cattle too old.

The government officials arranged a farm visit. Matsusaka, which is smaller than a Tokyo neighborhood, was soon receding in the rearview mirror of Chada-san's rented Toyota, and we began climbing a winding road that passed through manicured tea fields and along the Kushida River, which flows down the side of Mount Shirai. We parked outside a garage next to a cute house that had a well-kept garden with evergreen trees whose limbs had been pruned into bulbous shapes. A Matsusaka beef farmer of considerable repute named Kubo came out to meet us. Eight years ago, a cow named Satsuki won him first prize at a competition and was sold for 10 million yen, about $100,000. (He does not know who ate her.) The following year, he won first prize again. Two years ago, Princess 5 won him first prize for a third time.

Her sister, Princess 8, now resided in the garage, which is actually a barn, and was a few months away from qualifying as Matsusaka Special Beef. Kubo-san had not purchased her in hopes of winning another first prize—though he thinks there's a good chance she will do so. He bought her because he missed both Princess 5 and Satsuki. The very subject causes Kubo-san to come as close to misting up as a proud Japanese man is capable of doing.

Japanese cows do not wag their tails or pant enthusiastically, but Kubo-san's have probably considered doing so. When he entered the barn, nine horned, black, and fuzzy heads floated over the walls of nine wooden stalls, each one hoping for a chin scratch from her master. In terms of aroma, Kubo-san's barn has no equal. It smells honey-sweet, with notes of mint, citrus, and cedar, and standing inside it put me in the mood for breakfast cereal with cold milk. Kubo-san walked over to Princess 8 and gave the cow a head scratch that she appeared to enjoy greatly. "When you live with them for three years," he explained, "you become attached." Kubo-san sometimes looks at trophies from past winners, and is left with an "emptiness." When his cows are taken to the slaughterhouse, he feels very sad, even though he understands it is a part of business.

Kubo-san feeds his cattle hay, wheat, crushed soybeans, corn, rice straw, and barley. The grain is from Australia, and the wheat is from the United States. (Canada, land of inferior buckwheat, contributes nothing.) As far as the flavor of the beef is concerned, he told me, soybeans are very important.

No classical music was playing. I had heard that Japanese farmers pipe Mozart or Beethoven into their barns so as to soothe their cows between massages and buckets of beer, and promote even more marbling. Besides talking, the only sounds were cattle shuffling in their stalls and an occasional moo.

"Do they drink beer?" I asked.

"In the summertime."

"How much?"

"One bottle a day," Kubo-san said. The myths of Japanese beef cattle husbandry were falling apart before my eyes. "For Princess 8 only."

"What kind of beer?"

"Kirin. It is cheap."

Kubo-san explained that a cold beer can stimulate a cow's appetite on a hot day, but it seemed to me that the real reason Princess 8 was getting Kirin was because she was his favorite. The other eight cows in the barn, after all, didn't get a drop.

When I asked Kubo-san if he massaged his cattle, he giggled. Like Chada-san, he marveled at the idiotic beliefs foreigners carry in their heads about Japan. What Kubo-san did do, he told me, was brush his cattle, which didn't do a thing for marbling, but did make them look nice. He only ever brushed his cattle before entering them into a show.

"What about sake?" By now I was scrambling.

"In the past," Kubo-san said, "people sprayed some sake before they brushed, to make the fur look more sleek and lustrous. But sake can also make the fur appear red." Now farmers used something even better, he said. Kubo-san opened a closet and retrieved this wondrous substance: a plastic shampoo bottle displaying the words "Lux Super Rich."

Kubo-san hopped into Princess 8's stall to demonstrate, rubbing her flank in circular motions with a straw brush and sending up a cloud of sweet-smelling dust. Princess 8 obviously loved it. Her master did, too.

Like Bill O'Brien's feedlots, Kubo-san's barn is a place cattle are brought to get fat on grain. But there is a reason his barn is 0.002 percent the size of Texas Beef. There is a reason the air smells like potpourri, each stall has a window, and his cows become happy every time Kubo-san walks through the door. He believes that happy cows taste better. He has treated cattle well since he was twelve, when he asked his father for a pet cow and, unlike so many children who ask their fathers for ridiculous pets—I requested an elephant—actually got one. He has raised cows for sixty-six years and says the secret to good beef is very soft fat, and that you can tell good Japanese beef by placing a slice on a newspaper, because the fat will melt through. If you put young beef on a newspaper, the fat won't soak through to the other side.

"Do you use hormones?"

"Never!" Kubo-san said, crossing his arms on his chest and turning his face away in a pose suggestive of wounded pride, but also disgust, as though the mere mention of hormones had brought shame upon us all. Wagyu cattle are not so sensitive, fortunately. Princess 8 stuck her head out of her stall, nuzzled my elbow and then licked me, leaving a streak of saliva from the middle of my chest to my shoulder. Patting her head, I grasped her horn and in a state of mild shock announced, "It's warm."

"It is a sign of good health," Kubo-san said, his pride intact once again.

Everything I'd been told about Japanese cows was false. The accounts of sake-soaked massages, buckets of beer, and Mozart piano concertos were all myths. The cattle were just fed a long time. As steak epiphanies go, this one wasn't as deflating as I might have feared. I found it comforting, in fact, to know that the process responsible for fine Japanese beef was more like what went on in the wine cellar at Borgo San Felice than what takes place at some high-end spa.

I started thinking about dinner. Despite having overdosed on fat the previous night—not to mention my A3 beef lunch and a nagging case of vegetable hunger—I wasn't about to leave Matsusaka without tasting Matsusaka Special Beef.

Before leaving, Chada-san and I drove toward the top of Mount Shirai, parked the car, and took in the view. As in Switzerland, every square foot of ground in Japan seems to have been mindfully put to a specific use, even the country's limited wild patches, which are as bound by the hand of civilization as a putting green. The valley stretched out below us, as landscaped as any golf course, and equally inviting. Behind us, the paved road and the rectangular groves of tea plants gave way to a patch of wild forest that was home to a band of monkeys. It had never occurred to me that Japanese monkeys might be living so close to Japanese cattle—I assumed they had by now been relegated to nature reserves. I wanted very much, all of a sudden, to see Japanese macaques, which are famous for their penchant for luxuriating in hot springs. Chada-san explained that they weren't friendly and warned me that they might throw fruit, but this only made me want to see them more.

No monkeys appeared, unfortunately, with or without fruit. We drove down the valley and back into town for Matsusaka Special Beef, which was so tender I could cut it with chopsticks.

The list of people who have eaten high-grade Japanese beef four times in a little over two days is not long, but my name may now be added to it. If there are other names on that list, I doubt many of them are Japanese. Even Kubo-san, who professed a stronger love of steak than any Japanese person I've ever met, limits his intake to 100 grams (3.5 ounces) a week. (It would take Kubo-san almost five months to get through a Texas King.) The Japanese prize A5 beef beyond all other grades. Big corporations like Toyota or Sony will shell out tens of thousands of dollars for the prestige of serving an extremely well marbled carcass, but I believe their reverence for the A5 beef exceeds their love of the way it actually tastes. Of all the Japanese beef eaters to whom I spoke, only two men—the younger government official in Matsusaka and Kubo-san—claimed to prefer A5 beef. Everyone else thought it was too fatty. Everyone else preferred A3.

The day after my visit to Kubo-san, I visited a slaughterhouse near Nagoya—enormous by Japanese standards, but tiny compared to bovine-processing complexes stateside—where I sat down with a government meat official who'd been inspecting absurdly marbled Japanese carcasses for thirty years. He showed me a plastic color chart that displayed the spectrum of color for beef fat as a series of differently shaded white Chiclets, progressing from creamy yellow on one end to very slightly off white in the middle to perfectly white on the other end. Fat, he said, should be pure white, but he explained that beta-carotene in grass or hay can imbue it with yellow, which, to the Japanese, is a negative trait.

"Does yellow fat taste bad?" I asked. He said no. The problem wasn't how it tasted, but how it looked. "When beef is raw," he explained, "white fat looks better than yellow fat." Set against red flesh, white makes for a more pleasing contrast. He brought out a flesh chart that ranged from pale red on one end all the way to a deep carmine on the other. The ideal was in the middle—not too light, not too dark. Dark flesh, he said, could taste excellent, but it didn't look good.

Here was a man who knew his steak. If ever there was a true Japanese steak aficionado, it was the beef grader from Nagoya, a man at least in his fifties wearing designer jeans and a jean jacket.

"How often do you eat steak?" I asked, ready to high-five a fellow Beef Loyal.

"I don't like beef." He announced this matter-of-factly, like it was one of the more incidental bits of information he had conveyed to me that day.

The revelation led to deeper, more troubling questions. Did *anyone* in Japan like steak? What, for that matter, *was* steak? My working definition, thus far, was any piece of beef that was cooked quickly. That was now proving to be problematic. For one thing, by the terms of that definition the best steak I ate in Japan was a piece of A3 Matsusaka beef tongue. Could tongue be considered steak? It is a muscle, not an organ, and it comes from a cow. It was cooked quickly, and it tasted like steak.

If anything, the Japanese beef tongue was more steaklike than the so-called steak cuts—the rib eye, the strip loin—that were, basically, pieces of swirly beef fat transformed by intense heat into rich morsels of mouth-bursting smoothness. They were the beef equivalent of *otoro*. The tongue, at least, retained some degree of meatiness.

There is no sense of blood in Japanese steak. For the Japanese, steak is not about cutting through a piece of half-cooked muscle and gulping down its succulent juices. While Wagyu beef satisfies fat hunger, I'm not sure it satisfies meat hunger. It is, in other words, a texture thing.

This revelation descended after swallowing a mouthful of extraordinarily high-end Japanese tofu. I was back in Tokyo again, attempting to slake my still-unsated case of vegetable hunger. I found a family-run tofu operation that has been selling top-quality tofu for more than a century. Like almost everything else in Japan, tofu was brought from elsewhere—in this case, China in the eighth century—but the Japanese have elevated it to the loftiest of culinary heights. The curd, which I ate out of a little bamboo cup, was silky and so light as to be reminiscent of helium. A soy flavor was present, but you almost had to concentrate to properly savor it. The whole point of the food, it seemed to me, was its texture, a fact the gentleness of the flavor seemed to underline.

The rogue chef in Matsusaka—the one who said Matsusaka beef tastes the same as all the others—was almost right. The various brands of Japanese beef do taste rather similar. There *are* quality differences—the product coming out of Matsusaka and Kobe seemed more tender and juicy and didn't stick to the grill—but in terms of flavor, the differences between Kobe, Matsusaka, Gumma, Ohmi, and all the others are, at best, only minor. Matsusaka beef tasted somewhat sweeter to me than Kobe beef, although the sample size was hardly scientific. Good luck telling them apart in a blind tasting.

Laurent Vernet had warned me about this back in Scotland. He spent weeks in Asia eating meat and cautioned me against "the boredom of grain-fed beef." "You don't have variation of flavors in Asia," he said. "It all tastes the same."

And yet the Japanese have a sense of culinary subtlety more discriminating than that of any other nation on the planet. Japan is a land of absurdly delicate soba dough and handmade tofu. It is the land of discerning regionalists, where people get busted by the cops for lying about where their chicken is actually from. It is a land of pure savors—and that may explain why it is that the Japanese eat so little steak. Strictly speaking, their steak is not a *terroir* food. It reflects the people of Japan— their ingenuity, their unfailingly high standards, and their great farming skills. But when you take a slice of grilled black Wagyu beef fattened on Australian grain and American wheat and put it into your mouth, what nature are you tasting?

As I prepared to fly back across the Pacific, I felt the stirrings of ennui. The Japanese, I decided, are not weird. It is westerners, with their mythical tales of underwear-dispensing vending machines and cattle subjected to Swedish massage, who seem to wish that oddness upon them. The Japanese are, however, prideful. Like the French, they take their passions seriously. That was something I was going to miss. Americans talk marbling, but if marbled beef ever becomes an Olympic event, the Japanese will win every medal.

Before catching the bus back to the airport—the ride was as thrilling on the way out as on the way in—I went out and bought one last steak.

It was a slice of A4 rib eye and as perfect as a Japanese steak can be: wispy veins of snow-white fat permeating luscious, cherry-red flesh. Many months later, that steak is sitting on my desk next to my computer. I look at it while I'm typing. I stop, from time to time, to think about laying it on a 300°C rock, and imagine the burst of fatty succulence coating the walls of my mouth. But I don't eat it, and I never will, because my perfect Japanese steak is made out of plastic.

CHAPTER SIX

ARGENTINA

I had, by this point, crisscrossed the Atlantic Ocean three times, the Pacific Ocean once, and logged more than forty-five thousand miles, consuming somewhere on the order of fifty pounds of steak. Some of it was lean, and some was jubilantly fatty. Some of it was rare, most was medium, and the odd steak was well done.

There was, however, one steak that I could not get out of my head: that red slice of Scottish loin from the banks of the river Earn, barely marbled, silky even when raw, its fat the color of butter. Angus Mackay's Highland rib eye was the most flavorful steak I'd ever eaten. It was also the juiciest steak I'd ever eaten, and the tenderest, too. But I didn't think of it in terms of a score or technical superiority. What I remembered about that steak was the way it made me feel.

I would find myself stuck in traffic or falling asleep in bed at night, and my thoughts would turn to that meal and those furry cows with big horns grazing the green Scottish pasture. The memory invariably made me hungry. Eating the steak had changed me. I remember the thrill it gave me the same way I remember being kissed by a girl for the first time (in grade nine, in the back of a rented limousine on the way to a semiformal dance), or what it felt like to ski through chest-deep powder for the very first time. A simple piece of meat from a Scottish farmers' market had become almost mythical to me. I would sometimes wonder, Did that steak actually happen? But I snapped photos of that rib eye, and I would look at them from time to time to remind myself that it wasn't all just a dream. The photos, predictably, caused meat hunger. I wanted to eat that steak again.

What would West Texas think of Angus Mackay's Highland rib eye? It ran counter to everything the faculty of meat science at Texas Tech stood for. The steer it came from didn't eat so much as a kernel of corn, and its meat was hardly marbled. During its last winter, it ate hay, but in rainy Scotland hay isn't always good, so it also got a little barley—four pounds a day, at most, which is little more than a treat compared to the troughs of corn you find in a feedlot. For the last two months of its life, it ate nothing but grass. According to American meat science orthodoxy, it should have tasted terrible. It did not. And that meant Allen Williams— the disillusioned meat scientist I had met in Kansas—was right: grass *does* make for the best-tasting steak.

Williams is not the only one who believes this. Jim Cameron, the Scottish semen collector, says the best steak he ever ate—that Welsh Black strip loin that his fork "just fell through"—ate nothing but grass. I received the same gospel message at the Champany Inn, which is the best steak house in Scotland and one of the nicest on the planet. (A battalion of single malts stands at the ready behind the bar, above which hangs a diorama of a stuffed fox trotting away with a dead rabbit in its mouth.) The owner is a South African steak fiend named Clive Davidson, and he let me in on what he believed to be the secret to beef flavor: "It's the grass"—something to do, he said, with chlorophyll making beef taste good. At the Sagra della Bistecca in Cortona, after 2,500 steaks had been reduced to a midden of bones and everyone was dancing arm in arm to a man playing a Roland E-500 keyboard and crooning Italian pop, one of the organizers pulled me aside to talk. His great regret, he told me in a hushed voice, as though he were worried that someone might overhear, was that the quality of Chianina beef was, as he put it, fading out. "The best Chianina," he insisted, "should eat grass and only grass. But that is extremely rare now."

As it happens, there is a country where the cattle are famous for eating grass. It is a big country, the second biggest on its continent and the eighth biggest in the world. More than a fifth of it—an area the size of France—is grass-growing prairie of serious repute, an inland sea of pasture that locals refer to by an old native word, *pampa*. It is a country with fifty-five million cattle but only forty million people, and the reason its people keep so many cows is because they love to eat them. They are the world's greatest Beef Loyals.

The country is Argentina. By the end of February of any given year, a typical Argentine male has already eaten as much steak as a Japanese man will eat that entire year. By the end of July, he will have lapped an American. And by the end of December, a typical Argentine will have consumed no less than 150 pounds of beef. Argentines feel about steak much like the Plains Indians did about bison meat—it is the *only* meat. In Spain, the word for "meat" is *carne*, but if you walk into a butcher shop in Argentina and ask for *carne*, the butcher will present you with cuts of beef. Lamb, pork, and veal must be referred to specifically by name.

Argentina sounded like my kind of place. Then my mother broke a piece of news that made it sound even better: I was related to Mordecai Sternbach.

Some context:

Around the year 1780—half a century or so after Macelleria Falorni, the butcher shop in Greve in Chianti, opened its doors for the first time—a baby boy named Mordecai Sternbach was born in a town called Drohobycz, which was then part of Austria and is now in Ukraine. In 1806, Mordecai Sternbach had a daughter named Pessel who had a son named Leib Alter who had a son named Isaac who had a daughter named Mira who gave birth to my father's mother, Helen. But Mordecai Sternbach wasn't done having daughters. In 1825, his wife bore Ester, who had a daughter named Chaje Tille who had a son named Ignatz who had a son named Heinrich whose daughter, Vera, bore a daughter named Vicky, who, according to the laws of heredity, is my fifth cousin. (I'm pretty sure, anyway.) According to my mother—who, you will have by now deduced, has a penchant for genealogy that would put a Mormon to shame—there was a high probability that Vicky, too, loved steak and ate a lot of it. The same red tide of history that wiped out my father's family and returned aurochs to the forests of Germany had sent the few remaining members of Vicky's side of the family to Buenos Aires.

I had a fifth cousin, apparently, who lived in the country that had more cattle than people. She was a biochemist. She was married to a chemical engineer named Steve. Most important, she sent my mother an e-mail saying she was excited at the prospect of getting to know a person with whom she shared a great-great-great-great-grandfather and extended an invitation to me to pay them a visit, which included a promise to dine at a steak house. And so, thanks to the reproductively inclined Mordecai Sternbach, I found myself boarding an overnight plane headed south, over the equator and then some, to the land of steak.

By the time I woke up, Brazil was petering out and Argentina was moving into view, an unfurled sheet of green cordoned off into giant squares with the occasional river restating nature's preference for curved lines. It was an awesome display of agricultural horsepower down there, an expanse of ruminant-growing grassland that stretched unbroken to the horizon. In the relentless prairie, the only trees that grew were in fecund river basins, huddled in bushy little clumps that, from 39,000 feet, looked oddly like pubic hair.

Down on the ground in Buenos Aires, the similarities between my fifth cousin Vicky and me were uncanny. We both loved coffee, but neither of us could drink so much as a tablespoon after lunch without spending half the night staring at the ceiling. We both insisted on prunes at breakfast. And we both loved steak. (Which may explain the prunes.)

Vicky and her family eat steak a minimum of three times a week, but their beef loyalty is not restricted to consumption. Steak suffuses the family architecture. About thirty years ago, Vicky and Steve built a lovely brick home in a leafy suburb of Buenos Aires called La Horqueta. In the back garden they put in a pool, and behind it erected a handsome brick structure covered in vines that is dedicated to the cooking of steak. In one wall sits the greatest steak-cooking apparatus ever conceived by humankind. Picture a grand fireplace inside which hangs, suspended from chains, a grill that is four feet wide. Like the fabulous grills of Italy, its height is adjustable. A crank sprouts out of one wall, and if you turn it in one direction, the grill rises, and if you turn it in the other, it descends toward the coals.

If this were all there was to Vicky and Steve's steak grill, it would deserve a standing ovation. But my fifth cousin's grill solves the single greatest encumbrance to wood-fired steak cooking: the running-out-of-coals problem. When you cook a steak over wood, the wood has to burn down until it's reduced to glowing coals, because during the yellow-flame stage it emits all sorts of gases and particles that leave an unpleasant taste on the crust of a steak. But there is a problem with coals: they don't last very long. And when coals start fading, you're in trouble. You can't just add wood to the fire because it will burst into yellow flame and begin emitting unpleasant gases. If your steaks aren't finished cooking by the time your coals have expired, you may as well tell your guests to go home.

Unless, of course, you are cooking on Steve and Vicky's adjustable-height grill, because sitting immediately next to the grill is a metal basket that is a glowing coal factory. Fresh wood is placed in the basket and ignited; half an hour later, little glowing chunks start falling out the bottom, which can be moved into position beneath the hissing meat. More wood is then loaded into the basket, and the system thus provides you with a theoretically limitless supply of perfectly glowing coals.

Through a freak of historical accident and far-flung kinship, I now found myself in the home of two great steak fanatics in the most steak-loving country on earth. Their fantastic grill, they told me, had a name: *parilla* (pronounced "pa-rhee-sha" in Buenos Aires, "pa-rhee-ya" in standard Spanish). They fuel it with a special hardwood from the north of Argentina called *quebracho* that can be bought, of all places, at the supermarket. Whenever Steve or Vicky or any of their children feel the stirrings of meat hunger, they can go to the supermarket to buy steak and grab a bag of *quebracho* while they're at it.

All sorts of Argentines, it so happens, make weekly steak-and-*quebracho* runs, and the reason is that all sorts of Argentines have adjustable-height *quebracho*-fired grills, just like Vicky and Steve. To an Argentine, a *parilla* is about as unremarkable as a flush toilet, though perhaps more essential. If you are in the market to buy a home in Argentina and you go to an open house, you expect to appraise the *parilla* just as you expect to appraise the master bedroom and the kitchen. The lack of a *parilla* might give you leverage to bargain the seller down. It is not just leafy suburbs that have *parillas*. The shantytowns that house Buenos Aires' less fortunate have a simpler version of the device: a half barrel with a grill on top. Many of the apartment buildings in downtown Buenos Aires feature rooftop *parillas,* so that the residents are not denied the national birthright of grilling steak outdoors over wood. ("But this is still not one's *own parilla,*" Steve astutely pointed out.) Some buildings, however, have no *parilla* at all, and many Argentines would never consider living in these places.

We got in Steve's car and saw little *parilla* chimneys sprouting over the top of fences all over the neighborhood. A few had gray smoke curling out of their tops. It was early summer in Argentina, and jacaranda trees were in full bloom, but the sweet aroma floating through the streets of La Horqueta was a combination of sizzling steak and *quebracho* smoke.

This was all to be expected. I was, after all, driving through a nice suburb in the land of fifty-five million grass-fed cattle, where every steak promised to taste like Angus Mackay's Highland rib eye. *Of course* every house had a *parilla. Of course* mass grilling was taking place. Everything was finally making sense. That steak I had eaten years ago in the Peruvian restaurant in a mall in Chile was an Argentine steak, which explains why, when all that was left was a puddle of pink juice, I raised the plate to my lips and drank it. It explains why Argentines eat almost three pounds of steak a week. To eat that much steak, the steak, presumably, has to be tasty.

Vicky and Steve, still many ounces shy of their weekly three-pound mark, were driving, as they do on most Sunday nights, to their favorite neighborhood *parilla*—the word, it turns out, also refers to a restaurant with a *parilla.* When you walk into this particular *parilla,* the first thing you see is a very large grill half covered with red meat. It was like the dining room at Borgo San Felice, but on a grander scale—and much cheaper. This delighted me. I turned to Steve and asked, "Is it also a wood-burning grill? Or do the restaurants use gas?"

Steve's smile disappeared, and, hurrying me to the table, he sat me down, leaned over, and said, "Mark, there is something you need to understand: gas is an abomination in this country." We quickly moved on to a different subject: the *asado,* the name Argentines use for their beef-intensive version of a barbecue. If you invite friends to your house for steak, you are inviting them to an *asado*. Similarly, to visit a restaurant with a *parilla*, as we were doing, is to partake in the *asado*.

I scanned the menu. There were two to three times the number of cuts offered in an American steak house. Argentines love their rib eyes, strip loins, and tenderloins, but they love every part of a cow that can be successfully laid on a hot grill. There are quite a few, it turns out. Some of those parts weren't even muscle—like sweetbreads, which is the curious English word for a cow's thymus and pancreas glands. During an *asado*, they're served as an appetizer, along with blood sausage, chorizo, and other nether parts—all off the *parilla*.

The first steak cut we were served was one you don't find on North American grills. Argentines call it *tira de asado*, and it's one of their cheaper cuts, although some Argentines would pay more for it than for tenderloin. Americans know it as short ribs, a stretch of rib meat cut across the bone that isn't eaten as steak in North America, unless an Argentine happens to be in town. In Argentina, *tira de asado* is a blue-collar cut, but this does not bear a negative connotation. Tenderloin, which is the tenderest cut on a carcass, is often and justifiably derided as an old woman's steak among Argentines. Real steak lovers eat *tira de asado*. A year earlier, Steve had moved his company, which analyzes lubrication oils, into a brand-new, custom-built building. As a gesture to the builders, he treated them to an *asado* on the last Friday of every month. He gave some cash to the contractor, who insisted on buying the beef personally. The cut he bought his men was *tira de asado*. The workers constructed an ad hoc *parilla* by stretching wire over loose bricks, and they grilled *tira de asado* on this unsophisticated but highly functional grill *every day*.

The *tira de asado* arrived Maillard-brown and crossed with black. The meat was gray through and through, which was not surprising. As much as Argentines revere steak, they buck the near-worldwide conviction among steak-loving peoples that steak should be served pink or red in the center. Argentines prefer their steak well done. (I didn't believe it the first time I heard it, either.) While there is a loyal contingent that prefers it *jugoso* (juicy), they are in the minority.

From the looks of it, I expected the meat to be tough. This was a cut, after all, that the rest of the world deems a braising cut, and it had seen its share of cooking. My knife sliced through it with little difficulty, however, and I put this first morsel of Argentine grass-fed steak in my mouth. Tender. Moist. A big flash of beefy flavor. I waited for the note to gloriously build, but it vanished. I ate another piece, and it happened again. If the flavor were graphed, it would show a spike followed by a flat line that tasted mildly sour, but also of beef fat. It tasted remarkably like Texas feedlot steak.

I walked up to the *asador*—the man in charge of grilling—and asked where the beef was from, expecting him to name some quaint town adrift in that ocean of grass where there are five hundred cattle for every man, woman, and child. He held up a steak with cherry red flesh and flaky white fat. "The beef," he said, grinning, bursting with pride, "is pen-fed on corn."

I was eating feedlot steak.

I knew something like this might happen. Before leaving for Argentina, I had read a number of reports—all of them alarmist and depressed-sounding—that contended that Argentina was abandoning its grazing beef industry for the American model: growing corn and erecting Texas-size feedlots. And this was all due to the fact—apparently, oddly—that Argentines loved steak so much.

In 2001, the debt-laden Argentine economy crashed. When it began recovering, the price of beef started climbing. Farmers were making good money selling Argentine beef to Europe, Russia, and Israel, but Argentines were finding their three-pound-per-week habit was getting hard on the wallet. The price of steak got so high that at one point Argentina's president delicately suggested that his people might perhaps consider eating less beef, which, given the intensity of beef loyalty, was the political equivalent of asking eagles to give up flight. Sensing the darkening national mood, he realized the true source of all of his country's problems: foreigners. They were the true ones, he decided, who were eating too much Argentine beef, and this revelation moved him to do something more overtly political: he cut beef exports.

In theory, this should have flooded Argentinian butcher shops with cheap beef. For a while, it did, and the price of beef dropped by a third. But the flood of cheap beef was soon cut off by now furious, not to mention poorer, ranchers and farmers, who were so angered by their government's actions that they banded together and blockaded roads so that food-laden trucks from the countryside couldn't deliver to cities. The first thing to disappear from store shelves was steak, followed by pork, lamb, and chicken and, much later, pasta. Argentines rich and poor so detested the sight of empty butcher shops and bare *parillas* that a distinctly Hispanic political phenomenon known as a *cacerolazo* erupted. People leaned out of windows, hung off balconies, and stood on street corners banging pots and pans together to voice their anger. They marched to public squares with their pots and pans and banged them some more.

The ranchers backed down, in part because it had never been their intention to starve their countrymen, but also because the only thing worse than selling beef at a loss was letting it rot. Butcher shops were filled again; *quebracho* was lit. The policy worked. Cheaper steak was grilled and eaten.

The ranchers weren't done being angry, however. Thanks to the meddling government and an urban steak-loving populace who believed the countryside was overrun with fabulous wealth, their income was shrinking. Some were so strapped they decided to get out of the beef business altogether. Farmers who held the best land in Argentina, whose families had for centuries sneered at the very idea of crop farming, did what the law of supply and demand predicted: they cleared the cattle and planted crops. They laid down fertilizer by the ton and sowed corn and soybeans and wheat and anything else that was getting a good price on world markets. In a matter of months, Argentina was no longer using all its best land to fatten cattle but was raising corn and soybeans to fatten pigs in China.

The cattle had to go somewhere, and where they went was marginal land, land that had never been considered up to the task of finishing cattle. To get them fat, Argentines began herding them into pens and feeding them corn, which they now had in abundance.

It sounded like a crisis, all right. But thus far, the effects were still minor. I had heard that a couple of feedlots had sprung up on the pampas. This or that supermarket, people told me, was selling the odd feedlot steak. And yet here we were at Steve and Vicky's favorite *parilla,* eating feedlot steak. Had I come too late?

I did what any sane steak lover would do. I climbed onto the upper floor of an overnight bus, reclined my chair as far as it would go, and headed into that ocean of grass. Buenos Aires, a city of thirteen million people and *parillas* numbering in the hundreds of thousands (if not millions), gave way to the real Argentina—an unending monotony of fields. Cattle would appear in huge herds, followed by fifteen minutes of prairie, then a field of lumped hayrolls as tall as a truck scattered right to the horizon. The road was a strip of tar and pebbles painted on a sea of green, and it seemed as if a change in tide would bring the pampas flooding across it. As the summer sky began to darken and more fields rolled by, I drifted off into sleep.

I woke in a city called Santa Rosa, the capital of the province of La Pampa and, more important, the home of a meat scientist and grazing expert named Dr. Anibal Pordomingo. He pulled up to my hotel in a dusty, mud-spattered Chevrolet pickup truck, and we headed straight for a butcher shop. There was no way of knowing what kind of beef a *parilla* might serve, but at a butcher shop we could inspect raw steaks, which could give some indication of their provenance. We stood in front of a refrigerated display case and looked at steaks that were not so much arranged as piled in a manner suggesting that a lot of product would soon be moved. The flesh was a deep red and the fat was sufficiently yellow that it would win zero admirers in Japan—which is to say, it had a mild hue that only appeared yellow next to something that was pure white. Pordomingo knew the butcher, who invited us back to look at a half carcass hanging by a hook from the ceiling. He appraised the exterior fat, which was off-white and had a slightly glossy sheen. The beef *looked* grass fed. But would it taste that way?

We ate lunch at Parilla Los Caldenses, a big, airy joint with yellow walls that is, in itself, worth the price of a plane ticket to Argentina for one simple and gratifying reason: seven dollars buys you all the steak you can eat. It also buys you theoretically infinite trips to the salad bar, which was, more accurately, a salad and tongue bar, the latter poached, sliced, and dressed in either oil or mayonnaise. Argentine tongue doesn't approach Japanese tongue in quality, probably because poaching doesn't approach grilling, but it is satisfying nevertheless and every salad bar should stock it.

Our daily vegetable quota filled, it was time for steak. A waiter approached the table with a stretch of short ribs off the *asado*. In this case, *asado* referred to the fire, which was burning in the next room, and the meat was hung from metal crosses next to it. It was just one among many controlled bonfires raging indoors all over Santa Rosa, not to mention Buenos Aires, Córdoba, Chaco, Mendoza, and every other city, town, hamlet, and village in Argentina. This is a country where it is common to pass a restaurant window at ten thirty in the morning and witness a grown man lighting a very large fire, a scene that anywhere else would look like arson. Later, the same man will punch metal spikes into the sand next to the fire and hang beef ribs off them, so that the meat may absorb *quebracho* essence and heat without dripping fat directly into the flames. Argentines have mastered the contained bonfire. They have brought it indoors and made it mundane, and all because they love steak.

The short ribs had been cooking for something like two hours, which made them, in a technical sense, a roast, though I was not prepared to say they were not steak. Beef impaled on a skewer and roasted over an open fire is, in fact, what the word *steak* originally meant. It's an old word, borrowed from the Vikings, who undoubtedly relished a good steak. Originally, "steak" referred to meat that had been cooked on a stake in the ground. *Steak* comes from the same root as *stick*, and cooking the former on the latter may well be the oldest recipe there is. Magdalenian Woman cooked steak on a stick. So did the Vikings. The first Argentines to eat steak on a stake were the cowboys of the pampas, who are called gauchos, and whose level of mythological/cultural significance in Argentina is equal to, if not greater than, that of cowboys in America. Gauchos rode the plains chasing cattle. When they caught up to them, they cut their Achilles tendons with lances with moon-shaped blades on the ends. The gauchos were mainly after hides and took only as much meat as they needed, leaving most of it to rot. Because they could not drag heavy grills across the pampas, they drove spikes into the ground next to their campfires and cooked steaks, which they ate for breakfast, lunch, and dinner.

The oldest steak recipe in the world is a good one. Despite being cooked to well done, the short ribs had a crispy, smoky crust, a soft center, and a creamy finish. This was no feedlot steak.

"It's good," I said.

"It could be better," Pordomingo answered.

The waiter returned with a pile of other steaks, though these had come off the *parilla* (grill) rather than the *asado* (fire). They weren't as tasty, and according to Pordomingo, that had more to do with the steak than with the cooking. Argentine steak hadn't been giving him much to be happy about lately, and the weather was not helping. Autumn, he explained, sounding more like a rancher than a meat scientist, used to be the best season, agriculturally speaking, but now you couldn't rely on it. Spring wasn't rainy enough; summers were getting too hot and too dry. When all cattle eat is grass, the quality of their beef has everything to do with the quality of grass, which has everything to do with the weather.

Stuffed with *tira de asado*, we drove out to a field to see some weather and grass. In Argentina, grass is very often alfalfa, a legume related to peas and peanuts that offers a superb yield among forage plants. It looks more like a weed than a standard grass and has pretty little purple flowers. I bent down and tore off a piece and put it in my mouth. It tasted sour, but very slightly sweet, too. The weather was indeed terrible. It was so dry a dust cloud followed you when you walked. A herd of cattle was scattered among the alfalfa, but Pordomingo considered this to be a poor example of Argentine grazing.

On the next field over was an Argentine feedlot. Compared with Palo Duro Feeders, it was so small as to seem almost cute, with makeshift pens and feed bunks made out of blue plastic tarp strung over wire. The cattle had all been shipped off to the slaughterhouse a month earlier, but the pens remained a slick of mud and shit, its reek identical to that of Palo Duro Feeders. Pordomingo pointed to a puddle of foul water.

"That's going to get into the water table," he said. "This is why pen feeding is profitable here. Our environmental costs are lower, our wages are lower, and cattle here cost one-third the price."

"Are cattle happy in the pens?" I asked, remembering what Kubo-san had said about happy cows tasting better.

Pordomingo shrugged his shoulders. "How could they be?"

I went to a fancy *parilla* for dinner that night called Parilla Los Pines, which I had scoped out that afternoon, and stared at the *asado*, which I could see through a window next to my table. Drips of fat were falling from sheets of rib and landing with a small puff in gray ash. On the wall was a framed photo of an elk in a meadow, and another of a dog attacking a cougar. It was still early by Argentine dinner standards. There were only five customers in the restaurant, including me. All were men. All were eating steak.

The rib eye is Anibal Pordomingo's favorite cut. Welcome to the club. I ordered one for dinner, and it was so colossal that it made every other rib eye I've ever eaten seem two-dimensional. The enormous hunk of flesh was served on a white plate just larger than a saucer, a plate that seemed intentionally small, so as to exaggerate the sheer size of the steak.

Like the steak I ate at lunch, initial juiciness was good but trailed off. It was the same story with flavor—quenching and grassy, but fleeting. I was not disappointed, however. The meal, which included fries and a good bottle of red Argentine wine, cost a little more than three McDonald's Happy Meals back home but was exponentially more pleasurable.

The next morning, Pordomingo took me north to witness the agricultural engine that is the pampas turning at a higher rpm. He called out local forage as he drove—"Alfalfa . . . ryegrass"—reading the grassland the way a sailor reads the sky. One patch growing by the side of the road looked a little yellow. "Not green enough," he observed. "Probably low in phosphorus."

I brought up the delicate issue of the previous night's less-than-outstanding steak. "The steak doesn't taste as good as I expected," I politely told him, which is to say it didn't hold a candle to Angus Mackay's

Highland rib eye. Pordomingo wasn't surprised. Argentine steak in general didn't taste as good as he had expected, either.

The reasons were numerous. There was the weather, Pordomingo said, which was getting drier and drier, possibly due to global warming. For the last decade or so, Argentine beef cattle, he said, were slaughtered at a younger age, so that their meat now tasted more like veal—milder, more tender—than like beef. This trend was due in part to the cut in exports, which had made cash-pinched farmers try to fatten their cattle and move them to market in as little time as possible, the farming equivalent of just-in-time manufacturing. And then there was the problem of aging. In Argentina, aged beef is almost unheard of. Steaks from a cow slaughtered on a Monday can be in the butcher case by Thursday, giving the calpain enzymes hardly any time to break down fibers. There are people who will tell you that Argentines don't believe in aging, that they prefer the taste of fresh beef. But the truth is, most Argentines have never heard of aged beef. Argentine consumers—steak addicts, all of them—don't know that beef tastes better if it sits in the fridge for a week or two. They care only about the price, and aging makes the price go up.

More than two hours after setting out, we entered a zone of overcast drizzle not far from a town called Huinca Renancó. The fields rolling by became brighter and more verdant, with the alfalfa looking lush enough to toss with olive oil and vinegar. We pulled into one ranch where Angus heifers were grazing it hard. They were a long way from Scotland, but on pampa this moist the doddies had gotten fat by their fourteen-month birthday. A gaucho standing next to a wire fence was about to mount a magnificent-looking dun-colored horse to go check on the cattle. Instead, he hopped into the cab of Pordomingo's truck, and we drove over alfalfa. The fields were strewn with soupy patties of manure as flat as dinner plates, the Argentinian term for which is *abono*. When we got out of the truck, Pordomingo and the gaucho walked in deep conversation, using some sixth sense to avoid the *abono*. I let my guard drop and planted my left foot directly into a patty, and the way it coated my shoe, I may as well have stepped in a bucket of spaghetti sauce.

One heifer had eaten too much alfalfa. It had overfermented in her rumen, inflating it like a balloon, and now it was so puffed out that it was pressing on her lungs and making it hard for her to breath. She lurched in circles, panting. The gaucho tried to walk her through it, but the heifer collapsed and began hyperventilating. Pordomingo and the gaucho exchanged words in Spanish, then the gaucho unsheathed a large knife and stabbed the heifer.

It appeared as though the gaucho was trying to kill the heifer, but he was doing just the opposite. The tip of his knife punctured her hide and entered her pressurized rumen. When he pulled it out, gas-propelled alfalfa began spurting out, accumulating on the ground in a green, gooey mound. The heifer, looking relieved, sat there with her front legs splayed, like a cat, taking satisfying breaths of air as the alfalfa froth slowed to trickle and then a burble. A few other heifers walked over to have a look, sniffing the half-digested alfalfa, as though considering whether or not to take a bite, then sniffed their friend and walked off. According to Pordomingo, the heifer would likely make a full recovery.

Alfalfa bloat can be prevented in two ways. Either you can feed cattle the same antibiotic they get in feedlots, which is called Rumensin, and which kills gas-producing bacteria in the rumen, or you can cut the intensity of the alfalfa by planting some other grasses with it. This, of course, will reduce the output of the field, so for many Argentines it's easier and more profitable to grow lots of alfalfa and arm their gauchos with knives.

Alfalfa wasn't the only reason these cows had grown so big so quickly. Ranchers, Pordomingo explained, had gotten a lot better at choosing bulls that sired fast-growing calves. Like the Angus bulls advertised in the *Aberdeen-Angus Review*, these cattle got big in a hurry. As far as the ultimate effects on steak quality, Pordomingo was not enthusiastic.

For lunch, he intentionally took me to a restaurant that didn't do a lot of business, and so didn't have access to all that young, fast-grown beef. It was called Parador El Encuentro, and I walked in with my shoe and the cuff of my pants still covered in *abono*. We sat under a big air conditioner. At the far end of the room, most of the diners were gathered at a table near a big TV that was showing a daytime soap. Below the TV was yet another salad/tongue bar. "My hunch is that we'll get older meat here," Pordomingo said.

The steaks were a cut I had never heard of, *aguja*, which comes from the neck. Old neck meat, I suspected, would make for terrible steak, but I was wrong. That *aguja* turned out to be the best steak I'd eaten in Argentina—tender, smooth, but, most important, *beefy*. Pordomingo chewed, paused, and said, "They call this 'country flavor.'" It tasted, he explained, like the Argentine steak of ten years ago. I plowed through mine, flagged down the waitress, and ordered a rib eye. If the neck tasted this good, I could only imagine how good a rib eye would be.

I would never find out. We had driven so far north that we'd drifted into Córdoba Province, which is in a different time zone. The kitchen was closed, the waitress informed us. The *asador* had gone home, and the wood in the *parilla* had turned to ash.

I had been denied steak by a time zone. An artificial line drawn by the hand of man had taken potentially the best rib eye of my life out of my mouth, leaving a hole in my stomach that ached to be filled. I decided then and there to fill it at the best *parilla* in Santa Rosa. That evening, I would order a gargantuan rib eye. Now that I'd found Argentina's delicious grass-fed beef, it was time to really start eating.

My running total of steak consumption over four days was approaching three pounds. Stretched out to a year, that would amount to 275 pounds—not even double the Argentine average. It's hard to feel guilty about eating too much steak in Argentina. It's even harder after meeting Anibal Pordomingo's father, José Pordomingo.

He was sitting in his garden next to his *parilla* when I met him, looking distinguished, with a gray comb-over suggestive of inner youth. He was eighty years and two months old, with a mind that remains so sharp that when his son forgets a phone number, he phones his father, who may as well work for directory assistance. Physically, José Pordomingo has slowed. He used to run two ranches, but he got tired of the long drive between them both, so now he just tends one, which, by North American standards, is big: 740 acres. He checks in on his 250 cows every day. He pulls up to the gate, opens it, and walks two and a half miles of pasture.

The secret to José Pordomingo's good health, according to José Pordomingo, is exercise and a balanced diet. He recommends a lot of fresh fruit and green vegetables. He drinks one or two glasses of milk every day and watches his salt. He cautions against eating too much beef, which he himself consumes only once a day, every day—about half as much as he ate in his youth. His daily intake now stands at about 160 grams, which is more than most Americans eat and equals about a third of a pound, or a smallish steak, seven days a week, fifty-two weeks a year, for a yearly total of 130 pounds. His favorite cuts are rib eye and rump, but unlike most of Argentina—including his son Anibal—José Pordomingo prefers it *jugoso*. His wife, Elda, eats more beef than he does, but, at seventy-three, she is still in the eat-all-the-steak-you-want bloom of youth.

If it seems paradoxical for a man who eats that much beef to be in such fine health at such an advanced age, José is hardly an anomaly in Argentina. The whole country is something of a beef-eating cardiovascular paradox. Just as the French drink wine by the bottle, eat rich food, and seem all the healthier for it, so, too, do Argentines consume raging quantities of steak and yet do not all drop dead of heart attacks—not at the rate you might expect, in any case. In the United States, for every 100,000 men between thirty-five and seventy-four, 169 die of coronary heart disease. In Argentina, the equivalent 100,000 men will eat six million more pounds of beef a year than their American counterparts, but only 120 of them will die from coronary heart disease—30 percent fewer than in the States. In Argentina, the life expectancy at birth is seventy-five. In America—a country that spends vastly more per person on health care—it's seventy-eight. These numbers seem all the more amazing when you consider that the rate of smoking is almost twice in Argentina what it is in the United States. Roughly one in two steak-loving Argentine men smokes. More than half the population does not have access to adequate health care. Poverty is considered the greatest indicator of heart disease, and there is far more poverty in Argentina than in the States.

This is not to say that Argentina is the Shangri-la of coronary health, for it is anything but. Despite their seeming paucity of heart attacks, many an Argentine artery is stiff and clogged with fatty buildup. More Argentines die of strokes than Americans. But when you consider all the smoking, the poverty, and the poor health care, it doesn't look as if eating an average of 150 pounds of beef per year is all that deadly. Steak is not what's killing them.

This may have something to do with the kind of beef Argentines eat. Beef from cattle raised and fattened on grass is considered healthier than beef from cattle fattened on corn. Grass, which is a leafy plant, contains more vitamin E, vitamin B, and beta-carotene than corn, which is primarily rich in starchy carbohydrates (that's why it gets cattle fat so quickly). Vitamin E and beta-carotene are antioxidants, which neutralize substances called free radicals, and in so doing may help prevent maladies ranging from heart disease to Parkinson's disease, cancer, diabetes, and Alzheimer's. The most talked-about health advantage of grass-fed beef, however, is its fat.

A discussion of fat as it relates to health invariably revolves around the concept of saturation. Fats, basically, are chains of carbon and hydrogen molecules with a little oxygen at one end. A fat molecule that contains as much hydrogen in it as possible is said to be *saturated* with hydrogen. Certain fats, however, are missing some hydrogen atoms. A fat missing a pair of hydrogen atoms on each molecule is considered monounsaturated; a fat missing two or more pairs of hydrogen atoms is polyunsaturated. Of all the fats, the saturated ones have the worst reputation because they raise LDL cholesterol—the "bad" cholesterol, so called because too much causes heart attacks.

Cardiologists advise their patients to watch how much steak they eat because beef contains three saturated fats: myristic acid, palmitic acid, and stearic acid. Myristic and palmitic acid raise LDL cholesterol. Stearic acid, despite being saturated with hydrogen, does not, and the reason is that humans, just like black Wagyu cattle, produce the enzyme delta-9-desaturase, which grabs hold of stearic acid molecules and removes a pair of hydrogen atoms, converting it into oleic acid, which is monounsaturated and also happens to be found in abundance in canola and olive oils. Thanks to delta-9-desaturase, stearic acid is, from a cardiovascular health point of view, neutral. In grass-fed beef the ratio of saturated-to-unsaturated fat is lower than in corn-fed beef, but not by much. Grass-fed beef, however, does have more stearic acid and less myristic and palmitic acid. It is, therefore, better for you.

The subject of fat, beef, and human health does not end with saturated fatty acids, however. Within the world of unsaturated fats, a storm has been raging for some time now over two important kinds: omega-3 and omega-6 fatty acids. Both are considered *essential*—like the eight essential amino acids, the human body cannot live without them. Omega-3 fatty acids are believed to fight cancer, prevent heart attacks, soothe arthritis, and promote brain health (among other benefits). Omega-6 fatty acids are associated with healthy skin, vision, and immune system. Eating too much of one, however, makes it difficult for the body to process the other.

For this reason, nutritionists believe the human diet should contain a ratio of omega-6 to omega-3 fatty acids of about 4 to 1. Most North Americans, however, don't eat nearly enough omega-3 fatty acids, and their ratio is more in the area of 15 to 1, if not higher. The reason for this imbalance is grain, which contains a lot of omega-6 fatty acids, and not much omega-3. (This is one of the reasons that Ted Slanker, the grass-fed beef evangelist on Texas's Red River, believes grain to be "the atomic bomb of the American food system.") Although humans have been eating grain for ten millennia, in the last hundred years or so we have become very good at growing it and processing it into all sorts of edible products. We eat cornflakes for breakfast. We pour grain oil on our salads, or emulsify it into mayonnaise and spread it on sandwiches and hamburgers. Corn oil, which we use to fry potato chips and French fries and moisten our cakes and turn into margarine, contains an omega-6 to omega-3 ratio of 46 to 1.

We also feed corn to cows. In corn-fed beef, the omega-6 to omega-3 ratio can be as high as 20 to 1. The ratio in grass-fed beef is usually around 3 to 1 and is sometimes as low as 1 to 1, and the reason is that there are more omega-3 fatty acids in a field of grass than in a concrete trough full of corn.

A person in need of omega-3 fatty acids will get more of them from a plate of walnuts or flaxseeds or wild salmon than from a grass-fed Argentine steak. But walnuts and flaxseeds—and any other nut, leaf, fruit, or seed—have nothing on a steak when it comes to another recently famous fatty acid: CLA, which stands for conjugated linoleic acid, and which, in laboratory experiments, has been found to inhibit the growth of tumors. Grain-fed steak contains CLA, but grass-fed steak contains about twice as much. (The richest known source of CLA is kangaroo meat.)

Grass-fed beef is therefore healthier. In theory, at least. The problem is that it is easier to theorize about human health than it is to predict. It is easier to take a sample of ground beef, separate it into fat and water, vaporize it, and then analyze all the compounds using gas chromatography than it is to predict the effect that all those compounds—not to mention all the other compounds people eat—will have on the human body. The science of nutrition is, at best, imperfect. We know that when mice are exposed to a carcinogen, the ones who've had CLA spread on their skin develop fewer tumors. We know that people who consume omega-3-rich fish and fish-oil supplements appear to have a lower rate of cardiovascular incidents than people who don't. But we don't know how all these substances work together in the body. A nutritional scientist cannot predict how food will affect the human body the way an astronomer can predict when the next lunar eclipse will take place. The effect food has on the body is still something of a complex mystery.

Does eating grass-fed meat actually reduce your cholesterol? Will eating grain-fed steak give you—or, worse, *me*—a heart attack? Would the hearts of all those tobacco-smoking, steak-loving Argentine men begin infarcting if their yearly 150 pounds of beef came from feedlots?

To answer that question with certainty, you would have to raise thousands of people in identical settings and circumstances and feed them identical diets, the only difference being that half would spend their lives eating feedlot beef and the others would eat only grass-fed beef. At various ages, you would measure fat, cholesterol, and plaque buildup in the arteries, body mass index, and whatever other measurable metrics come to mind. You would wait out the decades and see who died of what, and when. Finally, when the last member of the study group expired, you'd have some serious data. Good luck getting that kind of funding.

In the real world, there are too many variables to make such comparisons easy. Argentines drink a lot of red wine. Many of their cars don't have catalytic converters and spew out noxious exhaust, and their health care system leaves much to be desired. Americans watch more TV and drink more soft drinks than Argentines. Americans also eat more feedlot beef than Argentines.

Only a single study, so far as I am aware, has ever attempted to compare the effects of feedlot beef with those of grass-fed beef. In 2006, the Cardiovascular Institute of Buenos Aires teamed up with a steak-friendly outfit called the Argentine Beef Promotion Institute and put forty-eight healthy people—twenty-four men and twenty-four women—on the same diet. For twenty-eight days—and this could only ever happen in Argentina—the men ate 200 grams of steak every day, and the women ate 150 grams. At the end of the twenty-eight days, there was a recess of twenty-one days, and then another twenty-eight-day cycle would commence.

There were four such cycles, all told, and during each one the subjects ate a different type of beef: grass-fed, grain-fed, or mixed (which means that the cows ate some grass, and a little grain, too). During the fourth cycle, one type of beef was repeated. At the end of each cycle, the subjects were measured, weighed, prodded, and blood was drawn from their veins and analyzed.

The results were what you might expect: when people ate grass-fed beef, their blood looked more like that grass-fed beef, containing more vitamin E and beta-carotene as well as more omega-3 fatty acids. HDL cholesterol (good cholesterol) was up slightly after a month on pasture beef, while LDL (the bad stuff) was down. The study did not yield the kind of earthshaking, eye-popping data that would have made grass-fed beef an instant nutritional panacea, as happened with oat bran in the late 1980s. The differences in the numbers were actually slight. That was most likely the case because the subjects ate lean beef—more fat may have resulted in more compelling data—and because twenty-eight days is not long enough for a diet to show dramatic effects. The data indicate a trend of the sort that would make a scientist say, *Hey, there's something going on here. Let's do another study.*

It is also worth noting that after the four cycles were completed, the forty-eight participants had lost, on average, two pounds and increased their muscle mass. A pamphlet published by the Argentine Beef Promotion Institute announced, "It may be assured that consuming beef once a day is healthy without any collateral effect whatsoever," which is all just a complicated way of saying the José Pordomingo diet is good for you.

Why would a country that loves steak more than any other nation give up grass-fed steak—which *appears* to be healthier—for feedlot beef? Why would Argentines, who had grass and cattle stretching to every horizon, decide it would be better to start laying down tons of fossil-fuel-based fertilizer, harvest corn, then crowd cattle into a pen and feed it to them?

I presented these questions to the man who runs the largest feedlot in Argentina. Miguel de Achaval comes by his expertise the old-fashioned way: he spent twelve years working in Texas for a feedlot company called Cactus Feeders, which is so huge it makes Bill O'Brien's two-feedlot operation seem rinky-dink. At any one time, Cactus Feeders can have as many as half a million cattle eating corn out of miles of concrete troughs.

De Achaval runs a 27,000-head feedlot four hundred kilometers north of Santa Rosa next to a town called Villa Mercedes, but he would like to open five or six more, including one with a 50,000-head capacity. He is still working for his old boss, Cactus Feeders, but he also works for Cresud, an Argentine conglomerate that owns shopping malls and office buildings, and Tyson Foods, the agri-behemoth that in all probability wholesaled the dry and flavorless rib eye I ate at the Big Texan. The three companies joined forces a few years ago here in Argentina and formed a company called Carnes Pampeanas.

De Achaval works at the organization's slaughterhouse and packing plant near Santa Rosa, where he sits behind an imposing desk in the largest office in the building, a sprawling map of Argentina on the wall behind him. As de Achaval sees things, Argentina is finally catching up to the rest of the world. Its agro-industrial awakening took place in the early 1990s, he told me, when the big multinationals arrived, and companies like Dow and Cargill began buying grain from farmers. They offered favorable terms—checks that paid in ten days, underwritten by companies that were in no danger of going bankrupt. Argentine meat-packers, on the other hand, took a long time to pay, if they paid at all. The price of grain on world markets, furthermore, was going up, and genetically modified varieties of corn meant farmers could reap bigger harvests than they thought possible. The multinational grain buyers even offered to help cattle ranchers with upfront costs, like fertilizer and pesticide, to help ease the switchover from cattle to grain. It didn't take long for Argentine ranchers to see where the profits were, and it didn't take long before all that grain they were growing began to be fed to cattle. "The world feeds cattle on grain," de Achaval said. "No one feeds cattle on grass."

The government, too, was playing its part. A few days before our meeting, de Achaval had met with a member of the governing party (known as Peronists after Argentina's longtime leader Juan Perón), who told him, "Every time a Peronist was in power and the citizens were not able to buy beef, the Peronists lost the election." In Argentina, steak is politics.

It was looking more and more as if Argentina's grass-fed steak days were behind it. The best beef land was churning out freighter loads of corn and soybeans. Cattle were grazing second-rate pasture, and the taste of their beef was, at best, inconsistent. Corn-fed beef, on the other hand, always tasted the same. Already, according to de Achaval, some-thing like half the beef the country produced was out of a feedlot. In ten years, he said, it would be more like 80 percent, and in twenty years, 100 percent, by which point the flavor of Argentine steak would be indistin-guishable from that of West Texas steak.

One aspect of de Achaval's account, however, didn't add up: If crops paid so well that all the best beef-fattening pastures were now grown over with cornstalks and soybean plants, how could it make financial sense to feed that corn to animals designed to eat grass? When it comes to pro-ducing meat by eating corn, cattle are notably bad performers. It takes about eight pounds of corn to get one pound of beef, which is a pathetic showing compared to that of a pig, which can do it on four pounds, or a chicken, which can do it on less than two pounds. Is it financially sound to grow cows the same way you grow pigs? If the price of corn keeps pace with the world's exploding population, will Argentina even be able to afford to eat steak? Or will Argentines suddenly find themselves throwing chicken legs and pork loins on their beloved *parillas*?

This nightmarish thought seems to have occurred to the Argentine government. They give the big feedlots something they do not give to the cattle ranchers: a subsidy. For every cow in de Achaval's feedlot, the government gives him 6 kilograms of corn and 3 kilograms of soybeans every day. If his company wants to export any of its beef, it must keep its fridges at 65 percent capacity. That, it seems to me, is a nice way of ensuring that steak remains both abundant and cheap, something that ought to help the Peronists the next time there is an election.

De Achaval himself is a believer in the free market. The mere concept of subsidies, he says, disgusts him. He claims, furthermore, that the cost savings resulting from all that free corn and soybeans is not helping his company. If those subsidies were abandoned, he said, the price of feedlot beef would not be affected; it would just lower the price of the steers he buys from small Argentine cow-calf farmers. "It is a very simple equation," he explained. "Purchase price plus cost of production equals selling price. When cost goes up, I turn around and kill the cow-calf guy."

This all sounded a tad odd. Why was a for-profit company taking a government handout and passing the cost savings over to the small farmers who sell steers? Why would a multinational be effectively handing cash over to little Argentine cow-calf farmers? I was about to ask as much, but I caught myself. I was getting caught up in Argentina's beef politics. I wasn't a rancher. I didn't run a meatpacking plant. All I wanted was a good steak. The real question about feedlot beef, it seemed to me, was, Did Argentines themselves actually like the stuff?

I put the question to de Achaval: "Would you say Argentine taste in beef has changed to be more accustomed to grain-fed beef?"

"Yes," he said. "No doubt."

"Is the taste for the old-style beef disappearing?"

De Achaval surprised me with what he said next. "I like the old-style *asado*," he told me—a shockingly candid admission coming from a guy who works for Cactus Feeders and Tyson Foods. He went on: "But I am not the one who buys the *asado*. I need to produce *asado* for the guy on the third floor in apartment B that goes to a restaurant. He has a fork and knife, and for him it needs to be tender."

It wasn't about flavor, in other words. It was about tenderness, world grain markets, consistent inputs (corn) leading to a consistent output (feedlot steak), and lean manufacturing. There I was, a steak fanatic ten years too late to Argentina. I may as well have been interviewing Henry Ford about the best horse-drawn buggies.

Argentine steak is presently undergoing the same process that transformed American steak after World War II. It is becoming a commoditized, fungible, industrially produced widget. It is even happening to what little grass-fed beef still remains. The realization hit me in Parilla La Colonia, the best steak house in Santa Rosa, which has an old-time elegant interior with plaid tablecloths and linen napkins folded inside empty wineglasses. On an average Wednesday night in high summer, it was packed with Argentine men in shorts and flip-flops tucking into gigantic steaks and drinking bottles of good yet astonishingly cheap red wine.

The steak did not live up to the setting. It had yellowy fat, indicating that it was probably grass-fed, and was tender and juicy, but it suffered from the same problem as the others: fade-out. There was a rush of beefy flavor, but then the flavor died, leaving only a mildly sour, mildly sweet residue that tasted, it seemed to me, a lot like the alfalfa I had chewed out in that field two days earlier. As steak fade-outs go, it was not as acute as that of a typical feedlot steak. But it was no Angus Mackay Highland rib eye, either—not by a million miles. Just like a feedlot steak, this steak came from a cow that had been fattened as quickly as possible and hurried to the slaughterhouse. It was created to be a cost-effective steak, not a delicious steak, a feat of business engineering that can be achieved using grass or corn.

I was beginning to have second thoughts. Maybe grass-fed steak wasn't what it was cracked up to be. Maybe Angus Mackay's Highland rib eye was an aberration. (That still didn't explain the excellent Angus steak from Hardiesmill, or the steak I ate with Anibal Pordomingo up near Huinca Renancó.) The doubt registered as a pinprick at first, but it began metastasizing, and I became riddled with uncertainty. I had traveled thousands of miles to five different countries and had learned precisely nothing about steak.

Two days later, that doubt evaporated instantaneously and totally at a steak house in Buenos Aires, where I ate an incredibly good grass-fed steak with yellowy, sweet fat that melted in my mouth and had zero fade-out. I have Miguel de Achaval to thank.

During de Achaval's withering indictment of grass-fed beef, he complained at length about its "astounding inconsistency." Some is good, he said, and some is terrible. So I asked him how it was that my brother, who had visited Buenos Aires more than ten years earlier, had managed to eat such good steak.

It was because my brother was a tourist, de Achaval said. Tourists, he explained, know where to eat good beef. Unlike native Argentines, they go to the good steak houses that practice the art of aging beef. (This is, to my knowledge, the world's only case of tourists knowing more than locals about where to eat well.) One of the steak houses my brother visited was called El Mirasol, believed by many to be the country's best. I hopped back on the overnight bus to Buenos Aires and made a lunch reservation. There, I ate one of the best steaks of my life. But not before eating the best testicle of my life.

In fairness, it was the only testicle I'd ever eaten, and that makes it, technically, the worst testicle I'd ever eaten, too. It did not taste like I expected testicle to taste, but I'm not sure the pastoral language school of flavor description is up to the task of describing either the imagined or actual taste of testicle.

Sitting next to me was a steak-loving local whose blogging name is Yanqui Mike and who is known in more official circumstances as Mike Skowronek. If the name sounds less Buenos Aires than Chicago, that's because Mike Skowronek is from there. On Valentine's Day 2000, he was in a bar in Havana, Cuba, where he fell in love with a green-eyed Argentine. He now lives with her in Buenos Aires just a few blocks from his mother-in-law, who eats steak every day and has done so for the past eighty-six years. He helps manage the family cow-calf ranch a three-hour drive southwest. (When I asked him if the big feedlots were passing on the value of the government feed subsidy to the cow-calf farmers, he laughed.)

Chicago is world famous for its grain-fed steaks, but during his many years there Yanqui Mike was never a big steak guy. Since he moved to Argentina, steak has become one of his favorite foods. "I preferred grass-fed steak ever since the first bite," he told me. What he remembers most of that initial steak is its flavor. It came off a T-bone so large it did not fit on the plate. When he cut into it he was stunned by the way it tasted. He kept on eating and eventually discovered that the entirety of meat had been transferred to his stomach, except for the few remaining fibers clinging to the bone, which he was picking off with his teeth.

Not long ago, Yanqui Mike's wife unknowingly bought a feedlot steak at the supermarket. "The steak sucked, and I didn't know why," he told me. The texture was mushy and the meat was greasy. "I started to get that feeling," he said, "like I'd eaten too much fat. I told my wife, 'I think I ate a grain-fed steak.'"

Yanqui Mike wrote about the experience on his blog, and since then he has been chronicling the alarming flavor implications of feedlots popping up all over the pampas. When he arrived in Argentina, every steak was great. Now, the duration between outstanding steaks is getting longer and longer. Great Argentine steak, he says, is disappearing.

He is as familiar with the reasons as anyone. Not long ago, a multinational company approached Yanqui Mike's family and offered cash in advance—U.S. dollars—to plant grain. "It was a no-brainer," he says. "We could not resist." Company men showed up at the farm, took soil samples, analyzed drainage, and eventually settled on his best cow-grazing pasture as the place to plant grain. "This was pasture that had never before been planted," he says. "Chemicals were sprayed. Fertilizer was laid down. They killed the grass, fumigated the insects, then planted. I couldn't be there when they broke soil. It broke my heart."

Yanqui Mike also enjoys a good testicle, and considered the ones at El

Mirasol to be "scrumptious." The testicles were from a lamb, not a cow, and ended a parade of stomach, intestines, and sweetbreads that made up the first course, all accompanied by glasses of crisp champagne.

The first cut of steak we ate was *entraña*, which Americans call a skirt steak and an anatomist calls the diaphragm. Yanqui Mike chewed, swallowed, and pronounced: "This flavor punch is what you try to communicate to people. You go through long stretches now where you can't find it. Then boom—you're back!" There was no flavor fade-out on the *entraña* at El Mirasol. It had the power of a trumpet blast, and it kept building. You could sit there with your eyes closed and meditate on the deliciousness raging inside your mouth. The flavor was big, bloody, salty, and just barely sweet.

The *entraña* was followed by *vacio* (flank steak), which had a prodigious flow of juice. Next came the *tira de asado*, the tenderest I had encountered so far, hugely juicy, and with a blow-your-hair-back flavor. I picked up each individual piece of rib bone and nibbled off every possible scrap of beef. I considered lifting the plate to my mouth and drinking the juice, but El Mirasol is a fancy sort of restaurant. Sitting near us were an elegantly dressed woman wearing an outfit heavy on the jewelry and a powerful-looking man in a suit, and I didn't want to cause a scene, but hindsight tells me that a scene—a full-blown shouting match with plates hurled across the room—would have been worth it to imbibe that amazing liquid.

I walked away from El Mirasol feeling as if I'd just eaten some precious endangered creature. The fact—the sad, unfair, and hard-to-believe fact—was that Argentina's great grass-fed steak is going extinct. My meal that afternoon would be a story to tell my children, a feature of the world consigned to history, something they could imagine but would never be able to taste. Oddly, I found myself smiling. The high would not wear off for several hours.

That night, I ate dinner—another *asado*—in the backyard of the house belonging to Vicky's brother Peter, my other fifth cousin in Argentina. Peter has one of the more unusual jobs you're likely to come across: he inspects oil tankers. We ate yet more steak and discussed the possibility of fitting big Saudi tankers with machine guns so that they could defend themselves against pirates off the coast of Somalia. (Which is to say, I suggested the machine guns, while Peter, who is exponentially more knowledgeable in such matters, gently dismissed the proposal.)

As wineglasses were drained, my thoughts turned to Mordecai Stern-bach. Would he be happy to know that his great-great-great-great-great-grandchildren had reunited over steak on the other side of the world? I think he would. But as far as my preference for grass-fed steak goes, old Mordecai would have shaken his head in disappointment. Mordecai Sternbach, it so happens, sold grain for a living.

Before I headed to the airport the following day, Vicky and Steve took me to see a store not far from their house called La Vaca Tuerta—The One-Eyed Cow. It is where locals go when they need a new *parilla*. The showroom is a wonderland of grills, grilling options, and grilling accessories. There were portable grills. There were hexagonal grills. There were grills the size of picnic tables. I found myself staring long-ingly at a three-foot-long number with grooved grill slats that carry away any melted fat so that it doesn't land on the coals and cause a grease fire. Steve informed me that a debate rages in Argentina over grill slats. Some believe the grooved ones are superior, but purists cling to the round-slat grill. I told Steve that if I lived in Argentina, my *parilla* would be half-and-half. He said, "What accessories would you pick?" and I wandered the aisles like an eight-year-old girl in a dollhouse emporium, pointing at a wood-handled barbecue brush, a basket for creating perfect grilling coals, and a crank system for raising and lowering the grill. I had just designed my dream *parilla*. Steve, who had been hovering near the cash register, handed over his credit card to the cashier and said to me, "We'll send it to you by FedEx." My dream *parilla* was now my actual *parilla*. Weeks later, a white FedEx truck pulled up in front of my office and unloaded a box containing both round and grooved grill segments. My plan was to assemble it at my family cottage on Little Hawk Lake, three hours north of Toronto, where I live.

A family, it would seem, can be separated by war, genocide, half a century, and an entire hemisphere, but genealogical traits—a love of coffee and prunes in the morning, grilled steak in the evening—somehow survive. When contact is resumed, kinship flickers back to life. Two people who were strangers five days earlier, whose children shared trace levels of DNA with my children, gave me a *parilla*. They had taken a beautiful feature of their own lives and made it one in mine. Every time I placed steak on its enamel-coated grill, I would think of them.

But was it really all that surprising? Vicky and Steve, you see, plan on taking a trip to my side of the equator. Being Argentine, they will enjoy eating steak cooked over glowing wood coals roughly three times a week. And when family is visiting from Argentina, cooking steak over gas is an abomination.

CHAPTER SEVEN

FLEURANCE

I wasn't sure I could handle one cow, let alone three, but when someone offers you three rare and potentially succulent cows for the price of two, even if you don't own so much as a barn, let alone a proper farm, it's hard to say no. That explains how, one crisp spring morning, a pickup truck towing a livestock trailer pulled in to a farm eighty-five miles north of my house, opened its gate, and released three bovine animals. One was brown, one was dun, and the last was a dark brown calf. I had six months, give or take, to make one of them delicious. The ground was still frozen, with remnants of fall grass flopped over and pasted to the cement-hard earth. This grass, I thought, had better start growing.

When I was little and grown-ups used to ask me what I wanted to be when I grew up, my answer was "house builder." Later occupational fantasies included ambassador, environmental lawyer, philosophy professor, lead guitarist of a popular and critically acclaimed rock band, and the greatest knuckleballer in the history of Major League Baseball. Farmer never made the list. I entered the cattle business for a single reason: meat hunger.

In hindsight, it would have been simpler to pack up and relocate to Bridge of Earn or Buenos Aires. But rather than move my young family partway around the earth just for the sake of good steak, I deluded myself into thinking there was primo beef closer to home. All I had to do was find it, and this proved easier said than done. For months, I was buying every kind of steak possible, hoping to strike a vein of beefy fantasticness. The results were all terrible, but varyingly so. Each steak seemed to be unpleasant in its own special way. I was becoming so frustrated that I was beginning not to want to eat steak at all.

The best steak I had eaten so far in the course of my search was grass fed. So was the worst. I bought it from a man I found on the Internet who raved at adjective-laden length about his pasture-raised Angus cattle. I dialed the phone number provided, and the woman on the other end assured me that the steak was indeed the finest she had ever tasted, no question about it, and that all their customers felt that way. Within seconds she had my Visa number, and two days later I possessed a piece of meat that was, technically, steak but looked, smelled, and tasted amazingly like liver—although describing it as such is unfair to liver, because there is such a thing as good liver, and this steak was not it. The flavor would convince anyone wearing a blindfold that he was eating organ—an old, atrophied, abscessed organ left in the trunk of a car sitting in a Miami parking lot for two weeks in July—not muscle. Tasting it made for an unexpected Proustian moment, as the memory of detesting liver as a little boy came flooding back. I was inclined to spit that grass-fed Angus steak into my fingers and surreptitiously toss it under the table and hope the dog found it before Mom did, which is how I dealt with liver back when I wanted to be a house builder. I had a sudden appreciation for the autonomy of adulthood. I was a big boy now. I stood up, dumped the steak in the garbage, and ordered pizza.

My brother bought steak from a Mennonite farmer selling pies by the side of the highway halfway between Toronto and Little Hawk Lake. The cow was grass fed, and seemed to have eaten its way through several acres of onion grass, judging by the taste. On the grill, the meat turned a whitish gray, and milky-colored gobs of fat dripped from it. At least it was cheap, unlike some grass-fed organic strip loins I purchased at a fancy butcher shop that were dry and tough and tasted like mold.

I visited a farmers' market where men with scraggly beards and women not at all in thrall to the beauty myth were sitting in the grass playing bongos and folk guitar, and where if I had spontaneously burst into "Kumbaya" someone would have broken into harmony by the third syllable. The grass-fed steak I bought there tasted very much like rotten fish marinated in tepid dishwater. Later that fall, I found another farmer at a different market selling grass-fed shorthorn. I bought a pair of good rib eyes—not El Mirasol good, but good all the same. The following May the market reopened after a winter hiatus, and I got more steaks from the same farmer. This time they were tough and gamy, which is a polite way of saying they had the kind of flavor that made you wince.

What was going on? Some—possibly even all—of the following: The cows weren't finished, which is to say they weren't fat enough before being slaughtered; they weren't grazing on the right kind of grass; the lean carcasses had been dry-aged too long, and mold had penetrated the meat and infected it with a bad flavor; the cattle had grazed on a type of grass called fescue that can be infected with a fungus that makes the meat taste off; the cattle grazed in spring on the wrong kind of grass, which, at that time of year, has too much protein in it and not enough carbohydrates, causing what meat scientists call an "off flavor" in the beef; the carcasses were too lean and became shocked by the abrupt cold of the meat cooler, which turned the meat hard; the beef came from "continental" cattle—Limousin, Charolais, and so forth—that don't do well on grass; the cattle weren't "on the gain" when they were slaughtered, which means they were getting skinnier, not fatter, a condition that makes them taste terrible.

How did I know all this? I had begun receiving a small but fascinating publication called the *Stockman Grass Farmer.* (Anibal Pordomingo is a regular contributor.) Part newspaper, part how-to manual, it's written for and by folks who farm the old-fashioned way. A typical *SGF* ad announces, "Get the Hay Out! If Bermudagrass or Bahia is your forage base and you are tired of making and feeding hay, then this unique Stockman Grass Farmer grazing school is for you!" A classified ad reads, "America's #1 source for powerful, easy-fleshing, beautifully uddered, maternally efficient Angus cattle." Its pages are filled with practical articles, a surprising percentage of which are about how to build the right kind of fences. But there are also uplifting accounts of the small prairie victories that go unnoticed, like the letter to the editor entitled "Evangelizing Grass-Finished Beef," submitted by a rancher who stunned pretty much everybody when two of her grass-fed cows were so marbled they graded Prime. (This is something the feedlot world will tell you is simply not possible without grain.) The *SGF* echoed many of the lessons I'd learned during my travels, like the fact that very young cows have no flavor, a concept the editor, Allan Nation, expressed thus: "Fine wines, whiskies and cheeses all have to have time to age. Exceptional flavor always requires what the wine maker calls 'the fullness of time.' This is why older animals taste better than young ones." It made for exciting if oddly discouraging reading, as the subtitle to every story may as well have been, "There are no easy answers." Raising delicious steak on grass, I learned, requires numerous kinds of expertise. You have to know your soils. You have to know your grasses. You have to know your cattle breeds. And you have to know how to get cows to eat the right grass at the right time until they become so fat as to appear inflated. The detail was complex and delivered in quantity that was sobering.

I phoned Allen Williams, the disillusioned meat scientist I had met back in Kansas, hoping he could put it all in more straightforward terms. Finishing cattle, he explained, is simple in theory: it's merely a matter of putting energy into them. The problem with grass is that it can have enormous amounts of energy or puny amounts, depending on factors like soil type, soil quality, the amount of rainfall and sunlight, and the time of year. Even *the time of day* can make a difference. A good grass finisher, he said, knows that on a sunny day a field of, say, bromegrass will have more energy in the afternoon than in the morning, and that it would be inadvisable to turn cattle out on it before lunch. In a month's time, however, that bromegrass could be dried out and woody, at which point the gamagrass might be entering its prime. Different grasses have different growth curves. A grass laden with sugars in May will be desiccated by July. To finish cattle, you need to provide at least one kind of grass in its lush, sugary prime at all times. In other words, to grass-finish cattle you need to be, above all, an accomplished grass farmer.

Grain, by comparison, could not be more simple. Grain is energy in a bucket, a bucket that contains the same nutritive value in February as it does in August. A moron can walk up to a cow and pour a bucket of grain in its feed trough. Grass isn't so easy. Williams likens finishing cattle to playing guitar. "Feeding grain," he explained to me, "is like knowing a few chords and playing an easy song. Finishing on grass is like being a virtuoso."

The problem with the steak I was eating is that it was made by ama-

teurs who thought they were virtuosos. It was the meat equivalent of bad
homemade wine. It was like an edible version of garage-sale art: an intimate glimpse of heartfelt ineptitude.

One snowy winter day, I visited a farm where the farmer was letting
the wrong kind of cows eat the wrong kind of grass. The farmer and his
wife were salt-of-the-earth types—three dogs, five kids—and lived in a
hundred-year-old farmhouse. Most of their cows were fed corn, but a few
of them ate grass and only grass, because growing numbers of precious
foodie types down in the city had been clamoring for healthy, earth-
friendly grass-fed beef. I drove back to the city with a grass-fed sirloin and
grilled it that night. When it was done, I cut a big hunk off, a hunk that
turned out to be much larger than my windpipe. While chewing it, I de-
bated whether the meat would make a better sandal or boot. My jaw wasn't
up to the task of pulping it, but for some reason I tried swallowing it anyway, and the meat lodged in the back of my throat like a golf ball in the
mouth of a vacuum cleaner. I couldn't breathe. Adrenaline burst, marking
the onset of panic, and a cascade of thoughts followed. My daughter, not
yet two, was there in the room with me, and I suddenly realized she would
grow up having witnessed her father choking to death on steak while writing a book about it. I envisioned gleeful headlines on vegetarian Web
sites about a steak lover's ironic demise. The clarity was Zen-like, and I
determined that my salvation lay in the steak's incredible stringiness. I
reached to the back of my mouth and clasped a ropy piece of fiber that
hung off the meat like a tail, tugged on it, and, pop, the steak was out,
allowing air to move into my lungs. I dangled the meat in front of my face
like a tea bag on the end of its string, then tossed it into the garbage dis-
posal and enjoyed the metallic gurgle of steak being shredded.

I went back to commodity beef. It was exponentially more tender
than that grass-fed sirloin, but on the whole not really that tender. What
it was, was consistent, and that consistency was astounding. All that
fourteen-month-old corn-fed steak tasted the same. It tasted of nothing.
This, I finally decided after one too many flavorless mouthfuls, is not
steak. It is corn-fed mature veal.

One day it occurred to me: What if corn-fed steak tasted bland because the genetically modified corn cows are fed is bland? This, of course, raises another question: What does genetically modified feed corn taste like?

Back at my farmers' market, I found a man with bushels of peaches 'n' cream corn for sale. "Do you grow feed corn?" I asked. He didn't, but his brother did, and the following week, as customers were picking over containers of heirloom tomatoes and potatoes still dusted with dark earth, I drove off with a bag of genetically modified feed corn. Shucking revealed a chunkier, yellower version of sweet corn whose kernels turned a rich, autumnal gold after ten minutes in boiling water. The corn itself was a chalky, pulpy, hard-to-swallow blob of gooey vegetable matter. It was the worst porridge imaginable, with only the merest corn flavor, in desperate need of raisins, nuts, and honey.

I felt sorry for the cattle that had to eat it. I wasn't alone. Allen Williams confirmed that cattle didn't much like it, either. If you give a cow two buckets, he said, one filled with modern super-starchy GMO feed corn and one filled with the kind of corn cattle were fed half a century ago, they will go for the old-time corn every time. It tastes better.

If I were a cow, the choice of food would be easy. Boiled GMO feed corn had nothing on the hay sauce I ate in Paris with Christophe Raoux. Hay is made out of grass; no wonder grass makes for more flavorful steak. If I wanted better steak, I was going to have to make it myself.

That's when I started phoning farmers and asking if they had any cattle for sale.

I had an idea: apples. I wanted to feed apples to cows. In parts of Europe, farmers feed apples to pigs, and the resulting pork is apparently delicious. Apples contain lots of energy—it's sugar, after all, that makes them so sweet. And while a bucket of apples doesn't approach a bucket of corn in terms of energy density, apples do occur in nature. Aurochs ate fallen fruit in the primeval forests of Europe and Asia, and any apple grower will tell you how deer invade their orchards and gorge on whatever they can reach.

Apples were also an elegant solution to the bad grass problem. If the grass wasn't sugary enough, the apples would make up for it. Apples meant I didn't have to become an expert on the growth curves of ten different kinds of grass. Apples meant I could finish a cow on grass with a little help from the trees. And juice apples, it turned out, are cheap, with a crate going for a little over a hundred bucks. A crate holds twenty bushels, and a bushel holds a little more than forty apples, which adds up to a lot of sugar. All I needed now—besides an actual cow—was some grass.

Let me tell you about my backyard, for which the term "yard" is generous to the point of fantasy. It is a capacious thirteen by twenty feet—which amounts to half of 1 percent of one acre. What little topsoil there is, however, is in no danger of eroding, not even in a tornado, thanks to a former owner with connections in the construction business who poured a six-inch layer of concrete over the top of it. Grazing options are limited to a wisteria bush on the east fence, a grapevine on the west fence, and some herbs growing in a planter. A ruminant no bigger than a goat could graze for an hour, tops. If I was going to raise a cow on grass and apples, I needed a farm.

Luckily, I do know a farmer. Besides raising lambs, chickens, and ducks—not to mention potatoes, cucumbers, carrots, and so forth—Michael Stadtländer is considered by many people to be the best chef in all of Canada. A native German, he emigrated in the early 1980s and quickly established himself as a trendy downtown chef of considerable repute. But he gave all that up in 1993 so he could be closer to his ingredients. Ever since he was a teenager, he had had romantic ideas about the pure Canadian wilderness. He bought a large parcel of it, named it Eigensinn Farm, and started treating it like *terroir,* extracting pure savors from earth where none had grown before.

Stadtländer is afflicted with the same obsession as Borgo San Felice: locality. He likes to catch brown trout in his trout pond and bake them in clay harvested from the bottom of the same trout pond. He will buy a Georgian Bay lake trout from a local native fisherman and wrap it in wild grape leaves that grow on a fence next to his barn and grill the whole package over burning wood from trees grown, cut down, and chopped on the farm. Decades ago, some forward-thinking soul planted apple trees on his land, and in the fall Stadtländer picks the apples and makes cider, which he reduces on the stove into a glaze that he pours over his pork chops, which come from heritage-breed pigs who live within snorting distance of the apple trees.

Stadtländer had excellent news: he also wanted a cow. But there was a problem, in that we couldn't actually graze a cow at his farm. He had tried it once before and discovered he didn't have the right kind of fencing. (He obviously didn't subscribe to the *Stockman Grass Farmer.*) He did, however, know another farmer who also wanted in on good steak. This farmer, who lived just down the road, raised organic turkeys and had eighty acres of unused pasture perfect for cattle. She also had superb fencing. Her name was Carla.

The only thing lacking now was a cow.

In every country other than Argentina and Texas (which often likes to believe it's a country), I ate local, in terms of breed. In France I ate Limousin steak. In Scotland, I ate Angus and Highland. In Japan, black Wagyu. And in Italy, Chianina and Podolica. Where did that leave things as far as my own country, Canada, was concerned? Was I going to have to hybridize an uptight British bull with an unwilling Catholic French cow to achieve something culturally correct? Fortunately, not. As it happens, there is an authentic Canadian breed of cattle with a very obvious name: the Canadienne.

The breed has been eating Canadian grass and suffering through the bitterest of winters for something like four hundred years. Not long after the French explorer Jacques Cartier discovered the land we now call Quebec, cows were rounded up from the French regions of Brittany, Normandy, and Gascony and shipped over to New France, as it was known back then. Those livestock were not of any specific breed—this was almost two centuries before Robert Bakewell and his ideas about purity and inbreeding came on the scene. Some died, and some thrived, grazing, breeding, and calving until they became a distinctive bunch of local Canadian cows. At one time, Canadiennes were *the* cow all the way from the mouth of the St. Lawrence River down to Detroit. Settlers heading for the New World didn't bring their own cattle with them, but would buy a few cows when their ships stopped in Quebec and then sail upriver to settle.

People stopped eating Canadiennes once Angus and shorthorns and other trendy beef breeds started coming over from Britain. And when dairy farmers began connecting their milking machines to the magnificently uddered Holstein breed—which produces gallons and gallons of unremarkable milk—no one had much use for a Canadienne anymore. The breed fell so far out of favor it almost went extinct. But in the last decade or so, artisanal cheesemakers in Quebec realized that Canadienne milk made fantastic cheese that, like the milk it comes from, is rich, creamy, and full of flavor. Canadiennes, furthermore, can take a winter. They can turn grass into milk without having to be supplemented with corn or protein-enriched feed. A Canadienne was starting to sound like a cow worth eating.

But really, a *dairy* breed?

Dairy breeds are the laughingstock of the beef world. What gets laughed at, specifically, are their skinny butts and small loins. They take too long to get big and walk around in hides that appear to be two sizes too large. But consider this: it has been scientifically proven that some dairy cows produce outstanding steak. For example, there is a documented relationship between milk with high butterfat and marbling. (Whether that's actually good or not depends, obviously, on how you feel about marbling.) The reason the beef industry doesn't like dairy breeds isn't because of the way they taste, but because their yield is terrible. The simple fact is, there's more money in cows with big butts.

Was it possible that a skinny-butt dairy cow might taste better than a chunky beef breed? A formerly famous dairy breed called the Jersey is renowned for being tender. Jersey is an island off the northern coast of France where some people still speak French, even though it has belonged to Britain for almost a thousand years. If Jersey's cows could speak, they'd speak French, too, because they originated in the same parts of France as Canadiennes, which look so much like Jerseys that some people call them black Jerseys.

Allen Williams told me that back in the old days, cattle ranchers selling beef breeds like Angus or Hereford would keep a Jersey steer for their personal stash. My father is friends with a man who can remember those days. He is today a meat enthusiast of the first order who can dress his own game, spends large sums on fine shotguns, and travels to the prairie every autumn to blast migrating ducks out of the air. The best steak he ever ate was back on the family farm more than fifty years ago. It came from a grass-fed Jersey, and nothing he's eaten since at any fancy steak house has come close. If Jerseys were that good, it stood to reason that Canadiennes would be, too.

Unfortunately, I couldn't have picked a worse breed. Not only are Canadiennes rare—fewer than two hundred purebreds presently walk the earth—but they are also dairy cows. When a calf is born on a dairy farm, two things can happen. If it's a girl calf, the farmer raises it as a heifer, breeds it to a bull, lets it calve, and then milks it. If it's a boy calf, the farmer sells it as quickly as possible for veal, because a bull calf literally suckles profits from its mother's teat. The chances of a dairy farmer having a full-grown steer to sell me were pretty much zero. The chances of a dairy farmer parting with a heifer were even worse.

I had a single faint hope: a barren heifer. Somewhere, I thought, there is a Canadienne heifer that's having trouble getting knocked up. The possibility, admittedly, was remote, but it was all I had. I called the largest Canadienne farm in Quebec, where a man with the thickest Québécois accent I've ever heard picked up the phone. I believe he understood my question, but his response was impenetrable, though his tone strongly suggested I should get off the phone and stop bothering him. I contacted another farm in Quebec where the accent of the voice on the answering machine was even stronger. I did not leave a message.

In my home province of Ontario, a grand total of five dairy farms were listed as stocking Canadiennes. Make that four. The lady at a farm near the town of Cannington didn't keep Canadiennes anymore because they didn't get along with her stupider but more productive Holsteins. She did have encouraging news, however: their meat was delicious. "Delicate," she said, "marbled, and wonderful." I phoned a farm farther north. A bull calf was available, but I didn't want veal—I wanted steak. The third farmer turned out to be a raging Canadienne enthusiast, who described them as "half cow, one quarter horse, and one quarter elk." This time around, I avoided asking the barren heifer question, because I was beginning to feel like an idiot. I explained my plight in the hopes that the farmer might take pity on me and offer up one of his fertile heifers. He suggested some nice bull calves instead. He was about to hang up when I blurted it out: Do you, by any chance, have a barren heifer you could sell me?

"Funny you should ask," the farmer said, "because I just happen to have two."

The deal was, if I bought two cows for $600, he'd throw in the bull calf free. A week later, they arrived at Carla's farm. One was big, one was smaller (though still big). The little calf had skinny legs and delicate, deerlike hooves.

The grass thawed and grew, the cows ate, and the first crate of apples appeared in June, by which point my little herd had names. The dun-colored one was Florimonde and the dark one was Fleurance. Both were named after members of the *filles du roi*, an ancient group of ladies sent to Quebec by the king of France so that the overwhelmingly male population of sexually frustrated lumberjacks, fur traders, farmers, and soldiers could have wives. A *fille du roi* named Florimonde Rableau married Pierre Chamard on October 13, 1665. (The Montreal phone book today lists fifteen Chamards.) Fleurance Asserin arrived two years later, but, sadly, never seems to have found a husband.

The two cows were a bovine version of *The Odd Couple*. Fleurance was curious; Florimonde was skittish. Fleurance got along with the other cows; Florimonde preferred to head-butt them. Fleurance loved apples; Florimonde wouldn't touch them.

Fleurance would stand in front of a pile of apples and eat one after another after another. After a few weeks of such gorging, her ribs disappeared beneath a layer of flesh. A crate of carrots, which are also sweet and full of sugar, was delivered, and Fleurance loved them, too. Florimonde wouldn't touch them. Florimonde was not as fat. This was good news for Florimonde, but not for Fleurance.

Grass continued growing. The cows would walk out, tear it off in clumps, and swallow. Later, they would hunker down next to a tree, regurgitate their meal, and chew it more—a bovine technique called chewing the cud (it helps break down cellulose). The grass would grow back, and the cows would chew, swallow, regurgitate, and chew some more. At this rate, my steak wouldn't be ready for several months.

I needed to deal with my meat hunger *now*. I needed interim options.

I found one at a farmers' market. It was a grain-fed steak and, to my great surprise, superb—so much so that I phoned up the farmer who raised it and asked him why his steak tasted way better than everyone else's. "If you feed 'em too much corn too young," he said, "they don't taste right." His cows got a mild grain feed, no antibiotics, and no growth hormones, a program his family has been using to raise beef since the mid-1970s. Before that, they were walking with the rest of the herd, so to speak, and treating their cattle with a growth hormone called diethylstyl-bestrol. But when it was linked to cancer, the family decided to raise beef the way they'd been doing it in the 1960s, which means no hormones and almost no corn, because corn requires too much fertilizer. His cows get an extra summer on grass, then spend a few months in a pen eating fermented barley grass along with some mixed grains the farmer grows himself.

As I waited for Fleurance to get fat, I kept my meat hunger at bay with more of that barley-fed 1960s-style steak. And I continued experimenting, not with the type of steak, but with cooking.

The world had proved to be deflatingly conventional when it came to preparing steak. Only Japan, with its kiln-powered rocks and blasting tableside grills, seemed interested in innovation. Everywhere else, it was either hot grill or hot pan, which seemed to fly directly in the face of all those high-tech steak cooking methods you see on TV and read about in magazines. Ruth's Chris Steak House, for example, doesn't so much cook steak as briefly incinerate it on a broiler that cranks up to 1,800°F (the melting point of silver). That, however, is laughably crude compared to how the British celebrity chef Heston Blumenthal treats a rib eye. He starts with a rib roast that he browns with a blowtorch and then places in a 122°F oven—so cool he could crawl in there with it if he wanted to—where the roast "cooks" for *eighteen hours*, minimum. After removing it, he lets the meat cool for four hours; he then cuts out the bone, trims bits of charred exterior, slices what's left into two-inch steaks, flash-sears them in a hot pan, and lets them rest. A day after igniting the blowtorch— during which time he could fly to New York, eat a steak, then fly back to London—the steaks are served.

My brother found a similar but pared-down technique in a cooking magazine, one among a recent flurry of stories claiming that standard hot-grill or hot-pan cooking was all a centuries-long mistake that resulted in meat that was overcooked and gray near the exterior and raw in the middle. (This is one reason why people tell you to let a steak rest, so that the fridge-cold interior has a few minutes to catch up to the scorching exterior.) According to this article, it was better to cook steak in a low oven for a long time until the entire piece of meat has been gently coaxed to an even medium rare, at which point you remove it, brown each side in an extremely hot pan, and serve.

I attempted it. I cooked a rib eye in a 180°F oven for forty-five minutes. When I took the steak out it was pink and oozing juice—one big chunk of medium rare. It tasted like warm carpaccio: bloody, savory, and juicy. But there was something missing: it didn't taste *steaky*. It was all yang and no yin. I flash-seared the steak as instructed and sampled it again. Now it tasted like steak. Now it had sweetness, roastiness, and nuttiness and that slight hint of bitterness I was expecting. The difference? Maillard reactions. The comparatively intense heat of the pan had caused a whole class of complex chemical reactions to occur. It was an object lesson in flavor chemistry.

I got to thinking about thickness. Thicker, everyone says, is better. A standard steak in Tuscany is thick, but a *bistecca alla fiorentina* is thicker still. No self-respecting Texas cowboy eats a steak thinner than his clenched fist. But are the Tuscans and cowboys right?

Every steak is a balancing act between the browned exterior and the bloody center. Up to a certain point, a thicker steak is not a better steak, it is, rather, a *different* steak. It is bloodier and meatier. But beyond a certain point—two inches, perhaps—a steak isn't a steak anymore; it's roast beef. The ratio of browned crust to bloody center is out of whack— there just isn't enough Maillard in the mix. (That, incidentally, is why when a family sits down to roast beef, there is a fight over the fabulously browned end slices. What everyone really wants is steak.) And when a very thick steak is cooked on a very hot surface, you find yourself with meat that's burned and raw at the same time. Burned is not the same as Maillard. Burned is mouth-puckering bitter.

The world can learn much from the Japanese about steak thickness. Their wafer-thin strips of beef cooked on extremely hot surfaces produce bite-sized bombs of juicy crust. Japan's message to the thick-steak-loving world is this: try going thinner—but not without adequate firepower. A thin steak cooked over a wimpy flame will be gray through and through and won't have any crust. There is, granted, one notable drawback to a thin steak: it's not always enough. But this problem has an easy solution: eat several.

As for the slow-heat method of cooking, I have doubts. My slow-cooked, flash-seared steak was good. But after finishing it, I took another raw steak and threw it on a standard hot grill. It was just as good, and it was ready in ten minutes.

The secret to great steak isn't the thickness, or ultra-low heat or ultra-high heat. It isn't dry aging, either, which is commendable but overrated—any rib eye that needs to be aged for sixty days isn't a good rib eye to begin with. The secret to great steak isn't salting the day before, marinating in olive oil, or any other lost technique from the old country. The secret to great steak is great steak. Start with good meat, and it will be good even if you boil it. That 1960s-style barley-fed Angus steak tasted good because it was good beef. Period.

But it was not *great* beef. Its flavor did not match the fullness of fine grass-fed steak. I never found myself in a state of euphoria and incredulity over how mind-bogglingly excellent it was, which is the effect good food—a great steak, a stellar peach, a superb cake—can have. My wife put it this way: "That steak was like a mediocre play or movie. Your mind starts to wander halfway through." But we ate and enjoyed those steaks, somehow forgetting about the greater beauty our mouths were being denied.

And then one day some rib eyes arrived from Washington State. They came from a creature called a beefalo, a cattle-bison cross that has slightly more cattle than bison in it, genetically speaking. The man who produced it, Mark Merrill, runs an outfit called Beefalo Meats. Merrill began raising beefalo so that people whose doctors had told them to stop eating red meat could still eat steak, because tests have found beefalo to have even less cholesterol and fat than roast chicken. But old-timers kept telling him, "Your beef tastes like what beef used to taste like." Merrill feeds his beefalo hay and alfalfa and, when he can get it, apple pomace, which is what's left over after you turn apples into apple juice. He sent me a box of rib eyes that had the kind of flavor we don't have the words for yet, flavor you can shut your eyes and think about, like you're listening to a story.

Grain-fed steak—even excellent grain-fed steak—is bland by comparison, and the reason is grain, which has a dulling effect on flavor. Used judiciously—as it is, for example, on the better farms in Scotland—grain can make steak raised on poor-quality grass palatable rather than disgusting. An oak barrel has a similar effect on wine. If you take a sour, mouth-puckering red wine and let it sit in an oak barrel for months, you will be amazed at how much easier it is to drink. The effect is similar to how a music producer with an arsenal of studio effects can put a tone-deaf yet sexy pop star in tune. But a young cow gorged too fast on too much grain is like an overoaked wine or an overproduced pop star: devoid of character. Ever since the 1950s, when we started feeding cattle corn by the truckload and killing them younger and younger, steak has been losing character.

Back in the days when steak had character, people didn't put much on it. At the most famous steak restaurant in American history, Delmonico's— which opened in New York in 1827, lasted just short of a hundred years, and was so revered for the deliciousness of its steak that it ultimately lent its name to a particular cut—a basic steak was seasoned with salt on both sides, basted with oil or melted butter, cooked over a "moderate fire," then set on a hot plate with a little maître d'hôtel butter (fresh butter mixed with chopped parsley, salt, pepper, and lemon juice) or clear gravy (a liquid similar to Christophe Raoux's beef *jus*). If desired, a fancy French sauce like *sauce bordelaise* could be poured over such a steak. Back then, fancy

French sauces were all the rage, but they were also *delicate*, made from ingredients like beef stock, mushrooms, wine, shallots, or bone marrow, ingredients that added to but did not mask the character of the steak. Call it the era of the gentle steak sauce.

There were no fancy sauces served at the greatest steak-eating extravaganzas in American history. These were called beefsteaks, and they were held in New York in the late nineteenth and early twentieth centuries. Men—and later, women—would get together in a rented hall, hotel, or restaurant, don butcher's aprons, and down ridiculous quantities of steak (as well as ridiculous quantities of beer, double lamb chops, and roast kidney wrapped in bacon). A top beefsteak butcher named Sidney Wertheimer was, by today's standards, a purist. He took whole strip loins, rolled them in salt, broiled them, sliced them, and piled the slices on day-old bread or toast. His sauce? Melted butter, pan drippings, and a few shakes of Worcestershire sauce. (Worcestershire sauce contains fermented anchovies, whose broken-down amino acids would have cranked up the umami in the pan drippings.)

Steak eaters of today do not know what they are missing. At the Big Texan, steaks are not only drenched in "au jus," they are dusted in Montreal steak seasoning. Montreal is 1,800 highway miles from Amarillo. The seasoning contains spices like coriander, red pepper flakes, garlic powder, onion powder, paprika, and dried thyme. The recipe, it is said, comes from Romania, where it was used to *cure* smoked beef. Jewish immigrants brought it to the New World and used the mix to spice beef briskets, but it eventually found its way onto bland commodity steak.

Some steak houses prefer intense, goopy sauces. Smith and Wollensky makes a steak sauce out of tomato puree, blackstrap molasses, malt vinegar, fresh horseradish, roasted garlic, and chili peppers. At David Burke's Primehouse, in Chicago, you can order a rib eye dry-aged for seventy-five days and obliterate whatever flavor there may be with a choice of sauces including "Sweet and Tangy Steak Sauce" and "3 Peppercorn Sauce," which your waiter will plunk down on the table seconds after he plunks down the steak.

Peter Luger Steak House has only two locations, but its intense, goopy sauce is sold in supermarkets and poured on steak all over the country.

According to legend, a waiter named Willie Wolfe developed the sauce as a *salad dressing* in the 1950s—the dawn of the feedlot era. Waiters at Peter Luger will urge you not to let the sauce touch any of their USDA Prime steaks, which are still cooked the old-fashioned way—salted, broiled, and brushed with butter. Their pleadings are ignored. Legions of diners show up at Peter Luger and order a big porterhouse. When it arrives, it is smothered in sauce.

Those diners are not totally stupid. The army of line cooks patting seasoning salt and ladling out "au jus" all across the land are not evil. They are dealing with flavorless commodity steak the only way they know how: by adding flavor. The steak in their hands is a red version of boneless chicken breast: a factory-produced protein-based texture vehicle sold on razor-thin margins. Assembly is required. Steak houses differentiate themselves not with steak, but with themes. Half are cowboy-themed, and the other half opt for an old clubby feel. But they all serve the same fundamental widget. They're not selling steak. They're selling a value-added flavor experience that is medieval in pungency.

The flavor of steak today is not the flavor of beef. It is the flavor of mass-produced seasoning blends and sweet-and-sour sauces. It is not a pure savor. And once you've tasted real steak, it's not a good savor, either.

Of course, it's easy to be a critic when you don't own cattle. Around midsummer, as the forage settled into serious lushness, the first waves of anxiety struck. On paper, things could not have been going better. The days were alternately sunny and rainy, the soil was moist, and the grasses were photosynthesizing superbly. I e-mailed close-up photos of Carla's fields to Anibal Pordomingo, master of forages. Nice pasture, he said, and went on to identify perennial ryegrass, annual ryegrass, orchard grass, smooth brome, alfalfa, white clover, mustards, and sweet clover. Mainly, he said, it was ryegrass. Fleurance was eating that grass. I should have been overjoyed.

For a time, I was. For a time, I walked around under the mistaken impression—a delusion, really—that Fleurance had, in a matter of weeks, become tremendously fat, that by the end of the summer she would have to be rolled off the pasture and over to the abattoir, where she wouldn't fit through the door. I sent a photo of her to Allen Williams, expecting him to respond with the e-mail equivalent of a standing ovation.

He did not. His assessment was painfully blunt. "She is quite a ways off from being finished yet." Visions of bulletproof lean meat appeared in my mind. I imagined a large table surrounded by friends and family, every last person choking on my signature shoe-leather beef. Fleurance was going to taste livery and disgusting. Grain, all of a sudden, had tremendous appeal. Grain was easy. Grain was risk-free.

Michael Stadtländer showed up at Carla's farm with some flax pressings, the stuff that's left over after you make flaxseed oil. Fleurance ate it; Florimonde did not. Carla bought another crate of apples, and we gave Fleurance as many as she wanted. (We also gave Florimonde as many as she wanted, which amounted to zero.) I had read in an old farming manual that too many apples will give a cow diarrhea, but if this were true, it was certainly not true for Canadiennes, because Fleurance's turds remained firm, shapely, and herbal.

I visited whenever I could. Since the arrival of Fleurance and company, Carla had bought three more Canadienne calves and a lactating mother cow whose impressive supply of rich milk—her udder hung like a medicine ball between her legs—quenched the thirst of all four calves. I would wander out into the field to study the herd. When I got too close to Fleurance, she would bolt, becoming momentarily undomesticated and deerlike. Carla phoned me one morning and reported that Fleurance had charged a pack of coyotes that were eyeing the calves. I called the dairy farmer who had sold me Fleurance and related her act of valor. "Good for her," he said. "That's my girl."

Anthropologists tell us that humans evolved on the African savanna, a vast plain covered in tall grass and well-spaced trees. Here, we hunted early ruminants and scurried up trees when lions came stalking. This may explain the soothing effect of prairie and why an afternoon spent lingering in a sunny meadow is as pleasant as one spent on any beach. By midsummer, I could get close enough to the cows to actually stand among them. I would spend long stretches studying them, listening to birdsong, inhaling the sweet aroma of wildflowers in bloom, and wishing I'd brought a lawn chair. The experience is something like scuba diving. Events take place in slow motion, language ceases, and any sudden hand movement will scatter the animals you are raptly observing. (Unlike in scuba diving, you never run out of air.)

Cows, I learned, don't actually bite off grass. They wrap their tongues around whole clumps, jerk their heads back, and tear it off. Cows are not clippers. They don't have any incisors on the upper row, only molars, which they use to grind fibrous grass down to the consistency of paste. (Sheep are the clippers, not to mention rabbits, which ought to be working for golf courses because they chew grass down to the level of suede.) Stand next to a grazing cow and close your eyes, and you will think someone is ripping the stitching out of an old couch.

Cows are also picky. They will select a particular clump of grass and then pointedly ignore apparently identical grass growing all around it, walking about for several paces before they again find appealing grass. Cows will disregard a stand of nettles for months, then wipe it out in a single afternoon, and then spend the rest of the season disregarding it again. Carla studied the fields every day. What the cows really liked, she said, were wild strawberry plants and wild turnips.

As Fleurance laid on fat, I found myself fantasizing about marbling, which made no sense, given that by now I had good reason *not* to believe in it. Angus Mackay's Highland rib eye—a life-changing steak—was, at best, USDA Select, and yet it tasted better than the Matsusaka Special Beef, which was so marbled it would have scored off the USDA charts. Never in my life had I eaten a USDA Prime steak that I considered great.

A steak arrived via airmail that verified my marbling doubts. It was from Wisconsin, raised by a man named Tom Wrchota who volunteered for the Peace Corps in Costa Rica in the early 1970s and fell in love with the local grass-fed steak. He now raises a Scottish breed called Galloway, which, looks-wise, is somewhere between an Angus and a Highland and is reputed to produce loins with a fine speckling of fat. The loins Wrchota sent me—out of his personal stash and representing the leaner end of his range—did indeed have fine speckles, but there weren't many of them.

And yet, like Angus Mackay's Highland beef, the steak broadcast a ma-
hogany-like depth. It walked softly, but it carried a very big stick. Marbling, clearly, had nothing to do with flavor.

But *a little* marbling seemed like a good idea. The steak that tasted
like old liver was as lean as a valentine heart. Ted Slanker's swampwater
steak was lean. And the sirloin I almost choked on was similarly without fat. If marbling indicated anything, it is this: you are eating a well-
fed cow.

I found myself staring at Fleurance's shoulder, following her spine as
it ran down her neck and flattened out along her back. Beneath that
brown fur, along both sides of that spine, were her rib eyes. I envisioned
wispy little curls and streaks of fat. If she had let me get close enough,
I would have massaged her, not that massaging has anything to do with
marbling, of course. But could it hurt?

By late September, the sun was losing power. Leaves were turning red
and yellow, and I began visualizing Fleurance's death. This was as much
a surprise to me as to anyone. I am, by nature, overly sensitive when it
comes to the death of animals. In the summer of 1981, I was inconsolable
when my father broke the news that a pet rock bass I'd been keeping in
a puddle during a family fishing trip would have to be returned to the
lake. At the age of eleven or thereabouts, my father shot a porcupine that
could have blinded the dog with one of its quills, and tears again flowed.
When a bird flies into a bay window, I will cradle its silenced body in my
hands and be stricken by a melancholy that can last for days.

Turning Fleurance into meat, I expected, would be the occasion for
another personal crisis. I dreaded it but stoically welcomed it, because I
felt that as a meat eater, I could no longer shield myself from the death
that is inherent in all meat. But now that Fleurance's death was nearly at
hand, my attitude was what management types call proactive. I didn't
want to kill Fleurance, exactly. I respected her. On some level, I loved
her. But the fact that she was going to die did not upset me. Death, after
all, is painless. It's pain that's painful. What I wanted was that Fleurance's death be fast and pain free. This was for her sake, but also for the
sake of my palate. Adrenaline and cortisol had to be kept to a minimum
so that her muscles would remain as tender and juicy as possible.

I began imagining myself crouched on the crest of a hill overlooking Fleurance's pasture with a cocked Remington 700 BDL .308 tucked into my shoulder. The crosshairs are centered just below Fleurance's shoulder, in the vicinity of her lungs and heart—what Scottish hunters call "the engine room." I pull the trigger, and before Fleurance has time to be frightened by the boom, a hot pain flashes through her midsection. She looks up, the world fades to black, and Fleurance is steak.

Anibal Pordomingo, of all people, told me an even faster death would be to calmly walk up to Fleurance, point a pistol between her eyes, and shoot. To a human, this might seem like nothing less than a gangland execution, but to a cow it would be instantaneous and painless.

In reality, numerous points of potential stress lay between a living, breathing cow and a fridge full of steak. I had to load Fleurance on a trailer. She had to endure a highway journey to the abattoir. She had to be unloaded. She had to be moved into the abattoir. And she had to be killed. Anything along the way—a loud bang, a dog barking, the smell of blood—could spook her. I had to engineer a way of getting Fleurance from the farm to the abattoir, and keep her happy the whole way.

By November, Fleurance was living in the barn. Her meals now consisted of hay, apples, and carrots.

And acorns.

Grass-fed purists will tell you not to use acorns as feed. They will tell you that acorns are like grain, an alien food form that will overpower a cow's rumen and saturate the fat. Grass-fed purists take things a bit far. When aurochs roamed the mature hardwood forests of ancient Europe and Asia, acorns rained from the soaring canopy, and aurochs hoovered down as many as they could find. Lewis and Clark witnessed something like this in person on September 16, 1804, when they were following the Missouri River northwest and came upon a wooded valley where all the animals were going crazy for acorns.

The acorns were now falling, and we concluded that the number of deer which we saw here had been induced thither by the acorns of which they are remarkably fond. Almost every species of wild game is fond of the acorn, the buffalo, elk, deer, bear, turkeys, ducks, pigeons and even the wolves feed on them.

Carla visited a nearby stand of oaks and filled a large wicker basket with acorns. Even Florimonde loved them, though her enthusiasm was nowhere near equal to Fleurance's. The supply was depleted in less than a week, so Carla called in reinforcements in the form of chestnuts, Persian walnuts, hazelnuts, and peanuts. That summer, Fleurance had eaten sweet potato, broccoli, beets, wild pears, apples, carrots, cooked potatoes, and corn on the cob (not a big hit), but her favorite food was nuts. According to Allen Williams, who does not cross the line into grass-fed zealotry, nuts were fine so long as we didn't serve too many. Nuts, he said, are lower in carbs and sugar than grains but higher in protein and oils. "Such food sources," he wrote me in an e-mail, "will be noted in an increased sheen in the hair coat and can certainly enrich the flavor and texture of the meat." Sure enough, Fleurance acquired a sheen. Judging by her appearance, Fleurance had started using conditioner.

In late October, I sent a photo of the now glossy Fleurance to Allen Williams. "She is getting there," he said. "I am starting to see some fat deposit in the brisket and across the ribs." Fleurance's body was starting to look something like the bodies of the cattle on the walls at Lascaux. She was fleshy. She was filled out. Fleurance was "finished."

Fleurance's last day on this world was a cold Thursday in early December. I planned to make it her best. My preparations did nothing, unfortunately, to keep my own cortisol and adrenaline levels from spiking. I didn't sleep the night before, and when I got out of bed it was too early to eat and I nourished myself with one too many coffees. The sky was still red when I walked up to Carla's barn. Inside, it was dark, and I stood there inhaling the smell of livestock and stared into the black. After a time, my eyes adjusted and I could make out two fuzzy ears in front of me. I pulled my cell phone out of my pocket and used the glow from the display as a flashlight. The ears were Fleurance's. She was waiting for me.

I had brought along four tall tins of Creemore Springs Lager, a pricey but excellent beer brewed just down the road from where we were standing. I poured two cans in a feed bucket and offered it to Fleurance. She stuck her nose in, sniffed, then removed it, unsure. She stuck it back in, but her nose was still dry when she pulled it out again. My plan was unraveling. *Fleurance*, I whispered, *this is no time to refuse beer.* I offered the bucket to Florimonde, who, uncharacteristically, started guzzling. Fleurance would have none of this, however, and she knocked Florimonde's head away, put her nose into the bucket, and took the most impressive gulp of beer I have ever witnessed. I handed her a chestnut, which she pulled into her mouth with her lips, and there followed a deep, loud, and immensely satisfying woody crunch. She ate chestnuts till there were no more and then ate hazelnuts and peanuts by the handful.

Carla appeared. The premise of the day hung heavy and unspoken in the air between us. "Do you want to give her some apples?" she asked. I grabbed a sack and walked over to Fleurance. In my other hand was the feed bucket, now filled with the final two cans of beer. She downed the brew in less than a second, pushing the bucket hard into my midsection as she tried to vacuum the remaining drops off the bottom. I took an apple out of the bag.

Humans have long believed that because we can express the experience of living in words, life for us is more richly observed and enjoyed. When a cow chews an apple, after all, it cannot frame the experience with concepts like sweet, sour, juicy, or peppery. Animals are stupefied by their own ignorance, or so we like to think. But of all the states of mind, none is simpler than pleasure. If you don't believe me, watch a cow eat an apple. The way Fleurance was chewing, it was evident that the apple was, for her, a 99, an A-plus, *a tart and crisp tour de force with notes of cinnamon, citrus tang, and apple blossom.* Her immersion in apple pleasure was total. She crushed it against her upper palate in a state approaching trance as juice ran out the corners of her mouth.

Deliciousness is a matter of survival. Ripe fruit tastes sweet to cows, monkeys, and humans because sweetness equals sugar, which equals energy, which equals survival. Meat tastes delicious to humans because meat equals umami and fat, which equal protein and energy, which equal survival. Evolutionarily, taste precedes language by millions of years. Deliciousness is more fundamental than eloquence. Fleurance loved that apple. She did not diminish the experience by trying to find the words to describe it. In a few hours, she would be dead, but at that moment I envied her pure and unmediated sense of pleasure.

The deliveryman arrived. He backed his livestock trailer to the barn door, and when we opened it, Fleurance made no move toward it. The knot of anxiety in my stomach tightened. I stood at the front of the trailer and tempted her with an apple. Nothing. The deliveryman got behind her and gave her a push and Fleurance finally took a step toward the trailer. Another step, and then another, until she raised a hoof and stepped up onto the trailer without so much as a rise in pulse. Fleurance walked forward and took the apple. The gate was closed.

Fifteen minutes later at the abattoir, my spirits nose-dived. The owner, Scotty, who is the loud and friendly type, was in a jokey mood. "Look how skinny she is," he said. "I'm going to have to sell you a bottle of barbecue sauce."

I was obsessing about a phenomenon called cold-shortening, which occurs when a warm carcass is chilled too quickly. It's the meat equivalent of a runner getting a cramp on a cold morning, as the cold causes the muscle to tense up and become tough and chewy. Cold-shortening is particularly common with grass-fed beef, because grass-fed cattle are often leaner and don't have as thick a layer of back fat as grain-fed cattle, which insulates against cold-shortening.

My adrenaline and cortisol were really flowing now. Events were happening in fast-forward. I paid the deliveryman, who said that he wished all his cattle were as cooperative as Fleurance. I spent a few minutes—or maybe an hour, I don't know—chatting with a guy who pulled up behind me with a bison in his trailer. There was a loaded rifle in the cab of his truck, because bison are so ornery they have to be shot dead in the trailer and then dragged out with chains.

It was time. Scotty walked me through the meat-cutting room through a door to what is known in packing parlance as "the kill floor." A food inspector was standing there wearing a yellow hard hat. A helper in a blue hard hat was holding a big knife. Scotty opened a door to the holding pen, and Fleurance appeared. She was in elk mode, ears pricked forward, alert, but not agitated. Without any coaxing, she walked into the knock box, which is something like a big cage. A metal gate closed behind her. She could not go backward or forward. She just stood there, looking curious.

Scotty picked up something that looked very much like a cordless drill but was actually an air-powered dart gun. He loaded a dart and walked over to Fleurance, who was bright and alert but calm as ever. Raising the dart gun to her face, he pointed it between her eyes, said something soothing, and fired. Fleurance dropped to the ground with the abruptness of a sack of flour pushed off the edge of a table. She was utterly still. The man in the blue hard hat walked up to her, bent over, and matter-of-factly slit her throat. The dart had left Fleurance unconscious, but as her blood flowed onto the concrete floor and into a drain she passed into death. Fleurance was no more. She was just a body now, meat that needed to be separated from bone, organs, and hide.

It felt bleak and harsh in there. Death is the most obvious fact of life, the gritty subtext to everything, which we spend all our waking hours pretending doesn't exist. There was no avoiding death now. Scotty cut off Fleurance's head. He lopped off her hooves and began pulling her hide off. Death was front and center.

As the hide came down, the mood turned. Scotty had good news. Beneath Fleurance's brown hide was a layer of creamy and glistening back fat. All morning, Scotty had been chiding me about my grass-, fruit-, and nut-fed lunacy. "It's gonna be lean," he kept saying. "I can tell." But Fleurance was not lean. Scotty walked up to me, holding Fleurance's warm liver in his hand, looked me in the eye, and complimented me straight up: "I'm impressed."

An hour later, we were all eating burgers. They were not from Fleurance, who had been cleaved into two sides of beef and was half an hour in to a scheduled two weeks of dry aging in Scotty's cooler. Fifteen minutes earlier, a tremendous boom had signaled the death of the bison, which was now hanging from its hind legs while we ate, its hide removed only halfway, looking as if someone had yanked down its pants. The bison's meat was red and muscly beneath its hide. It didn't have nearly the level of finish that Fleurance had.

Everything had gone according to plan. Fleurance had fattened on grass, fruit, and nuts. Her death was as smooth as death can be. I felt *good*. I drove back to the city above the speed limit, cranking classic rock from a local station. I phoned Allen Williams to tell him how well it had all gone down. There was still caffeine, cortisol, and adrenaline coursing through my system. It was a natural high.

A week later, the anxiety was back. I called Scotty to find out how the meat was aging, and the news wasn't good. A severe cold snap had set in, with the temperature outside falling to –18°C (0°F). "The cooler," Scotty said, "is running at just a hair above freezing. I'm not sure how much aging it's actually doing." Calpain enzymes are arrested by cold. If there had been any cold-shortening, the cold snap wasn't helping any.

In exactly a week, Michael Stadtländer would be hosting a Fleurance-themed dinner at Eigensinn Farm. Postponing was not an option; it was Christmas, and my brother had flown in from New York. I would be cooking Christophe Raoux's hay sauce, not for the steak—it may be years before I am able to adulterate steak with something other than salt—but for the fatty bone marrow, which Stadtländer loves as much as Magdalenian Woman did.

The morning of the dinner, I drove to Scotty's. He opened the door to the cooler and pointed out the two sides of hanging beef that belonged to me. Fleurance's fat was noticeably yellower than the fat on the other carcasses. He weighed a side: 288 pounds. It was time to start cutting.

The night before, I'd had a dream that Fleurance graded Prime. Now I watched as Scotty laid the side on his band saw and cut through it, revealing the virgin rib eye. We scanned the red surface for flecks of white. There were a few, but not many. USDA Select. Fleurance was in great company, eatingwise, but I was disappointed.

A few hours later in Stadtländer's kitchen, my mood spiraled again. I was making hay sauce, preparing a *jus* from Fleurance's rump, as Christophe Raoux had instructed months earlier in Paris. But when I immersed the hay, which had been cut in August, into the *jus*, Stadtländer's kitchen did not smell like a German hazelnut cake factory. The aroma was sweet, yes, but less so by orders of magnitude. *Sugar levels!* I thought, nearing panic. Carla's hay was not sugary enough. The forage did not contain enough energy. No wonder the rib eye wasn't marbled. Fleurance, it seemed certain to me now, was going to taste like swampwater. Or liver. Or perhaps an old shoe.

It was dark outside. The summer forage was a memory, covered by a blanket of downy snow. Flakes were falling from the sky, and the night itself looked marbled. Out on the highway, a wind was blowing the fresh snow into powdery little dunes. My brother and his wife arrived a little after 8:00 p.m., brandishing several bottles of red wine. Fleurance's tongue was chilling in a snowbank, because it's much easier to slice thin when it's half frozen. Stadtländer brought it in, laid it on a cutting board, and used a high-carbon Japanese blade to peel the skin off and cut the muscle into wafer-thin slices. His wife, Nobuyo, has infected her husband with the Japanese love of fine knives and marbled tongue.

Unlike the rib eye, the tongue was something to behold—by Japanese standards easily A3. It was the most marbled tongue Stadtländer had ever seen in North America. "It's beautiful," he said, arranging the slices on a platter that he brought to the dining room, which was lit only by candles flickering on the tables and licks of flame in the fireplace. It was the kind of fireplace an Argentine could love, because straddling a six-inch layer of glowing logs was a freestanding grill—height adjustable—that Stadtländer designed himself and had custom made.

Slices of tongue were laid across the grill, and fat dripped down, sending up flares. Only seconds passed when Stadtländer flipped them, and seconds after that he removed them to a plate where they swam in a puddle of melted fat and pink juice. He salted them and tasted the first piece. In flowery menu-speak, he was eating grass-, fruit-, and nut-fed Canadienne beef tongue, dry-aged and sliced Japanese style, grilled over hardwood embers in a hand-laid century granite hearth. But who needed words? Stadtländer nodded his head, muttering, "Mmm." He nodded his head again. "Mmm."

My brother reached for a piece. "That's good," he said. "*Really* good."

Stadtländer eventually found a vocabulary. "It's very nutty. And I like the way the fat comes out. I don't know where the fat is coming from, because if you look at the meat, it's lean. But the tongue is totally speckled."

My brother said, "I could eat this all day."

I placed a round of Fleurance's tongue on my tongue. The burst of fatty, mouth-filling juice was up there with the best stuff coming out of Matsusaka. The flavor was just as Stadtländer had described it: sweet and nutty. But also beefy. *Hugely* beefy.

Tongue, I decided right there, is a regal cut, the equal of rib eye. Why is it so underrated? Only Asians seem to revel in the joys of grilled tongue. Argentines boil theirs, and North Americans won't touch the stuff.

The rib steaks hit the grill next. A rib steak is a rib eye with the bone attached. (Some people call it a "bone-in rib eye," which is silly because the word *eye* denotes bonelessness, so they are effectively calling it a "bone-in boneless rib steak.") The rib steaks spattered, sizzled, and dropped fat. There were more Maillard-inducing flare-ups. Eating induced the following adjectives: "lovely," "tasty," "delicious." Stadtländer swallowed a piece and said, "The beef has all the hallmarks of great beef. It's sweet and nutty." But then he followed it with, "It just needs to be aged a little longer."

I barely registered the comment, as I was already swirling in my own funnel cloud of disappointment. I had picked up the same flaw as Stadtländer and the others: tenderness. The steak was not shoe-leather tough—no one was going to choke eating it—but it wasn't as tender as I had hoped. When you wanted to swallow, it still required a few chews.

My expectations, admittedly, were ridiculously high. It was unreasonable to expect my first-ever beef to be excellent. But that didn't stop me from hoping. After all, I owed it to Fleurance.

The good news was that there was still another side of beef aging in Scotty's gelid cooler. A week later, Stadtländer peeled off the tenderloin, roasted it for a New Year's Eve dinner, and proclaimed it to be as lean as venison, delicious, and—thank the Lord—tender. Three weeks later, after a grand total of six weeks of colder-than-normal dry aging, Scotty cut the other side. I took two rib steaks home and cooked them that night.

The weeks of hanging had imparted a not-unpleasant musty note to the meat, one you sometimes get in aged steak house steaks. (A lot of steak house types mistake this for genuine flavor in a commodity steak, which it is not.) More important, the calpain enzymes had worked their magic: the steak was now soft on the teeth. By the end of the meal, my wife—who was a vegetarian when I met her—was holding a rib bone in her hand and tearing off the last bits of meat clinging to the bone. She could have passed for Magdalenian Woman.

Every one of Fleurance's rib steaks was good. One friend even claimed her steak was the best he'd ever eaten. But over subsequent weeks and months, various imperfections announced themselves. The short ribs were too fatty, although whether this was a shortcoming or not depends on how you feel about fat. It was tasty fat, no question—nutty, smooth, and softer than warm butter. The sirloin was lean and challenging—anything over medium rare, and it was a goner. The strip loin was excellent but tiny. And there was too much gristle in the blade steaks. One evening, as my wife and I ate steak and watched hockey on TV, I found a small flap of meat on the inside of a rib steak that tasted like raw oyster. If you closed your eyes, it *was* raw oyster—pretty good raw oyster at that. I called Allen Williams, who explained that it was a product of dry aging. I had eaten meat that should have been trimmed off the carcass. No big deal, he said.

My daughter Greta, who formerly loved visiting Fleurance—"Daddy's cow"—to watch her eat apples, became a vocal fan of those rib steaks. When I would tell her we were eating steak for dinner, she would say, "Yay!" and clap her hands. The meat, she proclaimed, was "yummy." She would finish her little mound of precut rib steak morsels and say, "More steak, Daddy."

Almost three months to the day before Fleurance was killed, my wife had given birth to a baby girl, whom we named Violet, and a twin brother, Henry. By March, they were on solid food, and the first meat they ever tasted was Fleurance. The preparation was not one an Argentine would respect—the steak was pulsed in the blender and mixed with stewed mango—but the babies loved it. They finished the bowl and smiled, their cheeks streaked with bright orange and flecked with meat.

Feeding Fleurance to my offspring satisfied an inner desire I hadn't realized I possessed. It feels right and good to chop meat from an animal you have grazed personally and put it into little mouths. Supermarket meat now stared back at me blankly on Styrofoam trays. It seemed alien, all of a sudden. Where has it been?

Our own freezer was full of Fleurance. We ate rib steaks on weekends, braised short ribs, beef soup, and shank steaks cooked osso buco style. Some of the best steaks came on random weeknight dinners, when I would take inside round steaks, pound them with the flat side of a cleaver, sprinkle them with salt and pepper, dredge them in flour, and fry them. We call them fast-fry steaks, and my wife claims they are her number one choice for a last meal on death row. All the steak went down *clean*. You could not OD on fat with Fleurance's meat. It made you feel pure, as if you had just drunk spring water straight from the ground.

The human brain is about 12 percent omega-3 fatty acids, which is one more reason it felt good to feed Fleurance to my children. The growing brain of a young child goes through omega-3s the way a car factory goes through steel, and thanks to all that grass, Fleurance's meat should have been loaded with them. But I began to wonder how much omega-3 was actually in Fleurance. Had the nuts helped raise the level? Or were they fighting for the omega-6 team? For that matter, how saturated was her fat? It wasn't typical steak fat, being so soft that you could cream it with your tongue. Was I warding off heart disease by eating Fleurance? Or was I guaranteeing I would get it?

I phoned the Department of Nutrition at the University of Toronto, the institution that, years earlier, had granted me a highly unscientific BA in philosophy. I was given the number of one Richard Bazinet, a neuroscientist and nutritionist whose specialty is fatty acids, and who, I later found out, is descended from a *fille du roi* named Catherine de Seine (who arrived in Quebec in 1671, possibly on the same ship as one of Fleurance's ancestors). I invited him over for steak and served him grilled beefalo rib eye—hay-finished in Washington, dry-aged five days—because serving Fleurance seemed, somehow, incestuous. Bazinet is a steak lover, but, like many, he is frequently disappointed by the steak he loves. Weeks earlier, he had gone to Chicago to give a talk called "Recent Advances in the Neurochemistry of Brain Polyunsaturated Fatty Acids." While in town, he visited a famous Chicago steak house for a meal that was, like his research, rich in fatty acids. He liked the shrimp bisque, the creamed spinach, and the shoestring fries, but not the steak.

Bazinet, who also loves wine, was impressed by the beefalo's depth of flavor and long finish. When he finished the meal, he made the kind of observation only a fatty acids specialist can: "I found it interesting that when the beefalo steak cooled, it remained very tender. I wonder if the unsaturated fats in the phospholipids might influence this?" The steak he ate in Chicago suffered from the opposite condition: when it cooled, it became waxy and firm.

Bazinet, eager to investigate, made a proposal: Let's run some steak samples through my gas chromatography machine. A few weeks later, I showed up at his lab with four different samples of beef.

The first, which was standard supermarket corn-fed beef, scored pretty much as you would expect. The omega-6 to omega-3 ratio clocked in at a terrible 10 to 1. That was due mainly to a big spike in linoleic acid, an omega-6 fatty acid found in abundance in corn, and there was hardly any alpha-linolenic acid (ALA), an omega-3 found in grass, to balance it out. The beefalo was practically the opposite: less linoleic, but quite the spike in ALA, resulting in an omega-6 to omega-3 ratio of 2.3 to 1. The corn-fed supermarket beef was 47.5 percent saturated fat—the stuff nutrition scientists are pretty sure clogs up your heart and arteries. The beefalo came in at 43.1 percent—about 10 percent less. That may explain why Bazinet's beefalo didn't firm up while he lingered over his wine, because unsaturated fats stay liquid at room temperature. All that ALA likely had something to do with it, too, Bazinet told me, because as unsaturated fats go, ALA is *really* unsaturated. (It's missing three pairs of hydrogen atoms, for all you egghead chemists out there.)

Bazinet put the omega-3 findings in perspective. Despite the better ratio in grass-fed meat, the quantity of omega-3 acids was still fairly low. A grass-fed steak is not the omega-3 Shangri-la that a piece of wild salmon or herring is. And yet overall, Bazinet thought grass-fed beef made for a wiser food choice. "If you only eat beef once a week," he said, "it probably doesn't make a difference. But if you're going to eat it three

times a week"—if you're going to be a Beef Loyal, in other words—"I think
the numbers would start to have an effect. Someone should really do a
long-term study."

Fleurance proved to be quite the head-scratcher, fatty-acid-wise. Bazinet looked at her results and said, "Your cow is just really polyunsaturated. It's weird." Like the beefalo, Fleurance had a spike in ALA. But
like the feedlot sample, she had spikes in linoleic acid and another unsaturated omega-6 called arachidonic acid, bringing her omega ratio in
at a still respectable 3.1 to 1. This may have been due to all the nuts she
had consumed, but it likely had to do with the fact that the farmer from
whom I had bought Fleurance had fed her some corn. Strangest of all,
however, was Fleurance's sky-high level of the unsaturated oleic acid,
which, along with the ALA and arachidonic acid, made her fat so
absurdly soft.

Was it the nuts? Maybe. There's lots of oleic acid in hazelnuts, walnuts,
peanuts, and acorns, but Fleurance hadn't eaten *that* many—usually just
a few pounds a day, tops, and only for a few weeks. Bazinet wondered if
there was a delta-9-desaturase situation going on. Did Fleurance, like the
black Wagyu, produce enzymes that converted her stearic acid to oleic
acid? It's possible. But Fleurance actually had *more* oleic acid than a black
Wagyu. (So maybe it was the nuts. . . .)

How did I know this? For weeks I had been hoarding a sample of
pure black Wagyu beef and gave it to Bazinet with instructions that it
was not to be grilled. I did not part with it easily, as it was the rarest kind
of beef there is: grass-fed black Wagyu. It wasn't Japanese. It came from
Washington State. This particular type of Wagyu, which isn't even available in Japan, had an insane omega-6 to omega-3 ratio of 1.3 to 1, and its
fat was the least saturated fat of all the samples.

Grass-fed black Wagyu was something I'd been searching for ever
since the trip to Matsusaka. All I found were rumors, the foodie equivalent of urban legend, always starting with, "A guy I know in Colorado
knows someone who . . ." No one had seen actual grass-fed black Wagyu
grazing in person. No one had tasted their meat. I was beginning to
doubt they even existed, and then one day Sweet Grass Farm popped up
on a Google search. It was located on Lopez Island, a San Juan Island

bathing in cold Pacific water just off the coast near Seattle. The farmer was a former custom toolmaker named Scott Meyers, who sent me a rib steak by overnight courier.

Anyone who says cattle can't marble on grass should have seen that rib steak, which scored better than USDA Prime. Meyers told me his steak tasted like "beef times a hundred," which, if anything, is a tad conservative. The steak was so rich and flavorful I had to eat it slowly. It was so juicy and the taste so intense that I was reminded of extremely ripe fruit. It was to steak what espresso is to coffee. I couldn't even *cut* through it at normal speed. I found myself watching the slow and delicate action of my knife as it sawed across the fine-grained flesh and released juice. It was like steak with headphones on.

The next day, I phoned Scott Meyers to ask, Why is your steak so good? He started talking about forage growth curves. He said something about carbon levels in the soil and carbonic acid–releasing minerals. He told me about how he had developed an apparently ingenious technique to prolong the seasonality of a forage called Reed canary grass, which gets as sweet as grass can but is usually long past its prime by the time cows get onto it.

His husbandry techniques had placed my experiment with Fleurance in a whole different light. I was, I realized, a hack. I couldn't talk soil type or growth curves. I didn't know ryegrass from bluegrass. I had no idea about the levels of carbonic acid in Carla's fields. I had gotten lucky and made the steak equivalent of decent homemade wine. But I didn't know what I was doing.

There are people who do. There are people out there crafting steak of great beauty. It was time to go and taste some.

It was time to pay another visit to Allen Williams.

CHAPTER EIGHT

A RETURN TO
THE HEARTLAND

There is more than one way to tell how sweet a field of grass is. You can take a Brix reading, for example, which is what winemakers do when they want to tell if the juice inside their grapes is sweet enough. Grass doesn't give its juice up as easily as a grape does, however, which means you have to squeeze it through a garlic press and aim the drops onto a device called a refractometer, which tells you the Brix levels. A good reading is around 12 or 15, although Allen Williams will settle for 10. He hopes for better, though. He has seen grass that scored in the upper 20s, at which point it's as sweet as a ripe grape.

The meat scientist in Allen Williams loves the precision of a refractometer, which is why he was stooped over, tearing off clumps of Colorado grass destined for the garlic press while hot Colorado sun darkened his neck. The particular patch of Colorado grass in which Williams was standing is part of Maytag Mountain Ranch, which is situated in a stretch of naturally moist peat and glacial till sandwiched between the Wet Mountains to the east and the Sangre de Cristo Mountains to the west. The ranch's owner, a friendly, large-framed man named Russ Maytag, prefers a more traditional device than the refractometer: a dairy cow. "Let her eat the grass," he said, "milk her, and then drink the milk. If it tastes sweet, the grass does, too."

There was no milking cow out in the fields today, but Maytag was not out of options. He suggested I assess the sweetness of the grass the simplest way of all: by tasting it. "I eat the grass all the time," he said, and inserted two fresh blades in his mouth.

If the stuff growing at Maytag Mountain Ranch were in the produce aisle, it would be the heavyweight of the salad world. Arugula is iceberg lettuce, by comparison. I crunched a blade between two molars and a sweet, tealike liquid spread over my tongue. I tasted herbal, green, and peppery. The leaf itself was awful, as rough as a cat's tongue, but the stuff inside I could have savored all day. I spat out a pulpy wad and reached for another juicy blade.

Williams was not eating grass. He was staring, in a state approaching rapture, at a clump of manure. "You know you have too much protein when the manure is runny," he said. "But you know the mix is right when the turds are firm." He mushed it with his foot. "That's pretty good," he said. Turd observation, it seems, is another way of determining if grass is sweet or not. Williams didn't comment on the smell, but it was good, too: herbal, also floral. This cowpatty was another substance altogether from feedlot manure, so benign that you might well pass it off as cheap filler for potpourri.

Williams had not finished examining the manure. He drew my attention to its surface, which was strewn with little holes, as though someone had fired a shotgun at it. The holes were made by dung beetles, which lunch their way through a patty and drink down a liquid referred to, in some scientific circles, as "dung slurpie," in doing so cycling nutrients from the grass back into the topsoil. Williams used the toe of his boot to lift off the sun-baked shell from the top of the patty, exposing the moist interior to bright sunlight and sending dung beetles scurrying into their little holes. Williams turned to me and asked, "Do you know how few pastures you see this in?"

He now turned his attention to a patch of red clover, which had little red blossoms shooting up. "I like to see a good mixture of legumes," he said. All around the clover was grass, which looked to me like generic meadow. Williams urged me to take a closer look. The grass was, in truth, grasses. Some had thicker leaves, some had bushy tops, some was reedy, some was bunchy, and some of the grass was tall. The mix included timothy, orchard grass, intermediate wheat, brome, sedge, and bluegrass. The tallest plant in the field was not a grass, however, but a gangly weed called California false hellebore, which sounds pernicious, laid-back, and dubious all at the same time. What Williams liked about the California false hellebore was that it was getting trampled. "It's deep rooted," he said, "and when it gets trampled, it decomposes and releases minerals from way down below the surface up at the top." The soil itself, however well structured, mineralized, and cycled, was invisible beneath the grass, which was so thick that crossing the field was like walking through deep snow. "Just look at the density," Williams said admiringly. "You have to dig down to get to the ground. That's what I like to see."

Williams liked a lot of what he was seeing. But what he liked most of all wasn't in this field but over in the next one. There, a small convention of about a hundred forage aficionados, whose connoisseurship in the arena of delectable grasses surpassed that of Williams, were standing in a group and delighting audibly in the sugariness of long green leaves. Most were red Angus, but there were a few shorthorns and Herefords, and as they chewed they stared over at us, lowering their heads from time to time to reload. We walked over, and, as though picking up an old and ongoing conversation, Williams and Maytag began singling out the fattest ones. Williams pointed at a tubby red Angus steer. "That's a nice brisket," he said, fixing on its chest. Maytag called attention to the "buttons"—fat deposits—that were growing at the base of its tail. Then he pointed at a black heifer with a white face and commended the deposits in her ribs, which had disappeared under a layer of fat. The heifer was so plump that she looked as if she'd been inflated with a bicycle pump. "She's ready for sure," Williams said, nodding his head.

What she was ready for was eating, but before that could happen, she and the rest of the herd had to be moved off this field, which had been grazed for three straight days and reduced in height by more than two feet. The good forage—"ice cream," in grazier talk—had all been picked off, and now it was time to move into the next field. But only if that field was ready, of course, if its grass was sweet to the taste.

On this subject there was little doubt. It was 3:30 p.m., which meant the grass had been basking in solar radiation ever since the sun had peeked its head over the top of the Wet Mountains, its leaves photosynthesizing sugars. The refractometer rated it an eye-popping 21, whereas the field they were leaving was (a still very respectable) 16. The gate would be opened, the cows would roll in for three days of grazing, and then a different gate would be opened and they would move on to yet another field at the pinnacle of sweetness. Eventually, the field they were now about to leave would revitalize, and the cows would return to fill their rumens with grass and their briskets, ribs, and buttons with soft fat.

There is a term for when cows eat like this: managed grazing. It is the key—or, more precisely, one of a set of keys—to finishing cattle on grass. Williams explained how it works: "Cattle want the highest-energy feed," he said. "They're like me or you. They like their food to be sweet. On a grass plant," he explained, "the top growth is the sweetest and softest. That's what they always go for first." The problem with cattle is that, left to their own devices, they'll eat down the sugary parts of the grass, and then, when the grass becomes less sweet, they won't eat a thing. They'll just stand there, almost as if they were on a hunger strike, or they'll wander too much, as though the land itself were distracting them from eating. When you cordon off a big field into many little paddocks, however, and move cattle from one paddock to another, a mob mentality seems to take hold. They will eat everything, mowing the field almost down to the ground, if you let them. "When you move them," Williams explained, "they tank up on top growth. By moving them often, you can induce them to eat more than they would if you left the pace up to them."

(Note to self: Perhaps Fleurance should have been moved.)

The present pace was, if anything, a little tardy. The cattle were taking two or three bites off each grass plant, which didn't leave enough green photosynthesizing leaf matter left on the plant for the grass to recover quickly. Maytag was therefore not achieving "optimal solar panel effect," and he plans on installing more lines of fencing so the cattle can be moved to a new patch of grass every day.

The goal is to get his cows to take one bite per plant. At that clip, they will gain as much as three pounds per day, which approaches the level of gain a cow achieves on steamed, flaked, liver-destroying corn. Every day, Maytag's cows will find themselves standing in a fresh field of sweet and tender grass. It is the cow equivalent of eating steak all the time.

Grass quality is Allen Williams's number two problem in life. He is the chief operating officer at Tallgrass Beef, a company that produces about 5,500 steaks a week, every one of them from cattle that have not eaten a single kernel of grain in their entire lives. Put up against one of the big packing companies, Tallgrass's output is minuscule, not so much a drop in the bucket as a drop in a lake. But in the young and vigorous world of American grass-fed beef, Tallgrass is a heavy hitter. It sells what's known in the industry as boxed beef. Tallgrass supplies restaurants and supermarkets. People visit the Tallgrass Web site and enter a credit card number and days later a FedEx truck delivers a package of vacuum-sealed rib eyes, strips, burgers, short ribs, and hanger steaks to their front doors. Almost every Tallgrass skirt steak is claimed by the celebrity chef Rick Bayless, who serves them at his Chicago restaurants. To produce that many skirt steaks, you need a lot of cows and serious acreage of grass. Tallgrass works with two hundred ranchers in five states. Russ Maytag was one of them, until the local meatpacker wasn't able to cut steaks to Tallgrass's standards. But Williams hopes he will be again, and it's not hard to see why, considering what the refractometer thinks of Maytag's grass.

Bad grass equals bad steaks. And grass, as I'd learned, can be bad so many different ways. Soil, too, is crucial. It can be too dry or too wet. It can lack minerals, such as calcium and phosphorus, and the grass won't be able to synthesize sugars, a problem that will show up in the flavor of the meat. Williams puts roughly a hundred thousand miles on his truck every year, a good deal of them spent taking him to Tallgrass finishing fields, so he can monitor soil quality, keep an eye out for onion grass and bitterweed, monitor Brix levels, and, of course, look at flanks, briskets, and buttons.

And yet grass is still only Williams's number two problem. His biggest problem makes the task of growing good grass seem like a mere inconvenience. It not only keeps him up at night and infects his dreams, it sends him monthly back and forth across the country in search of a solution. As often as not, he comes home empty-handed.

Allen Williams's number one problem is finding good cattle. America's beef herd currently stands at roughly ninety million, but Williams estimates fewer than 10 percent of those cattle would taste good after four months on good grass. They are too tall, for one thing. They grow too fast and are bad at converting grass to meat and fat. Some of them don't even know how to graze anymore. They just stand there in a field and bellow for the feed bucket.

Allen Williams has himself to blame.

"You go off to college and think you're so smart," Williams told me as we pulled out of Maytag Mountain Ranch and headed north in the hopes of locating a few first-rate cattle. "I was learning all this stuff from my college professors, and I'd go back home to the farm and tell my dad and uncles how to do things: 'We gotta use hormone implants and all the modern vaccines.' 'We have to supplement with protein feeds and grain because grass just isn't good enough.'"

Williams's family had been farming on South Carolina's Piedmont Plateau since 1842, when, in the early 1980s, they got into the feedlot business and eventually owned two feedlots of about fifteen thousand head. They didn't want the short, fat British cattle—Angus, Herefords, shorthorns, Galloways—that American cattle ranchers traditionally raised. Like everyone else feeding corn to cattle, they wanted taller cattle that grew quickly and got fat on corn. They wanted yield. By the time Williams was in graduate school, he was helping create those cattle.

He was working at what's known as a bull test station, where pedigree bulls were placed in a feedlotlike environment and fed incredible volumes of flaked corn in the hopes that they would gain a fantastic amount of weight. Bulls that got the fattest the fastest produced semen that would, in turn, sire offspring that also got fat fast on corn. Advertisements for such semen promised "high average daily gains," and it sold for big money.

Producing that semen wasn't easy. Some of the bulls were so obese their scrotums got fat, which raised the temperature of their testicles and shut down sperm production. And that was if they even survived the fattening period. Bulls would come down with the all the sundry feedlot illnesses—acidosis, ketosis, founder, lameness, respiratory disease, foot rot, bloat—but because each bull was worth thousands of dollars, "mortality" wasn't an asset impairment anyone wanted to see on his balance sheet. So Williams and his fellow grad students performed veterinary triage twenty-four hours a day. "It was like critical care in a hospital," Williams remembers. "You didn't want any of them to die. But even with twenty-four/seven monitoring, some still died." Williams always carried a bloat tube, and he became an expert at inserting it down a bull's throat and into its rumen and finding the pockets of gas. "You'd know it when you hit it because there was this *whoosh* of air coming out, and boy, did it smell."

It was all justified in the name of "improvement": the weak were being selected out. In genetics classes, Williams had learned about the perils of single-trait breeding. But they were selecting for only a single trait: high average daily gains on flaked corn. It was evolution in fast-forward. What thousands of meat scientists, grad students, and cattle breeders accomplished was to change the way the American beef cattle process feed. Thanks to their grand effort—which is still moving decisively ahead—America's cattle inched a few notches over on the evolutionary map. Compared to the cattle of fifty or a hundred years ago, they are now a little more like pigs, which aren't good at eating grass. They've gotten better at converting corn to beef. Their muscle fibers are bigger, leaner, and less tender than they used to be.

The "utter ridiculousness" of what was going on at bull test stations all across America finally struck Williams one cold winter night in 1989. He was on the meat science faculty at Louisiana Tech University, where he ran the school's bull test station. A grad student phoned him in the middle of the night with bad news: a bull had come down with a bad case of bloat and looked as if it wasn't going to make it. Williams drove to the station as fast as the law permitted and found a bull lying on its side in pouring rain, breathing fast, its head in the mud. He and his students got down and kneeled in a cold slurry of mud and manure and tried to lift the bull upright, but it wouldn't budge. They were soaked with rain and covered in filth, the temperature was a few degrees above freezing, and a prized bull was about to die. A thought occurred to Williams: What the hell are we doing?

The following year, Williams decided to keep the bulls on pasture and feed them less corn. They still got sick, but not as sick. The year after, he fed them even less corn. In time, grass became a bigger and bigger part of Williams's approach. In the world of American meat science, where corn is very much king, Allen Williams became a rogue.

It had nothing to do with flavor. Williams's mission was to improve the lives of cattle and the farmers who raised them. He saw grazing as a means of reducing the crippling expense of vaccinations, growth hormones, antibiotics, grain, protein supplements, vet bills, and dead cattle.

That changed in 2001. Williams was now working for a livestock cooperative in New England that had asked him to develop something that was extreme even by Williams's standards: a "grass-only" method of raising beef. He helped them find good cattle, plant the right grasses, finish the animals adequately, and so forth. Eventually, it came time for Williams to put his steak where his mouth was. The hope was that the newfangled grass-fed beef would merely be *competitive* with feedlot beef. The plan was to win the hearts and dollars of consumers with the environmental, health, and animal welfare benefits of grass-fed beef. The taste only needed to be "acceptable." Would it be? Williams didn't know, as he had never eaten a "grass-only" steak before. The meat certainly looked good—marbled, decent fat cover, nice-sized rib eye.

Williams and some farmers gathered in a kitchen in Maine one evening and cooked a rib eye, a strip loin, a tenderloin, and a sirloin. Williams sliced into a steak, put the morsel in his mouth, and after a few chews, began silently revising the business plan. It was no longer about being competitive with grain-fed steak; it was about being *better* than grain-fed steak. Suddenly, it was about flavor.

In 2004, the television news personality Bill Kurtis—host of *American Justice*—asked Williams to become a partner in his new company, Tallgrass Beef, whose mission was to raise cattle on grass and create, as Kurtis put it, "the best beef out there." Williams knew their single biggest problem would be finding good cattle. The only way they could consistently produce delicious beef on grass was to find old herds of British breeds that had somehow remained free of the taint of commercial breeding. He began a series of journeys into the heartland, chartering planes and logging hundreds of thousands of highway miles, traveling as far north as Canada and as far south as Mexico in the hopes of turning up pockets of old-time genetics.

Williams found some very good cattle on the eastern slopes of the Rocky Mountains in Montana. They were black Angus with short legs, barrel-shaped midsections, and flesh that ran deep and thick. On his way to a farm in Kentucky one morning, he looked at the fields alongside the highway and saw more superb Angus cows grazing. He tracked down the farmer and bought some. He found outstanding Herefords in Kansas and an excellent herd of British White cattle—a rare breed—in Minnesota. Some of the best cattle he has ever come across was a herd of outstandingly retro Herefords in the remotest Sierra Madre in Mexico.

Those were the good cows, and they are all too few. Eight times out of ten, Williams will show up at a ranch and find feedlot cattle that are too big, tall, or "hard fleshing," which means they won't get fat on grass. The vast majority of them wouldn't taste good even on the best grass.

As we covered mile after mile of highway, we passed cattle grazing on fields next to the highway. Williams would look over and say, "Angus. But you can tell there's some Charolais in there." He spotted fields that were overgrazed and others that were deficient in minerals. Most of the rangeland, however, looked just superb. We would cross over a rise, and the land before us would be a ruffled carpet of green all the way to the horizon. "This is excellent pastureland," he would say, "just excellent." Near Denver, the sprawl of malls and track homes poured into the rangeland like fungus. Williams looked at the big-box stores and the generic houses that are the same in Colorado as they are in Mississippi, Maryland, California, and New York. "This could be Anywhere, USA," he said.

We spent the night at a terrible motel in Laramie, Wyoming. The next morning, after several cups of the weakest coffee in the West, Allen Williams went looking for some seriously old Herefords.

Incest is a way of life in rural America. The word "incest" is rarely uttered, but what is happening—son on mother, uncle on niece, nephew on aunt—is incest. The term of choice is "linebreeding." Only livestock do it. Most people have no idea it's taking place, and those who do don't think it's a bad thing.

Linebreeding is when you take a heifer with, for example, a very full brisket, plump rump, and short legs and mate her to her uncle, who also has a very full brisket, plump rump, and short legs. The intent is to obtain offspring with those same desired qualities. If a farmer has a herd of cattle that possess favorable characteristics, he linebreeds them—with great care, mind you, putting much consideration into which uncle should be put with which niece—so none of those characteristics will be lost. Any outside genetic influence, after all, will change the herd. Robert Bakewell, the man who invented cattle breeds, is considered the father of linebreeding, but the practice likely dates back to the dawn of cattle, when tame aurochs were bred with their tame siblings to produce even tamer aurochs.

The Laramie Plains of Wyoming are a high, dry stretch of dusty, flat-as-a-bed rangeland, in the midst of which sits Flying Z Ranch—home to the kind of incestuously bred herd that makes Allen Williams spend nights in lousy hotels that serve terrible coffee. They are Herefords, a breed that was once the most famous in America. Back when Texas was overrun with longhorns, Herefords were brought in to "improve" them and reigned until feedlots started sprouting up all over the Midwest. All that corn made them too fat, so they were bred to be taller and more muscled. Breeders often accomplished this, Williams believes, by quietly crossing them with non-Hereford cattle—European breeds like Simmental, Charolais, and Chianina—and claiming nevertheless that the offspring were pure Hereford, thereby ruining Hereford genetics. The scheme doesn't seem to have worked, however, because today no one has much time for Herefords.

But these Herefords were unique. They seemed to have just stepped out of some kind of time warp, and it was all thanks to a man named Bob Gietz, who has been deceased since 1962. An easterner by birth, Gietz was lured to Wyoming in 1919 to become a cattleman. By 1925 he presided over a herd of Herefords that he judged to be of such outstanding quality that they were, henceforth, never to be corrupted with the genetic influence of any other cow or bull. They have since enjoyed almost a century of controlled incest. Genetically speaking, they are the same now as they were the year Adolf Hitler published *Mein Kampf* and Calvin Coolidge swore his oath of office.

Gietz's daughter, Janet Talbott, greeted us in the driveway, and within a few minutes Williams was in the corral appraising her bovine anachronisms. The cattle were short, the way doorframes in very old houses are short. The tallest came up to my bottom rib. "Look at the moderate frame size," Williams said in the same tone of voice he uses when in the presence of excellent forage. "They're definitely older style."

Beauty is only hide deep, however. Only weeks earlier, Williams had tried and failed to eat a roast from the Grand Champion Steer at the Dixie National Rodeo and Livestock Show. That steer, which looked better than hundreds of other contestants, was so tough and gristly as to be inedible. Williams asked Talbott to bring a few of the Herefords into the barn, because he wanted to take a look inside them—a task that called for neither rubber glove nor scalpel, but a high-tech device called an Aloka SSD-500 V, an ultrasound machine of the same type that obstetricians use to scan pregnant women to examine the fetus.

First up was a white-faced heifer with curly hair between her eyes. The area behind her left shoulder was shaved and rubbed with vegetable oil, and when the scanner was placed upon it, an image appeared on the screen: live rib eye. It appeared as a long tube of muscle running just under the heifer's hide.

The first thing Williams looked for was marbling. The heifer scored 2.89 percent. USDA Choice is 4 percent or better, but it was, nevertheless, a good showing, because the heifer was being kept on dry and dusty rangeland, not lush, sweet grass like back at Maytag Mountain Ranch. If she could score almost 3 percent on marginal terrain, she'd do well on good grass.

Next, Williams examined the bundles of muscle fibers, which are surrounded by sheaths of chewy connective tissue. He examined the angle at which they ran through the steak—if connective tissue runs even somewhat across the grain of the muscle, it makes a steak hard to cut and chew. He looked for connective tissue that was too thick. He found neither. The heifer scored an impressive 2.3 on tenderness. "If you slaughtered her today, she'd be tender," Williams said. "There's no gristle."

The heifer scored even better—1—on stress, an index that is Williams's own invention. Animal scientists have long known that when a cow is stressed, marbling is the first fat to disappear. But Williams has personally noticed that marbling is burned up in a particular pattern. A cow pulls fat out from the top of the rib eye first and works its way down. By examining the way marbling is deposited—if any of it is missing on top, basically—Williams can infer whether or not the cow is stressed, which is to say sick, agitated, on poor feed, running around too much, and so forth. The heifer's marbling appeared as a dusting of white, not unlike the appearance of the Milky Way on a clear night, and the muscle was as cloudy on top as on the bottom. "This girl is showing no stress," he said.

Williams now snapped a cross section of the rib eye, cutting it right where a butcher would. Appearing on the screen was an image of a steak that, despite being rendered in gray scale, looked so real you almost expected to see a grayscale baked potato and vegetables sitting next to it. There was, all told, 7.6 square inches of rib eye area—decent. Back fat was good, too. So was shape. "She's performing well," Williams dryly announced.

The next heifer performed similarly, and the bull that followed did, too. His rib eye featured less marbling, and the marbling was notably absent near the top. He was showing signs of stress, in other words, but that was to be expected in a young bull who was, as Williams put it, "spending all his time chasing the ladies." Williams examined two more bulls and three more heifers, and they all scored pretty much the same. They were "uniform." That is linebreeding for you.

When the testing was done, Allen Williams and Janet Talbott stood outside the barn and chatted. "Are you pleased?" Talbott asked, sounding nervous.

"Yes," Williams said. "Your cattle seem very consistent. That's what we look for. They're tender. They have excellent muscle shape."

In front of us, the flatness of the Laramie Plains was interrupted in the far distance by Jelm Mountain, which is home to one of the world's leading infrared telescopes. Above it, a blue sky was crisscrossed by white contrails of now-distant airliners. Over in the corral, Bob Gietz's Herefords were mooing like it was 1925. Genetically speaking, Allen Williams hit the jackpot.

•　　　•　　　•

All those rib eyes on the screen of the Aloka SSD-500 V reawakened a steak craving that had gone unquenched ever since Maytag Mountain Ranch. Two more hours of driving took us south to Fort Collins, Colorado, where we came upon a steak house called the Charco Broiler in whose fridge, at that very moment, sat five Tallgrass rib eyes, shipped at the behest of Allen Williams.

We kept right on going. There was a woman in Fort Collins I needed to talk to first. I had a question that I still hadn't quite answered, and she was the only person in the world who could help me. It was the question Bill O'Brien asked me at Texas Beef, when we pulled up to one of the pens in his feedlot: "Do these cattle look unhappy to you?" I didn't know then, and I didn't know now.

From the point of view of flavor, at least, it didn't matter. I knew what steaks tasted best: the ones raised on grass. Were those cows happy? I assumed yes. As so many people had told me, grass is a cow's natural environment—which isn't quite true, because evidence suggests that aurochs spent something like half their time in forests. But was it possible that cattle were actually happier in feedlots? Was a feedlot a kind of junk-food paradise where the cows that didn't come down with bloat, acidosis, founder, and such were immeasurably pleasured as they gorged themselves on the cattle equivalent of doughnuts and potato chips?

The woman with the answer is Temple Grandin. She is one of the world's highest-functioning autistics as well as one of the world's foremost experts on the inner lives of animals. The two are connected. Because of Grandin's autism, a condition of the brain, she thinks differently from neurologically "normal" people. "The problem with normal people," she writes in her book *Animals in Translation*, "is they're too cerebral." They parse everything they see and hear into concepts, she says, and have a habit of making the world yield to the concepts in their heads. The non-autistic strike her as walking "abstractifiers."

Grandin thinks in objects. Her mind is a whir of *detail*, an ongoing festival of free association. Animals think the way Grandin does—in images. If a cow was abused by a man wearing a white hat, for example, that cow would henceforth be afraid of white hats.

This similarity of mind has given Grandin an ability to step into the minds of animals. A slaughterhouse once came to her and asked why their cattle were all getting big bruises on their chests right before slaughter. No one at the plant could figure it out. Grandin stepped into the chute and walked through it as a cow would and discovered a sharp metal bar sticking out, into which the cattle were walking. She saw detail to which others were blind. She visited another slaughterhouse where workers were constantly using electric prods to get pigs to walk down a certain chute that they did not want to enter. "What is the pigs' problem?" everyone wondered. Grandin got down on her hands and knees and headed down the chute, where she saw what the pigs saw but the plant managers could not: a wet floor. Light was glinting off it and spooking them.

Over the past few decades, Grandin has single-handedly revolutionized the way animals in North America's food system are treated. She has designed better feedlots and slaughterhouses. She has reduced the use of electric cattle prods. She has developed a scoring system by which slaughterhouses can themselves be graded. Cattle in a Grandin-designed slaughterhouse never have any idea where they're headed. They calmly follow their friends single file into a big building, and soon after their world abruptly fades to black. If there were a dial measuring all the fear, pain, and anxiety experienced by the animals North Americans eat, the dial would be much closer to zero now than in the past. The reason is Temple Grandin.

She was waiting for us at the front door of the Animal Sciences Building at Colorado State University, wearing a western-style shirt featuring a scene of horses standing in a snowy field done in airbrush and an ascot tied around her neck, looking something like central casting's idea of a prairie grandmother. She took us down to a basement boardroom that was still cool and damp in the heat of July and, despite the institutional setting, smelled like a suburban basement in summertime.

Grandin was in the mood to talk steak. She is a big-time beef eater, and will consume steak as often as three or four times a week when she's on the road and dining in restaurants. The night before, she had been stuck at an airport hotel in Dallas due to a missed connection, and she used the meal chit provided by the airline to order a tenderloin. ("Lean and good, but not as juicy as it should have been.")

Temple Grandin believes the quality of steak is going down. She first noticed there was a problem with meat when she attended a banquet some years ago and was served pork from a heritage breed of pig. "The hotel tried very hard to ruin it," she said, "by keeping it under a heat lamp all day and letting it get all dried out. But it was still absolutely delicious. And it had a very fine muscle fiber." Not long after, she visited a client who was raising genetically modern pigs with giant, fast-growing loins. "Tough as hockey pucks," she said. "I didn't realize how bad pork had gotten. Some of it you need a steak knife to cut." After that, Grandin got into the habit of ordering a pork chop and dissecting it to see how big the fibers were.

"Quantity and quality are two opposing goals," Grandin pronounced, neatly diagnosing the central problem of today's meat industry. It didn't matter how quantity was cranked up—hormones, genetics, drugs—there was always a price to be paid in quality.

One of Grandin's major concerns of late is a drug called beta-agonists used in feedlots to make cattle gain muscle mass. The cost is tenderness. There are, presently, no controls on beta-agonist doses, and Grandin has walked into feedlots and found cows jacked up on them sitting down on the ground and panting like dogs. Beta-agonists make cattle sore-footed. "They act like they're walking on hot metal," Grandin says. And lately she has seen cattle dying in strange and unheard-of ways. "I went to a plant and saw a perfect black heifer that was just dead. That never used to happen. She had no snotty nose, she wasn't bloated, no broken leg. Such a pretty little heifer." Even moderate doses of beta-agonists can make cattle jittery, as if they've had too much coffee to drink.

If happiness is the opposite of stress, what makes cattle happy?

It comes down to core emotional systems, Grandin says. In all mammals, including humans, there is a primitive part of the brain called the subcortex that is home to basic emotional and life-support systems. "The emotions are down deep," Grandin said. "They're the motivators. An animal will run from a tiger because it's afraid of it. It'll seek out grass because grass is good." The subcortex is roughly the same size in the brain of a cow as it is in the brain of a pig, and a human subcortex isn't much larger. "The main difference between us and animals," Grandin explained, "is that we have this big great computer sitting on top, which greatly increases the complexity of how the emotions are expressed." But our basic feelings are the same basic feelings as a cow's, and include emotions like fear, separation anxiety, rage, sexual lust, and nurturing. The subcortex is also home to pleasure and reward. If a human brain is scanned while that human eats something delicious, the subcortex lights up and sends signals, like forked lighting, up into the cortex. Anatomically speaking, it is the home of satisfaction and joy.

Like humans, cows enjoy eating tasty foods such as sweet grass, apples, or grain. What they don't like, Grandin said, is to have fear, rage, or separation anxiety turned on.

We decided to head out to the countryside to observe basic emotions in action. As we drove, Grandin repeated much of what she'd said in the boardroom, often word for word, which is a common trait among people with autism. She talked again about how bad pork has gotten and then, seemingly from out of nowhere, mentioned romaine lettuce. "It used to be green," she said. "Now it's like iceberg lettuce. I think they're breeding for rapid growth." (All of which has disturbing implications for lovers of Caesar salad.)

Fifteen minutes out of Fort Collins, we pulled into Horton Feedlot and were met by the very same reek that invaded my nostrils in West Texas and that corn-feeding pen in Argentina. It was tiny by modern standards, housing around ten thousand cattle. Half of them stood at the feed bunk, dipping their heads down to load up on flaked corn feed.

"Are these cattle happy?" I asked.

Her response surprised me: "They don't look unhappy to me." None of the cows looked sick, she pointed out. "No one here is panting." She examined the feed and saw that it contained a lot of roughage, which meant the cattle were less likely to suffer from bloat or acidosis. Williams agreed. As feedlots go, he said, this one was pretty good. The cattle got to sit around eating sweet treats all day, which undoubtedly qualifies as some people's idea of paradise. If anything, the cattle looked bored, although boredom and contentment are never very far apart.

Even in a small feedlot like this one, the pens of cattle stretch farther than the eye can see, so I hopped on top of a feed trough to get a better view. This spooked the cattle, which took off in every direction, kicking up a huge cloud of dust, then stopped and, as if on cue, began coughing in unison. We walked farther down the alley and neared the hospital pen. One cow had a cough that would not quit. "Pneumonia," Grandin said. We got closer, and another cow started to panic, running back and forth from one side of the sick pen to the other. The cow was experiencing fear, and Grandin stopped us from going farther. If we spooked the sick cow bad enough, she said, it might try to jump the fence.

We'd seen enough by this point, in any case. Most of the cattle, it seemed, were not suffering. But Grandin is under no illusions, and says that if feedlots are well run, they are, as she put it, "acceptable." "It's like living in a really cramped apartment in Tokyo," she explained, which is something that twelve million Japanese willingly do.

On the way back into town, we passed a herd of black Angus grazing by the side of the highway and pulled over. The contrast verged on the absurd. Birds were singing. The air smelled like cedar. The grass looked so soft and green you wanted to walk on it in bare feet. There was no coughing, no dust, and no reek, and we lingered, lulled by the periodic pauses in highway traffic.

Grandin has written that in large slaughterhouses, it's important to rotate jobs so that the same person doesn't end up doing all the killing. It can be unhealthy, she explained, to be around death all the time. "These people get warped," she told me. "They get nasty to the cattle and they have to be removed." As we stared at the grazing cows, I was reminded of Fleurance and the happy hours we spent together on pasture. I thought about her death and remembered how unexpectedly reassuring and positive it was, for me at least. It still pleased me to think how stress free her beer-and-apple-filled last day was, and that surprised me.

I mentioned the experience to Grandin. "That happens all the time," she said. When people raise an animal and kill it responsibly, they find it uplifting, apparently. "I think you can also get too far away from death," she observed. What people are getting too far from is nature, she believes, explaining that people in big cities are particularly susceptible. They have no connection to the meat that sits on Styrofoam trays on supermarket shelves. The mistake that vegetarians and vegans make, she told me, is that they confuse death with suffering.

We looked at the pasture again. I asked Grandin, if she had to be reincarnated as a cow at Horton Feedlot or a cow eating grass on this field, which would it be? She didn't take long to respond. "I think I would choose being in the field." Not all pasture is nice, she pointed out. Some cruel farmers leave their cattle outside all winter with not much to eat and little in the way of shelter. Then she returned her gaze to the field and said, "But this right here is cattle heaven."

The problem is "scaling it up," as Grandin put it. It's one thing to look at a bunch of cattle idyllically grazing. It's another to feed a nation of three hundred million that likes its steak. It comes down, once again, to quantity and its battle against quality.

Allen Williams believes the two goals don't have to be incompatible. Tallgrass partners with ranchers in Kansas, Georgia, Alabama, California, and Nebraska to finish cattle, and every single fat cow that comes off its roughly fifty thousand acres of pasture receives an ultrasound. Stress is a deal killer. Any cow with a stress score worse than 25 is herded into a special pen and taken to the auction barn, where it's sold to someone with less rigorous standards. Tough meat is similarly not tolerated. And if a cow tests mediocre in every category, it, too, is sold to the highest bidder. But of all those fat Tallgrass cows, less than 5 percent fail. The rest become steak.

It was time, at long last, to head for the Charco Broiler to eat. The restaurant was Grandin's choice. She likes it because it isn't part of a chain and because if you order a steak medium rare, it will arrive that way, a feat of culinary expertise beyond the reach of all too many steak houses. The Charco Broiler served its very first steak in 1957, and the present owner is the nephew of the man who opened the restaurant. In more than half a century, it has been through numerous renovations and additions, but its sunken lounge, which has little round tables, low seating, and subdued lighting, is as fine an archaeological relic of the 1970s as the caves at Lascaux are of the Upper Paleolithic.

The waiter came out and presented the raw steaks. They were a deeper red than feedlot steaks and marbled enough to grade Choice, one step below Prime. These hailed from Kansas, finished on a stretch of grass next to the cabin featured in *Little House on the Prairie*, where the book's author, Laura Ingalls Wilder, lived with her family. (The original cabin is gone, but a replica stands as a local tourist attraction.) Tallgrass packaging does not, at this point, specify pasture of origin, although the company is considering including that. It nevertheless keeps all the information in-house—as well as a DNA sample of every single cow—which is how Williams knew the steaks we were about to eat might taste something like steaks Laura Ingalls Wilder ate more than a century ago.

After the salad course, the steaks were returned to the table sporting a gorgeous Maillard crust. Temple Grandin took a bite and did not waste much time abstractifying. "Mmm," she said. "That's good. That's *really* good. This reminds me of the beef I ate in Argentina," she said, which she'd earlier told me was the best she'd ever eaten. She took another bite. "You sure get lots of flavor."

Where was that flavor coming from?

Not marbling. Grade-wise, the Tallgrass steaks were low Choice. And yet the steaks had a rich, almost smoky flavor, one that was exponentially deeper than the USDA Prime I ate in Oklahoma, or even the Matsusaka Special Beef I had in Japan.

I believe I knew the reason why. I now felt I understood, at least dimly, the food I had been chasing and eating for so long. I had formulated what you might call the Grand Unified Theory of Steak.

Humans evolved into meat eaters millions of years ago. We became good at catching and killing animals, but our ability to eat them and digest them never caught up to our skill as hunters, perhaps because we never gave up on fruits and vegetables. We don't have the teeth of a carnivore, which is one reason we mastered fire, because cooking makes meat easier to digest. We never evolved the right enzymes to digest high doses of protein; too much lean meat will kill us. That's not something

we worry about these days, because we have access to more fat and carbohydrates than nature ever thought possible. But back when Magdalenian Woman was walking around the south of France, fat was all humans
thought about.

We like fatty meat because fatty meat was the purest form of dietary
energy available back in the days of hunting and gathering. Fat meant
survival, which is why fat receptors on the tongue trigger a pleasure response in the brain. The human requirement for fat may have even
played a role in the evolution of intelligence. Unlike eagles, wolves, lions,
snakes, and so forth, humans don't hunt anything that moves. Humans
hunt fat, which meant we had to become visually discerning. That explains the corpulent aurochs on the walls at Lascaux.

Our palate is even more discerning than our eyes when it comes to
fat. We love umami, but if meat is too lean, it won't taste good no matter
how much umami it contains, because 100,000 years ago, that meat was
potentially poisonous. (And by "lean," I refer to the kind of fat-free flesh
only hunters, polar explorers, Lewis and Clark, and the odd farmer—or,
for that matter, someone who's bought underfinished grass-fed beef at a
farmers' market and found the close-to-unchewable meat tastes like fish
and/or liver—have ever tasted. Boneless chicken breast, however low in
fat, comes from well-fed birds.)

Fat cows taste better, period. It isn't the fat that's yummy; rather,
there seems to be something in the process of growing fat that makes a
cow taste good. Williams stressed repeatedly the importance of cattle
being "on the gain" when they're slaughtered, warning that the palatability of a cow—even an exceedingly fat cow—will suffer if the cow has
been losing weight. The prestige that marbling commands to this day in
North America and Japan, where governments award it their most lauda-
tory grades, is a testament to our love of plump animals.

But marbling is not where flavor resides.

An interesting thing happened while Richard Bazinet, the nutritionist who studies brain fatty acids, ran the fatty acid profiles of the steak I
gave him. In all four samples he tested—feedlot beef, grass-fed black
Wagyu, the hay-finished beefalo, and Fleurance—the visible fat didn't

look all that different. The trim and marbling on the feedlot piece was white, whereas it was slightly off-white on the other three.

To run the fatty acids in his chromatography machine, however, Bazinet had to extract the fat from the meat and store it in test tubes. And when he did that, something unexpected caught his eye. The feedlot-beef fat looked like it did in the steak—white. But the other three samples were now considerably darker: the black Wagyu fat was the color of apple juice, the beefalo fat was just north of a dark broth, and Fleurance's fat looked like tea. The color, it seemed to me, actually matched the flavor to some degree. The beefalo, which tasted deep and brooding, had the deepest, darkest fat. The black Wagyu and Fleurance, on the other hand, tasted brighter and sweeter, and the appearance of their fat corresponded.

Something was going on with the fat. It didn't appear to be happening in the visible fat—the marbling or the trim—because it wasn't colored. It had to be something else. But what?

I asked Bazinet. He thought it must be internal fat, either structural fat found in cell walls or fat stored as energy inside the muscle cells. Something in the grass the cows had eaten, it seemed, was making its way into the muscle.

Bazinet seems to be on to something. A British food scientist named Don Mottram concluded as much back in 1982. He conducted an experiment in which he removed various kinds of fat from beef, then cooked the beef and had a panel of thirteen people smell it to see if the aroma had changed. (He also put it through a chromatography machine, so as not to rely on smell alone.) When he removed the triglycerides—the kind of fat you find in marbling and trim—and cooked the beef, the smell was barely altered. Stripped of the marbling and trim, in other words, steak still smelled like steak. But when Mottram took out the structural fats—scientists call them phospholipids—and cooked the beef, suddenly it didn't smell like steak anymore. It wasn't as "meaty." (There was two hundred times less 1-octen-3-ol. There were fewer alcohols and aliphatic aldehydes, but a rise in benzaldehyde levels.)

Mottram believes alpha-linolenic acid—the unsaturated omega-3 fatty acid found both in grass and in grass-fed beef—is the key. When combined with intense heat, protein, sugar, fat, and everything else you find in a steak, ALA is highly prone to forming the complex aromatic compounds associated with beefy flavor. ALA, in other words, comes alive during Maillard reactions.

In British meat and flavor science faculties, it is grass that equals flavor, not marbling. Mottram described the relationship between grass and flavor as "one of the few correlations we're sure of." All marbling adds, he told me, is succulence. Succulence is good, of course. Marbling adds richness to a steak the same way butter adds richness to pastry. But succulence without an underlying flavor to enrich is, basically, lard.

Harold McGee, the author and expert on the chemistry of food, supports a different theory. In *On Food and Cooking,* he claims that what gives grass-fed beef its flavor is a substance called terpenes. Microorganisms in a cow's rumen convert chlorophyll into these aromatic chemicals, which are related to the aroma compounds that give herbs and spices their intense flavor. (When people sprinkle spice rubs on feedlot steaks, they're applying terpenes that should have been there in the first place.)

McGee's theory resonates with the steak I've eaten—the best illustration being raw steak. When a feedlot steak is raw, it is almost totally without flavor. A raw grass-fed steak, on the other hand, has depth—not the depth of a cooked grass-fed steak, but enough flavor to enable you to taste and enjoy the meat you're eating. There is no browned crust, obviously, in raw steak—no complex aromatic compounds, in other words— and therefore it cannot be the ALA providing all that flavor. It must be terpenes.

Judging by the rich color of Bazinet's harvested fat samples, my guess is that there is even more than terpenes in grass-fed steak: flavonoids, carotenoids, and who knows what other kinds of 'oids. We can't, as yet, call them out by name, but we can taste them.

Flavor, however, can't simply be reduced to grass. I know this because three days after eating the *Little House on the Prairie* steaks, I ate another A-plus steak and scaled another lofty peak of gustatory fulfillment. This one came from a cow that had spent the summer mowing a verdant carpet growing in Idaho's Pahsimeroi Valley. It had eaten basically the same kinds of grass as Tallgrass cows, and yet it tasted different.

That could only mean one thing: the flavor of those steaks wasn't about the grass the cows ate so much as the soil that grass had been growing in: soil.

Glenn Elzinga is one of America's last unironic cowboys. He wears a Stetson because it shields his face and neck from the sun when he's on a horse, which is often. He wears cowboy boots because the heel stops his feet from slipping through a stirrup, and the tall, rigid sides protect his ankles and calves from rattlesnake strikes. He can tie a lasso and throw it around a horse's neck, which is important, because otherwise he'd have a tough time wrangling his horse in the morning.

Elzinga owns a worn-out pair of chaps, pulls calves from mother cows struggling with birth, and rides up into range country once or twice a week with his lunch in a leather saddlebag. To properly experience a steak at Alderspring Ranch, he told me, would take two days. No restaurant has that kind of time to set the mood. Neither does Elzinga, who has a ranch to run, after all. But he made an exception for me.

And so it was that within minutes of parking my rental car, I found myself standing next to a man in a Stetson and boots and twirling a lasso above his head. A minute or two earlier, Elzinga's horses had been standing with their noses to the ground happily eating grass, but now they were all wound up, running in circles around him and letting out the odd neigh. The only way he was going to halt one of those horses, it seemed obvious, was by landing the lasso around its neck. But each horse eventually slowed down and willingly took a halter. Except, that is, for a defiant chestnut mare named Missy, who had to be apprehended by rope. "This one's your horse," Elzinga said, turning to me. At twenty-six, she is the oldest horse I have ever met, but she was just a pretty young thing compared to Bonnie, a white and formerly wild thirty-five-year-old mustang that is so gentle a ride she is reserved exclusively for children.

Missy, Elzinga told me, had never fallen down, a fact that I found reassuring until one of Elzinga's daughters—he has seven—corrected him. "Actually," she said, "there *was* that one time. . . ." Then she reminded her

father that a few weeks earlier, a visiting photographer from the Nature
Conservancy had hopped onto Missy's back, at which point Missy tore off
into a gallop and did not stop.

"Wouldn't it be simpler to just stay here and eat steak?" I asked.

Yes, it would, Elzinga said.

Before getting into cattle, Elzinga sought perfection in backcoun-
try powder snow. He sounds more like a ski bum than a rancher—on
the spectrum of dude talk, his inflections and vocabulary are somewhere
between cowboy and surfer. He also doesn't look like the ranching type,
Stetson and mustache notwithstanding. He stands six foot five and is
leaner than a lodgepole pine, wears round eyeglasses that are more in
keeping with a university library than with the ruggedness of his surroundings, and looks like a man who could get blown clean off the side
of a mountain. There have been several wipeouts, including a legendary
near-fatal spill in 2005. And there have been several injuries: he has
broken ribs three times, and a bull once rammed a gate Elzinga was trying to shut, striking him in the head. He thought he was fine and drove
into town to buy some groceries. As he was entering a supermarket, some
friends approached. "They were like, 'Hey, Glenn, did you know your
ear is about to fall off?' The whole bottom half was flapping around in
the wind." Like almost all of Elzinga's anecdotes, asides, and full-blown
tales, this one climaxed with laughter.

Elzinga pointed at a mountain off in the distance. Way up on the side
of it, so far as to seem abstract, some cows were grazing the wrong creek
drainage. There would be no steak until we rousted them out and sent
them into the next valley, where the grass was better.

So Elzinga, his daughter Linnaea, and I piled into a 1977 Chevrolet
Sierra Grande, and around midnight we rolled into camp, which consisted
of a horse corral and fire pit on the side of Taylor Butte next to Big Hat
Creek. The sky was black and it appeared as though someone had turned
up the brightness dial of the stars to eleven. I stepped out of the truck and
almost on the head of a rattlesnake, whereupon Elzinga grabbed a shovel
and tried to kill it, but it slithered off.

The horses were put in a corral for the night with some hay, and
Elzinga made a fire over which he warmed up a pot of the best beans I

have ever eaten. (The secret to which, he says, is crumbling in yesterday's leftover hamburgers.) In a separate pot, Linnaea baked a peach cobbler. We stared into the fire as we ate, and afterward Elzinga unfurled a tarp for us all to lay out our bedding. I looked at the sky one last time, turned over, shut my eyes, and listened to the water moving down Big Hat Creek and wood crackling in the fire.

Come morning, Elzinga was heating up a pot of cowboy coffee— coffee in which the grounds are not filtered, and so must be poured with a steady hand. He toasted some tortillas in the gray coals and fried some eggs and beef sausages in a pan. We ate our fill.

By nine, the horses were tacked up, and the three of us were on their backs, gaining elevation as we clopped up a U.S. Forest Service road under a canopy of aspens and Douglas firs. At some opening in the trees visible only to himself, Elzinga turned left, and soon we found ourselves climbing a treeless, rocky slope, beginning our ascent of Taylor Butte in earnest.

Halfway up, Elzinga paused and said, "This is where the crash happened." He was referring to the legendary crash of 2005. His horse, Ginger, got spooked and bucked Elzinga off, stomped on his chest, then tumbled a hundred yards down the mountain. When she finally came to a halt, she was covered in puncture wounds and her front leg appeared to be dislocated. Elzinga came close to shooting Ginger that day, but he managed to walk her back to camp, where he fed her water warmed over the campfire to keep her from succumbing to shock. A few weeks later, a vet told him that Ginger would never recover, but years later here she stood, a gorgeous buckskin quarter horse, ready to go herd cattle.

It would be a good idea, Elzinga mentioned almost in passing, if I pointed my heels down on the steeper pitches, so that if my mount went over I could land squarely on my foot and so be poised to leap out of the way of a tumbling horse. For the rest of the day, my heels stayed down, as though pulled by rare earth magnets.

Some pitches were so steep we had to get off and walk, leading the horses by the reins. The grass grew here in little tufts, islands of green surrounded by loose rock and dry ground, but it was lush and tender. When I stopped to catch my breath, Missy would tear off a clump and chew. "Horses are not nearly as good as cattle at digesting grass," Elzinga said. "You can tell by looking at their turds." Like Allen Williams, Elzinga is a veteran turd observer. "There's more undigested grass in it," he explained.

Horses nevertheless do fine on grass. A band of feral horses lives on Taylor Butte, and grass is all they eat. Elzinga sees them all the time, as well as a band of mustangs that lives a few valleys over. (Mustangs are horses that have been feral so long that, like the Texas longhorn, they have original Spanish blood in them.) His daughter Melanie had recently been with her mother, Caryl, a PhD botanist, looking for rare plants when she spotted a small orphaned mustang far off in the distance. Melanie crawled through tall sagebrush on her belly, commando-style, and tracked it for half a mile. When she got home, she phoned the Bureau of Land Management to tell them they had an orphaned mustang colt on their land. A day later, they phoned back and said, "Do you want it?" He now goes by the name of Chance and lives in a corral at Alderspring Ranch with Ginger and Missy and the other horses. In time he will be climbing Taylor Butte, tearing off grassy tufts and looking for cows.

Elzinga listened for moos. Nothing. We kept riding and dipped low to cross a creek, where the grass was ultra-green and the soil was so soft the horses' hooves sank down deep into it. As we approached the water, trout darted out of our way.

Cows will not finish on range grass, but they are well nourished by it. It contains so much protein that a mother cow can feed herself and her growing calf. Elzinga had, all told, 160 mothers and calves in his fifty thousand acres of rangeland, which is owned by the Bureau of Land Management and the U.S. Forest Service, but which he has the right to graze. His cattle spend spring, summer, and fall here. When snow hits the ground and the creeks freeze up, the cattle are herded the twenty-six miles back to the ranch. The trip takes three days, and it is the living legacy of a herding culture that stretches back to Spain and Scotland. By the time the cows hit the Pahsimeroi Valley, they know where they're going. They know there are fields of green, sweet grass and mountains of nutty hay waiting for them, so they break into a run and do not stop.

At the moment, most of those cows were up over the other side of the butte, grazing Big Hat drainage. But a few stragglers—fifteen or twenty cow-calf pairs—were wandering around Park Creek drainage. The U.S. Forest Service had notified Elzinga that it was time to give Park Creek drainage a break from foraging, and that the cows would have to be moved.

Every hour or so we would come across a few patties, and Elzinga and Linnaea analyzed them for freshness. The most recent was two days old, and the rest were disappointingly sunbaked. It went on like this until lunch, which we ate next to the creek in a cool grove of pines that smelled sweet and minty. We stretched out in a clearing, dining on prunes, nuts, and chicken out of a can, drinking cold water from the creek. I lay my head back and noticed it was inches from an old cowpatty, but it was as fresh as the creek-cooled air.

By mid-afternoon, the absence of cows was becoming something of a problem. Where were they? "Do you think they might have gone over to the other side of the butte by themselves?" I asked Elzinga.

"It's possible," he said, "but I doubt it." We kept riding. When the land flattened out, we would canter, and when it steepened we would slow down so as not to tire out the horses.

After another two hours, we found ourselves on the crest of a ridge, high enough that magnificence spread out in every direction. The Pahsimeroi Valley rolled away beneath us, looking as if it was covered in horsehide, and off in the distance you could just make out Alderspring Ranch. The sun was blazing, a breeze was blowing, and a few hundred feet in front of us a golden eagle was soaring. On the other side of the valley, the tops of the Lemhi Mountains were covered in snow that, even in July, looked as thick as toothpaste.

A cow mooed. Then another. The slope was steep, and the herd was somewhere below us. If they headed downhill, we would have to loop around and come at them from below to chase them back up and over the ridge, through a gate into the next valley. It struck me as the kind of situation tailor-made for a spectacular wipeout. Our horses broke into a gallop. The cows bolted. They were aware of the plan, evidently, because they made directly for the gate. All we had to do was run up behind them and shut it.

The sun was low in the sky by the time we got back to the ranch. Elzinga made a fire in an outdoor grill from some old, dried-out fence posts, explaining, "You get a good smoke." Before he laid a steak on the grill, he put a sheet of black iron over it, because Elzinga does not believe in grills. He thinks too much moisture drips away between the slats. I believe he is wrong about this, but I am no enemy of a pan, or sheet iron, for that matter.

Nearer the river, cattle were grazing and slapping flies with their tails. The grass grows well at Alderspring Ranch because the soil is thick with minerals like calcium and magnesium. The West has always had a reputation for good steak, and some argue that it's because back when American cows ate grass, the mineralized soils of the mountainous West produced better-tasting meat.

Three hundred and fifty million years ago, Alderspring Ranch was under fifty feet of warm seawater. The land was then pancake-flat, but that changed fifty million years ago when the Pacific Plate collided with the North American Plate and caused what geologists, who have a great gift for understatement, call "uplift." Volcanoes burbled mineral-rich lava for millions of years. Mountains made of ancient, dead marine creatures rose from the ground and reached high into the sky. Millennia of glaciers, snowmelt, rain, and wind have moved all that lava, limestone, dolomite, and quartz—grain by grain, pebble by pebble—down into the valley. The roots of Elzinga's grasses needle their way through it, nourishing themselves on minerals, water, and sun.

We talked genetics. Elzinga used to have three Limousin cows, but their offspring were never tender, so he sent them down the road. Elzinga doesn't own an ultrasound machine, so his diagnostic instrument of choice is his mouth. He eats at least one strip loin off each cow. Lack of flavor is hardly ever an issue. Very rarely, tenderness isn't what it should be; he won't sell those steaks. Elzinga has been culling a cow here and there over the years, pushing the herd's genetic makeup in the right direction. In twenty years, he figures he'll have the herd he wants. The one he has, however, tastes very good.

The sheet of iron was now so hot that he poured water on it to cool it down, for fear that the meat would burst into flame. The water did not even dance on the hot metal. It turned instantly into steam and drifted away.

Two handpicked rib eyes were sitting on a plate facing a sky that was nearing them in color. Elzinga loves skirt steaks, culottes, hanger steaks, shoulder tenders, rump steaks, you name it. The only cuts he doesn't have time for are "those super-duper lean jobbers, like tenderloins or London broils." Rib eyes, however, hold a special spot in his heart, and another in his stomach.

The ones sitting on that plate were marbled enough to grade high Choice. More than half his steaks come out that way, and Elzinga is thinking of creating an ultra-premium line, for which he would take sides of beef from his fattest steers and heifers, sides with the thick back fat and snowy rib eyes, and dry-age them for an extra two or three weeks. "I'm talking about steak that walks on water," he said. "I'm talking about steak that rocks everybody's world." His steak, I can attest, already walks on water and rocks worlds, so Elzinga is in need of a more powerful metaphor. But that should not stop him from trying.

Back in Scotland, Laurent Vernet had warned me that a wet steak can lead to boiled flavors in the meat. I mentioned this to Elzinga, and he patted the blood off the rib eyes with a paper towel. When he flipped them, the cooked side was an even, gorgeous brown.

I looked up at Taylor Butte, the outline of which seemed to glow on the horizon. I thought about the asteroid that, sixty-five million years ago, smashed into the Yucatán Peninsula and put the world on course for steak. Fifteen million years later, the Pacific Plate bumped into the North American Plate and raised the mountains that give Alderspring steaks their particular flavor. Two million years ago, hominids discovered that meat held over a fire turns brown and delicious, and ten thousand years ago their descendants, now featuring bigger brains and smaller jaws, tamed the tastiest beasts roaming Europe and Asia, the aurochs. For all this, I was thankful.

Over the past many months, I had visited seven countries, all told, to eat steak. Considering there are 195 countries in the word, that's a rather meager percentage. I had witnessed a mere handful of geographical points on a planet whose immensity and diversity defy comprehension. I did not visit Ethiopia, for example, but I wish I had, because Ethiopians are fond of a very lean steak tartare called *kitfo*. I would like to visit the grass-growing paradise that is New Zealand for its "steak of origin competition" that attempts to determine, on a yearly basis, which farm is raising the most outstanding beef. On the way there, I'd drop in on Australia for a steak or two. Uruguay is up there with Argentina in terms of steak consumption, and I have heard stories about Uruguayan steaks served with the hide still on—I need to see and eat such a steak in person. Koreans have their own breed of ultra-marbled cattle called Hanwoo, which, despite being the color of suede, are related to Japan's black Wagyu. Koreans consider their steak superior to any other, but those steaks may be on the path to ruin because recently they have taken to crossing their Hanwoo with big and tall Charolais cattle, all in the name of improved yield. Lament not, however, because there are pictures on the Internet of North Korean Hanwoo cows eating grass and pulling wooden carts. They appear to survive off mangy forage and I have fantasies of airlifting a herd to Bridge of Earn and leaving them in the care of Angus Mackay.

In Mongolia, cattle survive on land so dry and barren it looks like the moon. Could they marble like a black Wagyu or a Hanwoo? Is their meat finer grained than a Highland's? How saturated is their fat? What would a Mongolian cow taste like after twelve months under Allen Williams's supervision? No one seems to know. Another Asian breed said to fatten very well on grass is known as an Aulie-Ata. That's a name I would like to see on a restaurant menu, but chances are I won't.

Steak remains a mystery. Its greatness is, at best, only dimly understood. The one secret the world has mastered is how to produce steak in the greatest possible volume. But a few people—Glenn Elzinga, Allen Williams, and Angus Mackay among them—have taken up the fight for quality, for less-saturated fatty acids, slow-twitch muscle fibers, terpenes, flavonoids, carotenoids, and flavor. Perhaps one day ranchers will walk through mountain valleys collecting soil samples and sporting refractometers, all in the hopes of finding land on which to create sublime steak. The story, really, has just begun.

Elzinga reached down and tested the firmness of the rib eyes with his index finger. They were firm, but not too firm, gorgeously browned on the outside but still red in the middle. Like the two humans that were about to eat them, their outward crust concealed a core that remained primitive and bloody. We went inside to eat.

I would like to tell you how that steak tasted, but the truth is, we lack an adequate meat vocabulary. The flavor that burst over my tongue with each chew was comparable to a symphony, but any attempt to describe the individual notes would sound pretentious and be meaningless, I fear. As I ate, I thought about Fleurance and the near trance she entered while chomping that apple back in Carla's barn. That's how I felt now. My mouth wasn't in the mood to form syllables. It wanted to chew. I let it.

What I can tell you about that steak is how it made me feel. The flavor reached deep into my subcortex and uncorked a sensation that bubbled up and drowned out every other thought, concern, and anxiety drifting through the chaos and endless dialogue that rage in the mind. I chewed, swallowed, cut more steak, and chewed, sustaining my state of mind with each bite. It is the feeling that no human, or animal, for that matter, ever tires of experiencing. It is a feeling that makes life, for all its pain, frustration, and sadness, worth living. The feeling is joy.

AFTERWORD

A few weeks after the final character of the book you see before you was typed—a period, predictably—I found myself in a bar talking to a lawyer friend. He couldn't wait to read my book about steak, he told me, because he was, as he put it, "really looking forward to finally learning how to properly cook one."

He then launched into a description perhaps too rich in detail of the various ways he and his wife had desecrated countless expensive beef cuts over the years. I barely took in a word. In my head, I was scanning over the roughly 106,000 words I had written over the preceding months. Nowhere among them was there what you would call a recipe for cooking steak. Apparently, *How do you cook a steak?* was the big question people wanted answered. (In my friend's case, the *only* question.) A book entitled *Steak*, you might think, would answer it. But it did not.

Cooking a steak is simpler than boiling an egg, yet somehow it remains a feat everyone from lawyers to steak house chefs gets wrong with regularity. So, from someone who's both witnessed the cooking of steak and cooked rather a lot of steaks himself over the past many years, here is a step-by-step guide.

How to Cook a Steak in 15 Easy Steps

1 steak
salt
heat
Serves 1

Step 1. Find a source of tender, juicy, and, above all, flavorful steak (by far the most difficult step in this recipe). Frozen steak is fine, so long as it's good frozen steak.

Step 2. Decide on a cut.

There is a rather large selection to choose from, as you will have noticed: strips, flank steaks, rump steaks, tenderloins, rib eyes, and so forth. And don't forget about those rare "butcher's cuts." At least once a year, every men's magazine will run a story on steak that tells you, in the coolest language the writer can muster, that these are the cuts that steak insiders eat, and that by putting a skirt steak, hanger steak, or flatiron steak on your grill, you will distinguish yourself from the strip-loin-consuming masses and attain the dude-simple purity of a cattle rancher or an old-time New York butcher.

My guess is that you'll like a rib eye most of all. But here's a little secret for you: they're all good. So long as you follow Step 1, that is. Every steak cut is delicious, and some of the "braising" cuts are, too. Try them all. Get to know each cut as intimately as your pillow. If you follow Step 1, any and every cut you get will be eminently palatable. But follow Step 1.

Step 3. Choose a thickness.

Don't fall into the trap of believing that bigger steaks are always better. Thin steaks are plenty good, too. You just need to cook them properly, on a very hot surface, so that you can brown the outside without overcooking the middle.

Step 4. Examine the steak.

Prod it. Poke it. Pick it up in your hands, or with tongs, and waggle it. Try to memorize the suppleness of the flesh. You'll understand why when you reach Step 12.

Step 5. Choose a cooking surface.

It can be a grill or it can be a pan. Both are fine. That's right, *both* are *fine*. If you're cooking with a grill, you might prefer wood or charcoal, because they impart a subtle but enjoyable flavor to the meat, to gas. But gas is fine, too, so long as you follow Step 1.

Step 6. Let the steak warm to room temperature.

Don't cook a cold steak on a hot grill or pan. And never cook a frozen steak.

Step 7. Wipe the steak dry.

Pat both sides of the meat dry with a paper towel. A dry piece of meat will form a better crust. A wet steak, no matter how it's cooked, may end up tasting like it was boiled, and that would be terrible, especially if you've followed Step 1.

Step 8. Salt the steak.

Take a pinch of whatever salt is currently trendy—anything other than standard iodized salt is fine, although even it is acceptable in a pinch—and sprinkle both sides of the steak. You'll need one to two pinches per side, possibly more if it's a thick steak. Only experience will tell you how much is enough, and it's always better to err on the not-enough side, because too much salt is a disaster. Salt five minutes before cooking, unless your steak is less than a quarter of an inch thick, in which case don't salt it until it's cooked, because the salt will draw out moisture.

Step 9. Figure out how you want it cooked.

Don't be one of those people who run around uttering bombastic statements like "I have no respect for anyone who eats a steak over medium rare." Roughly three quarters of all Argentines eat steak well done, and they probably eat more steak than you do. My own preference is for medium rare, although on certain days I demand rare. But that doesn't matter to anyone but me. What matters is *your* preference. Figure it out. Stand by it.

Step 10. Cook the steak.

Make sure your pan or grill is hot. You want to brown the exterior of the steak, but you don't want to burn it. Browning happens when heat causes chemical reactions to take place on the surface of the meat. This starts at 70°C (158°F). Burning happens at much higher temperatures. A charred crosshatching from the grill is nice—a bitter hint of the fire the steak cooked over. But a black steak will taste bitter. A black steak is what happens when rich men with big barbecues—loudmouth types, usually—cook thick steaks on a torrid grill for too long.

Step 11. Flip the steak.

After the first side has browned, which could take anywhere from one minute to eight minutes, flip. If you're cooking a very thick steak and the first side browned quickly, turn down the heat—after you flip it—because you're well on your way to a burned piece of meat.

Step 12. Assess doneness.

Examine the steak again. Poke the surface with your index finger. (It's not that hot.) As a steak cooks, it becomes firmer, so you should start to feel some resistance. Pick up the steak with your tongs and waggle it. It should show signs of beginning to stiffen. When little droplets of red liquid start to form on the surface of the steak—I call this beading—the steak is approaching medium rare.

If you poke your steak and find that it feels like a cutting board, you've overcooked it, in which case you might try moistening it with the tears dripping off your cheek. But that probably won't help, so revert to Step 1 and begin again.

Incidentally, don't expect this method to work the first time you try it. But by the tenth time, you should have the hang of it. I hope.

Step 13. Rest the steak (optional).

If you've cooked a steak any thicker than an inch, you can rest it for a minute or two, or longer for very thick steaks. Resting allows heat from the exterior to radiate inward and cook the meat in the center, which releases the all-important steak juice. But resting is overrated. It is acceptable and often quite enjoyable to cut into a steak that's raw in the middle. If your one true desire is for a steak with an evenly cooked interior, turn the heat down on your grill. So long as you follow Step 1, the steak will be delicious whether it's rested or not.

Step 14. Resist the temptation to smother your steak in a sauce or rub.

Steak sauce is like crystal meth—habit forming and ruinous. There's no point in following Step 1 if you're going to cover your steak in intense seasoning and smother it in a sauce so tangy as to make ketchup seem refined. Some sauces—particularly those from France—celebrate a steak's flavor without masking it. But if you're dealing with good steak, then the flavor of steak will be the best thing on your plate.

Step 15. Eat the steak.

A fine steak knife is not always essential, but using one is fun.

ACKNOWLEDGMENTS

Despite the single name—*mine*—appearing on the spine of this book, *Steak* was nonetheless a collaborative endeavor. I will be forever grateful to Rick Kot at Viking, who gave a Canadian writer his first book contract, and who, along with Laura Tisdel and the rest of the fine Viking team, invested so much in making it better. This book would never have happened if not for the efforts of my agent, Richard Morris of Janklow and Nesbit. You are a fine representative and a better friend.

Steak is a far bigger subject than I ever realized, involving everything from animal science, meat science, flavor science, human evolution, and ruminant evolution to the history of crop farming in Argentina. The list of people who have helped me along the way is long, and the collective effort is huge. Thank you: Dr. Alberto Alves de Lima, Elizabeth Andoh, Jan Busboom, Dario Cecchini, Seiichi Chada, Nirupa Chaudhari, Rufus Churcher, Anne and Clive Davidson, Carolyn Dmitri, Dorothée Drucker, Susan Duckett, Anne Effland, Karen Eny, Cinzia Fanciulli, Kevin Good, Dr. Juan José Grigera Naón, Andrea Grisdale, Claude Guintard, Andrew Isenberg, Randy Jackson, David Kasabian, Steve Lantos, Douglas Law, John Leffingwell, Paul Link, Jim Logan, Vicky Lux-Lantos, Hazel McFadzean, David MacHugh, Emily Maggs, Charlotte Maltin, Stephen Mennell, Markus Miller, Holly Neibergs, Mari Okada, Alan K. Outram, Emmanuelle Perrier, Bob Pickering, Keith Redpath, Don Reeves, Jerry Reeves, Alan Richman, Andrew Smith, John D. Speth, Craig Stanford, Mike Steinberger, Helena Tchekov, Julia Turner, Cis Van Vuure, Tommy Wheeler, and Hanya Yanagihara.

Thank you, Klara Glowczewska, and the rest of the excellent staff at *Condé Nast Traveler*, for helping propel me on my worldwide quest in ways that only you can.

A special thanks to Wes Brown for waking up at 5:00 a.m. on a Saturday and driving three hours with his ultrasound machine. Thank you to the many good people of Texas, including Markus Miller and the rest of the faculty at Texas Tech University, and to Bill O'Brien, for reaching out to a big-city journalist to show him a feedlot from the inside. Thanks to the generosity of Glenn and Caryl Elzinga, I slept in their home and spent more than a day on a horse exploring Idaho as it ought to be explored. Thank you, Christophe Raoux, Alain Ducasse, Laurent Vernet, Charlotte Maltin, Jim Cameron, Keith Redpath, Russ Maytag, Carla Hanisch, Ted Slanker, Michael and Nobuyo Stadtländer, and Temple Grandin. Thank you, Richard Bazinet, for bartering nutrition science for steak. And thank you, Allen Williams, for the hours of Meat Science 101 you so patiently visited (and revisited) with me.

Years ago, I wrote a story for Slate.com about steak. Not long after, I received an e-mail from a Wyoming cattleman named Paul Butler. Thus a long-distance, steak-obsessed e-mail relationship was born. Thank you, Paul, for your encouragement, your knowledge, your wisdom, and your enduring faith that great steak is out there, waiting to be tasted. The day will come when you create a truly beautiful beefalo steak. I will be there to taste it.

Fleurance, I don't know what to say other than that I miss you. Thanks for everything (literally). I have your hide to remember you by, and I think of you often.

Writers have a reputation for being anxiety-riddled catastrophists, and I am guilty of confirming the stereotype. For support, I thank my friend and editor Ted Moncreiff for his reassurance, enthusiasm, and tack-sharp editorial insight.

This book—not to mention my life—could not have happened without my parents, Valerie and Joe Schatzker, who have always believed in me, even when I have not. Thanks to my brothers, Erik and Adam, for taking part in my steak quest and sending invaluable notes from the field. To my children, Greta, Violet, and Henry: your excitement is infectious, and you make me smile at the most unexpected times. Thanks for the levity.

There is only one dish I know of that tops steak: my wife, Laura McLeod, whose mere smile gets me through the valleys and back up the mountain. Laura, for a former vegetarian, you sure have eaten a lot of steak. You may not be quite up to three and a half pounds of beef a day, but you will always be my Magdalenian Woman.

BIBLIOGRAPHY

For a list of where or how to buy some of the steaks described in this book, visit www.steakthebook.com.

Ackerman, Diane. *The Zookeeper's Wife: A War Story*. New York: W. W. Norton, 2007.

Aiello, Leslie C., and Peter Wheeler. "The Expensive Tissue Hypothesis." *Current Anthropology* 36, no. 2 (1995).

Allen, Lewis F. *American Cattle: Their History, Breeding and Management*. New York: Taintor Brothers, 1868.

Bailey, M. E. "Maillard Reactions and Meat Flavour." In *Flavor of Meat, Meat Products and Seafoods*, 2nd ed., edited by F. Shahidi. London: Blackie Academic and Professional, 1994.

Barthes, Roland. *Mythologies*. London: Vintage, 1993.

Bellisle, France. "Glutamate and the Umami Taste: Sensory, Metabolic, Nutritional and Behavioural Considerations. A Review of the Literature Published in the Last 10 Years." *Neuroscience and Biobehavioral Reviews* 23 (1999).

Blumenthal, Heston. *In Search of Total Perfection*. London: Bloomsbury, 2006.

Bocherens, Hervé, et al. "Isotopic Evidence for Diet and Subsistence Pattern of the Saint-Césaire I Neanderthal: Review and Use of a Multi-Source Mixing Model." *Journal of Human Evolution* 49 (2005).

Breidenstein, B. B., et al. "Influence of Marbling and Maturity on the Palatability of Beef Muscle. I. Chemical and Organoleptic Considerations." *Journal of Animal Science* 27 (1968).

Brewer, Susan. *The Chemistry of Beef Flavor—Executive Summary*. Prepared for the National Cattlemen's Beef Association. University of Illinois, 2006.

Cassell's New Dictionary of Cookery. London: Cassell and Company, 1912.

Cordain, Loren, et al. "Plant-Animal Subsistence Ratios and Macronutrient Energy Estimations in Worldwide Hunter-Gatherer Diets." *American Journal of Clinical Nutrition* 71 (2000).

Dimitri, Carolyn. "Agricultural Marketing Institutions: A Response to Quality Disputes." *Journal of Agricultural & Food Industrial Organization* 1 (2003).

Drucker, Dorothée, et al. "Determination of the Dietary Habits of a Magdalenian Woman from Saint-Germain-la-Rivière in Southwestern France Using Stable Isotopes." *Journal of Human Evolution* 49 (2005).

Finch, Caleb E., and Craig B. Stanford. "Meat-Adaptive Genes and the Evolution of Slower Aging Humans." *The Quarterly Review of Biology* 79 (2004).

Frevert, W. *Rominten*. Munich, Bern, and Vienna: BLV-Verlag, 1957.

Goodson, K. J., et al. "Beef Customer Satisfaction: Factors Affecting Consumer Evaluations of Clod Steaks." *Journal of Animal Science* 80, no. 2 (2002).

Grandin, Temple. *Animals in Translation*. New York: Scribner, 2004.

———. *Animals Make Us Human: Creating the Best Life for Animals*. Orlando, FL: Houghton Mifflin Harcourt, 2009.

———. "Assessment of Stress During Handling and Transport." *Journal of Animal Science* 75 (1997).

Hammond, P. W. *Food and Feast in Medieval England*. Stroud, UK: Sutton Publishing, 1995.

Harris, Marvin. *Good to Eat*. Long Grove, IL: Waveland Press, 1985.

Heck, Lutz. *Animals: My Adventure*. London: Scientific Book Club, 1954.

Heseltine, Marjorie, and Ula M. Dow. *The New Basic Cook Book*. Boston: Houghton Mifflin, 1933.

Hill, Janet McKenzie. *Practical Cooking and Serving*. Garden City, NY: Doubleday, Page, 1927.

Hopkins, John A., Jr. *Economic History of the Production of Beef Cattle in Iowa*. Iowa City: State Historical Society of Iowa, 1928.

Jordan, Terry G. *North American Cattle-Ranching Frontiers: Origins, Diffusions, and Differentiation*. Albuquerque: University of New Mexico Press, 1993.

Kerr, William, et al. *Marketing Beef in Japan*. New York: Hathern Press, 1994.

Lawrie, R. A. *Lawrie's Meat Science*, 6th ed. Cambridge, UK: Woodhead Publishing, 1998.

McGee, Harold. *On Food and Cooking: The Science and Lore of the Kitchen*. New York: Scribner, 1984.

MacLeod, G. "The Flavour of Beef." In *Flavor of Meat, Meat Products and Seafoods*, 2nd ed., edited by F. Shahidi. London: Blackie Academic and Professional, 1994.

Maga, J. A. "Umami Flavour of Meat." In *Flavor of Meat, Meat Products and Seafoods*, 2nd ed., edited by F. Shahidi. London: Blackie Academic and Professional, 1994.

Mennell, Stephen. *All Manners of Food: Eating and Taste in England and France from the Middle Ages to the Present*. Urbana: University of Illinois Press, 1985.

Mitchell, Joseph. *Up in the Old Hotel*. New York: Vintage, 1938.

Mottram, D. S., and R. A. Edwards. "The Role of Triglycerides and Phospholipids in the Aroma of Cooked Beef." *Journal of the Science of Food and Agriculture* 34 (1983).

Outram, Alan K. "Hunter-Gatherers and the First Farmers: The Evolution of Taste in Prehistory." In *Food: The History of Taste*, edited by Paul Freedman. Berkeley: University of California Press (2007).

Prince, Joseph M., and Richard H. Steckel. "Nutritional Success on the Great Plains: Nineteenth-Century Equestrian Nomads." *Journal of Interdisciplinary History* 33 (2003).

Ranhoffer, Charles. *The Epicurean*. New York: Dover Publications, 1971.

Reischauer, Edwin O. *Japan: The Story of a Nation*, 4th ed. New York: McGraw-Hill, 1990.

Roeber, D. L., et al. "Implant Strategies During Feeding: Impact on Carcass Grades and Consumer Acceptability." *Journal of Animal Science* 78 (2000).

Romans, J. R., et al. "Influence of Carcass Maturity and Marbling on the Physical and Chemical Characteristics of Beef. I. Palatability, Fiber Diameter and Proximate Analysis." *Journal of Animal Science* 24 (1965).

Rosen, Amy. "Water Worker." *Toronto Life* (May 2005).

Sacks, Oliver. *An Anthropologist on Mars: Seven Paradoxical Tales*. New York: Vintage, 1996.

Schor, Alejandro, et al. "Nutritional and Eating Quality of Argentinean Beef: A Review." *Meat Science* 79 (2008).

Skaggs, Jimmy. *Prime Cut: Livestock Raising and Meatpacking in the United States 1607–1983*. College Station: Texas A&M University, 1983.

Speth, John, et al. "Energy Source, Protein Metabolism, and Hunter-Gatherer Subsistence Strategies." *Journal of Anthropological Archeology* 2 (1983).

Stanford, Craig. *The Hunting Apes: Meat Eating and the Origins of Human Behavior*. Princeton: Princeton University Press, 2001.

Tatum, J. D., et al. "Carcass Characteristics, Time on Feed and Cooked Beef Palatability Attributes." *Journal of Animal Science* 50 (1980).

Thomas, Lately. *Delmonico's: A Century of Splendor*. Boston: Houghton Mifflin, 1967.

Thurman, Judith. "First Impressions." *The New Yorker* (June 23, 2008).

Van Vuure, Cis. *Retracing the Aurochs*. Sofia, Bulgaria: Pensoft, 2005.

Wobber, V., et al. "Great Apes Prefer Cooked Food." *Journal of Human Evolution* 55 (2008).

INDEX

Williams, Allen (*cont.*)
  grass feeding praised by, 36–37,
    172, 204, 222, 237–38, 242
  on Jersey steer, 209–10
  on Lascaux paintings, 58
  manure examined by, 236, 260
  on nut diet, 222

wine, 102–3, 110, 112, 130, 142,
  144, 190
Wrchota, Tom, 219–20

yakiniku, 150, 159
Yanqui Mike, 196–98